THE BOOK
of
HEDGE DRUIDRY

About the Author

Joanna van der Hoeven is a Druid, Witch, author, and teacher. She has written several books on Druidry including the best-selling introductory book *The Awen Alone: Walking the Path of the Solitary Druid*. She has also written countless articles for Pagan magazines and websites and spoken at conferences, fairs, festivals, and more. Joanna is the co-founder of Druid College UK, which offers a three-year training programme, and she is also the director of her own dance company.

Joanna was born in Quebec, Canada. She moved to the UK in 1998, where she now lives with her husband in a small village near the coast of the North Sea. She has a BA (Hons) English Language and Literature degree. In her spare time, Joanna enjoys reading, walking and singing back to the land.

Praise for *The Book of Hedge Druidry*

"*The Book of Hedge Druidry* is a beautifully written exploration of the world of the Hedge Druid. Joanna van der Hoeven digs deeply into the core theories that inform the practices of the solitary Druid with a sensitivity and depth of insight that reveals the richness of this path. Joanna freely shares her extensive knowledge and experience and offers the reader a wealth of useful practical suggestions; everything from ritual creation, prayer, and meditation to the study and application of ogham, herblore, and spellcraft. In the skillful presentation of both theory and practice, Joanna provides a working template for the Hedge Druid, encouraging them to develop their own path, one that has true resonance and personal meaning. This wonderful book is an invaluable resource for those new to Druidry but will also bring inspiration and a deeper understanding to those already on the path. Highly recommended."

—Philip Carr-Gomm, author of *Druid Mysteries*

"In *The Book of Hedge Druidry*, Joanna van der Hoeven has deftly woven together various strands of wisdom to craft a tapestry that is accessible, foundational, and inspirational to all who are drawn to the path of Druidry. She offers insightful practices, heartfelt rituals, powerful tools, and resonant meditations that are infused with tradition and informed by experience; clearly Joanna has walked the pathways she now illuminates for others to explore as well! This is a practical guide that encourages seekers to immerse themselves in the work of the Hedge Druid—a spiritual path that values direct participation with, and first-hand knowledge of, the worlds within us, around us, and beyond us."

—Jhenah Telyndru, author of *Avalon Within: A Sacred Journey of Myth, Mystery and Inner Wisdom* and *The Mythic Moons of Avalon: Lunar and Herbal Wisdom from the Isle of Healing*

"Joanna van der Hoeven eloquently offers tools, theories, techniques, and her inimitable wisdom to guide the solitary Druid practitioner through the dappled groves of tradition. This is the perfect ally to those new on the path and seeking a genuine voice to accompany them."

—Kristoffer Hughes, author of *The Book of Celtic Magic*

THE BOOK
of
HEDGE
DRUIDRY

A Complete Guide for the Solitary Seeker

JOANNA VAN DER HOEVEN

Llewellyn Publications
Woodbury, Minnesota

FIRST EDITION
Fifth Printing, 2023

Cover design by Shira Atakpu
Editing by Brian R. Erdrich

Llewellyn Publications is a registered trademark of Llewellyn Worldwide Ltd.

Library of Congress Cataloging-in-Publication Data
Names: Hoeven, Joanna Van der, author.
Title: The book of hedge druidry : a complete guide for the solitary seeker
  / Joanna van der Hoeven.
Description: Woodbury : Llewellyn Worldwide. Ltd, 2019. | Includes
  bibliographical references.
Identifiers: LCCN 2019023274 (print) | LCCN 2019023275 (ebook) | ISBN
  9780738758251 (paperback) | ISBN 9780738758312 (ebook)
Subjects: LCSH: Druids and druidism.
Classification: LCC BL910 .H55 2019 (print) | LCC BL910 (ebook) | DDC
  299/.16--dc23
LC record available at https://lccn.loc.gov/2019023274
LC ebook record available at https://lccn.loc.gov/2019023275

Llewellyn Publications
A Division of Llewellyn Worldwide Ltd.
2143 Wooddale Drive
Woodbury, MN 55125-2989
www.llewellyn.com

Printed in the United States of America

Dedication

To my mother, father, sister, brother, and extended family—you all mean so much to me.

To my readers for being with me on this journey and supporting my work. My deepest regards and thanks.

Disclaimer

Contents

PART THREE: STUDY

PART FOUR: SKILLS AND TECHNIQUE

Introduction

*S*he walks toward the hedge, the boundary that separates the farmer's field from the village, a line that runs down to a wooded area and the heathland beyond. When she reaches the hedge of hawthorn, blackthorn, and dog rose, a triad of wild and native plants that hold ancient and special meaning, she smiles and reaches out to stroke a rose hip. The cool autumn breeze plays in her hair, whipping it around her face as the sun spills its light in waves across the landscape, the sky dotted with huge fluffy clouds. It is harvest time, when nature's abundance is at its peak. She feels the strength of the ancestors flowing through her blood and bones and hears their song in the wind. She says a quick prayer to the ancestors and blesses the land and the ongoing harvest, even as the sound of heavy farm machinery floats upon the breeze.

She turns and follows the hedgerow down to the little woodland, a special place that bursts with bluebells in the spring. In this place she stands for a moment, utterly still, listening to the sounds of the spirits of place: the robins and blackbirds, a pheasant squawking, a hawk crying high overhead, riding the thermals. This is the edge—where the hedge meets the wild, where the known meets the unknown; the civilised comes up against the wild. Here, at the edge, is the special place, the in-between place. This is where she belongs.

Inviting the power of the ancestors to flow through her, inviting the gods and goddesses that she loves, inviting the spirits of place to join with her intention, she turns three times anticlockwise and sings. Once she has stopped, she knows that she walks between the worlds, that the Otherworld is all around her and she can seek its wisdom and guidance, while testing her courage and her wits. Here she will find the answer to help her in her quest. Here she will find the inspiration, known to the Druids as awen. Here is where the magic happens. Here she walks as a Hedge Druid.

Druidry is a deeply fulfilling earth-based spirituality. Western spiritual traditions often differ from, say, Eastern traditions in that they can be a more solo affair. Our mythology is filled with tales of a hero or heroine on a quest, and it is that quest which seems to be a recurring theme. There are challenges and people to help along the way, but on the whole the quest must be fulfilled by the seeker and the seeker alone. With Buddhism, one often has a community, a sangha, a teacher to go to, monasteries and abbeys, and more. Western Paganism is a bit different, but fast growing with events, organisations, festivals, schools, colleges, and more. Perhaps in our lifetime we will see the equivalent of Pagan monasteries and abbeys, where the priesthood or those wishing to live a life entirely dedicated to their Pagan religion is sanctioned, widely accepted, and has community financial support. However, the point remains that the solo quest has been and most likely will always be central to Western Paganism.

This quest can be seen in many different ways. It could be a quest to find the true nature of the self. It could be a quest on behalf of another person, or a spiritual quest to find communion and integrate with the gods, a form of mysticism if you will. Often we are seeking to bring disparate parts of our own soul back together, to find the whole once again, to bring a holistic view into our ever-increasing disparate and isolationist society. When we find the whole within our own self, we find the whole within the community and the world.

Druidry is no exception. Druidry is the quest to find our place in the world and to work in the world in balance and harmony. It is being a part of a functioning ecosystem, to learn its ways and find how we too can be a contributing member. We might be seeking the divine in order to build that bridge that allows us to understand how to find our place in the world, or we might be trying to connect with our ancestors and their knowledge of the world. We might look to the spirits of place or to the Fair Folk for guidance and inspiration on how to walk in this world and the Otherworld, in balance and for the benefit of all. For the Otherworld is also a part of this world, overlaying it and offering a different perspective on the nature of things. We need this different perspective in order to step outside of our narrow human-centric perspective, to enable us to see the bigger picture. And so we might quest to the Otherworld as well, to gain this broader viewpoint, finding guides and companions that can provide knowledge and insight for us to take back into this world.

What is most important is that one actually begins the quest. So often we can just think about it, contemplate it, talk about it, but not actual *do* anything about it. We must be bold and take those first steps and then have the fortitude to see it through. Should our paths turn away from our original goal, then we must pursue those if we feel that is the right thing to do. But as long as we are walking on the path, as long as we are actually doing the work and not just thinking about it, then we are on the mythic quest that is so much a part of our Western heritage.

Along the way, we will find great joy and sadness, great courage and great fear. We will face those parts of ourselves that we would rather hide away. We will also acknowledge our gifts, talents, and abilities and be able to use them to their best advantage. But we cannot do it if we are not actively engaged on the quest. So be bold, take those first steps and see where they may lead, for no one else can walk the path for you. Great adventure awaits!

I hope to share with you in this work the inspiration and knowledge that I have received over the years. May you find the path rise to meet your feet; may you walk it with integrity and honour.

An áit a bhuil do chroí is ann a thabharfas do chosa thú.
(Your feet will bring you to where your heart is.)

Part One
THEORY

Here is where we explore the theory behind Druidry. We will look at who the Druids were and who they are today. We will look at different concepts and cosmology in the Druid tradition, such as the awen, the gods, the ancestors, the Otherworld, and more. We look more closely at what it means to be a Hedge Druid and the importance of the Hedge in the tradition. We also look at the festivals celebrated in Druidry, following the Wheel of the Year as well as the cycle of the moon. We will also look at meditation, prayer, magic, and animism within the Druid tradition. These concepts form the basic grounding of the Druid tradition; the theory behind the practice.

Chapter 1

The Druids

There weren't always Druids in the world. The Druids have had their name from the Iron Age onward. What they were called before then we simply do not know. What we do know is that they held a high status in the community, advising kings, divining auguries, healing the sick, and more. The accounts that we have are still rather scarce, however. The Druids followed an oral tradition, believing strongly in the power of memory and recall in order to follow their path. What was written down was done so by often opposing forces, such as the Romans, and therefore we have to take what was said about the Druids with a pinch of salt.

I think that it is fairly safe to assume that before Druidry there was a sha-manistic/animistic religion or spirituality practiced here in the British Isles and even before they became an island nation. From the retreat of the last Ice Age, when the land known as Doggerland (that connected Great Britain to the continent) became flooded beneath the North Sea on the east coast of England, there has evolved a different people, a different way of life. The people that lived in the British Isles became changed from those on the continent, though they still held very similar beliefs. Sharing an ancient prehistoric ancestral root, they still continued to evolve and adapt to their surroundings and so their religion was shaped by the new islands upon which they lived, as all religions are shaped by their environment. One theory is that Druidry evolved from the indigenous spirituality of the British Isles and was influenced by the Celts.

There is another theory that the Celts brought Druidry with them as they traversed westward across Europe. With this theory, Druidry did not originate in Britain. There are a couple of schools of thought on that matter. One point of view that meets halfway is that there still continued to be a religious practice on the British Isles since the Stone Age and beyond, which then evolved much later into Druidry with the influence of the migrating Iron Age Celts, an amalgam that eventually evolved to what we have today. In this theory, there is no unbroken lineage of Druidry per se, but an evolution of religious practice much like everywhere else in the world. The Celts may have brought ideas with them that shaped the Druidry of the Iron Age, as other religions today influence Modern Druidry, such as concepts from Native American animistic traditions or even exploring the Indo-European shared roots through the Vedic traditions of the East. Others might say that the Celts came to these islands and brought their fully fledged Druid tradition with them. Neither theory has been proven or unproven, though the former feels more correct to me.

The megalithic stone temples and prehistoric monuments were built right up until around 1400 BCE before the Celts arrived in Britain. It is still debated whether the proto-Celts (who may have arrived around 2000 BCE) were associated with these temples or not, but if so, then it is possible that a form of Druidry associated with them has existed since before recorded history began. However, opinion is still divided and many scholars seem to hold that the Celts came to these isles in waves of "invasions," who had no recent link to the Stone Age or Bronze Age Britons of the time or to their religious traditions. We have no definitive answers and can only go by our instinct based upon the evidence we have.

Druidry historically can be found throughout the British Isles, as well as in other places throughout Europe such as ancient Gaul, an area that covered a large region of Western Europe during the Iron Age period. It was inhabited by Celtic tribes and encompassed present-day France, Luxembourg, most of Switzerland, Belgium, and Northern Italy. It also contained parts of the Netherlands and Germany on the west bank of the Rhine.

Julius Caesar and Diodorus Siculus recorded their perceptions of the Druids in the first century BCE. From these Classical sources, much of Modern Druidry draws its knowledge. The Druids were the priest caste of Celtic society, exempt from service in war among other privileges. Indeed, the image of the wise Druid worshipping in a grove in a forest comes from these Classical sources. So too, of course, does images of burning people alive in wicker constructs and horrible other means of sacrifice. We just don't know what is truth and what is fiction, what is fact and what is Roman propaganda.

Christianity came to these shores in the fifth century, and another layer of gloss was added to the story of the Druids. Many earthly energies and powers of nature became canonised as saints, such as the goddess Brighid becoming Saint Brigit. Churches were built upon ancient pagan sites of worship. Some claim that a form of Druidry merged with Christianity, forming a Christic path known as Culdee. In Ireland at this time, Christian monks began recording the ancient laws, for which we are very grateful, but again we have to accept that it is from a differing perspective and religious tradition that they are derived, with its own biases and prejudices. We also have to recognise what they don't say, what they haven't recorded. Much of the Welsh mythology was recorded and written down at this time, and we have to differentiate the older teachings and nature-based ways of being from these Christianised accounts.

The seventeenth and eighteenth centuries saw the Druid Revival, stemming from a Romantic notion of Druidry in an era when industrialisation of the country was becoming rampant. It was a reaction to the factories as much as a longing to return to the ancient traditions of these isles. Coloured by pastoral poetry and art and led by early proto-archaeologists such as William Stukely, they jumped to many conclusions while creating a very structured nature-based religion. However, the gods of nature and nature itself are never as ordered as we would like to have them.

In more recent history—the 1940s and 1950s—two men, Gerald Gardner and Ross Nichols, joined the Ancient Druid Order, which began in the early twentieth century. Between them they came up with the eight festivals that are now celebrated in modern Western Paganism, largely in the traditions of Druidry and Wicca, based upon their knowledge and research of older, pre-Christian traditions mainly from a Celtic source. Gerald Gardner became the father of modern Wicca and Ross Nichols became the figurehead for Modern Druidry and chief of the Order of Bards, Ovates and Druids (OBOD). Gardner and Nichols were good friends and shared many thoughts and beliefs, hence you will see many similarities today between Modern Druidry and Wicca. An example of this is in the three strands of Druidry (Bards, Ovates, and Druids) found in OBOD and other Druid systems and the three levels of initiation found in modern Wicca (first, second, and third degree Witches). The eight holy days are shared, four of which are ancient Celtic festivals, as well as the honouring of the phases of the moon in most traditions. Much of the mythology stems from British/Celtic sources and concepts. There is a similar belief in reincarnation and the afterlife which is also apparent in both traditions. The list goes on…

So, how old is Druidry then?

Modern Druidry dates back to Ross Nichols in the middle of last century. How long does the spirit of Druidry go back in time? Who knows! A religion is always evolving, adapting, and changing, especially a religion of nature. Nature changes with the seasons, times of light and darkness, and the ebb and the flow of the tide. We could follow some of those threads all the way back to the Stone Age and beyond if we wished, but they are only threads and not the whole tapestry.

There was a school of thought, which is now changing, that antiquity equated to validity. Yet just because something is old doesn't mean it's right or relevant. The threads of Druidry could be very ancient indeed, as ancient as the first time humans walked upon these lands or older, because the powers of nature are as old as nature itself, regardless of whether humans have worshipped it or not. We must learn all that we can from history, even when it is ever-changing with new light and facts coming to the fore. But we should not confuse antiquity with validity on a spiritual path. Things evolve all the time. Things become outdated, irrelevant, and sometimes even illegal.

Modern Druidry is seeing a large increase in numbers, especially since the 1990s and the coming of the new millennium. There are many more writers on the subject being published and many more different voices being heard. From the late nineties onward, women's voices began to be heard again in the community (for there were always female Druids in ancient times, though during the Victorian era and to the latter half of the twentieth century era, men dominated), offering their perspective, their experience, and their knowledge, both academic and experiential. Today we very much have a balanced form of Druidry, where men and women are equally represented, but that hasn't always been the case. Starting with the coming of the Romans and then Christians, women in religion, politics, and many other places have taken a back seat, not holding any authority or power. But today we are seeing the balance being redressed in Modern Paganism and in Druidry, despite women's power still being under secular threat from governments even such as our own today.

The world stands at the precipice, where the urge to hold on to power without service provides one with the empty comfort of rewarding the ego. Those rewards are sugary little sweets that have no substance, no meaning. They are empty, devoid of nourishment. Only when we take responsibility for all the damage that we have done and seek to redress the balance will we ever survive. Even though we claim assurances from modern science, still we are very afraid, very afraid of everything. We think we are not afraid of nature; that we have controlled it, but anyone witnessing a tsunami or earthquake knows otherwise. We are still monkeys, running around scared for the most part, reacting to our world instead of acting with intention. We react to protect our egos, our sense of self. But only when we realise that there is no separate self, that we are all related, will that fear leave us.

That is the essence of Druidry. It is connection, being part of an ecosystem, weaving the threads of inspiration, and finding our place in the world, in the here and now, in harmony, and with respect.

The Hedge Druid

The Hedge Druid is a more recent term that applies to someone who walks the Druid path for the most part alone, using their wit and intelligence, the wisdom gained from long hours of research and practical experience in order to create their own tradition that is right for them and their environment. The term "hedge" when applied to Druidry stems from the nineteenth-century term "hedge priest," which denoted a priest of the Christian faith who did not follow a particular or established tradition, had no church per se and who preached "from the hedgerow." The term was first applied to Witchcraft in Modern Paganism and popularised by the author Rae Beth. The term then spread to Druidry and became synonymous with solitary practitioners, who were not part of any order, grove, group, or other established sect. Not all solitary practitioners of Druidry would call themselves Hedge Druids; however, it is a term that is growing in popularity. In this work I shall show how Hedge Druidry goes beyond the notion of a solitary practitioner into something that is deeper and more connected to the natural world.

The Hedge Druid is also one who rides the Hedge, who travels between the worlds, who works with boundaries and the liminal places where the edges blend and meet. The term "hedge riding" is a practice found in the Pagan community, mostly in Witchcraft traditions. It stems from the German word *hagazissa,* which means "hedge sitter." The Saxon term is *haegtessa* and both are where we get our word "hag." Someone who rides the Hedge can straddle the worlds, this world and the Otherworld, to bring back wisdom and information to use in our world, the Middleworld. We will learn more about the importance of the Hedge and also hedge riding in later chapters. Suffice it to say that the work with the boundaries of the civilised world as well as that which lies beyond the hedgerow is the world of the Hedge Druid, connecting and weaving together those threads to shape the world and find balance and harmony with the whole. It is the known world and the wilderness beyond that shapes and informs our earth-based tradition.

For me, Druidry is mostly a solitary path, though I do belong to some Druid orders and networks and celebrate the seasons with a few friends. But the everyday Druidry, the currents of intention that flow through me, my home, and the landscape where I live, is my main focus. It is a mostly solitary pursuit. Like learning, I always preferred to do it on my own, rather than working with a group, for I found that my concentration was higher and I could have a deeper level of experience than I could with the influence of others upon my work. The day-to-day living of my Druid path is what is most important, punctuated by the celebration of the seasons and festivals with others.

Of course, we are never truly solitary creatures, but in this sense I am using the word "solitary" with regards to other humans. I am never truly solitary, for I am always surrounded by nature and all its creatures every single second of my life. I am always a part of an interconnected web of existence. Living this connection, weaving the threads of my life to that of my environment and all that exists within it, means that there is no separation, no isolation. Yet, when asked to describe my path, I use the term solitary or Hedge Druid in the sense that I prefer to find such connection on my own, without other humans around. Why this should be so is perhaps due to my nature: naturally shy and sensitive to noise, light, barometric pressure, and other phenomena; it is just easier to be "alone" most of the time.

It is similar to the path of the mystic or a monastic. The path of the mystic is much the same; a solitary path where personal connection to the divine is the central focus. Some would say that the mystic path is the search for the nature of reality. For me, Druidry is the search for reality within nature and so the two can walk hand in hand down this forest path. There are many elements of mysticism in my everyday life, where the songs of the land and the power of the gods flow through me, the knowledge from the ancestors deep within my blood and deep within the land upon which I live, rooted in its soil and sharing its stories on the breeze. To hold that connection, day in and day out, to live life fully within the threads of that tapestry is what I aspire to do, each and every moment. Sometimes a thread is dropped and it requires a deep mindfulness to restore it, but practice helps when we search for those connecting threads, becoming easier with time and patience both with the world and with your own self.

The monastic, however, retreats from the world to connect with the essence of the divine. There is a deliberate intention to be separate from the so-called "mundane" world or secular culture. However, within Druidry we realise that there is no such thing as mundane, and the duality between the physical and the spiritual is something that is anathema to the tradition. Learning how to be in the world is of great value, even as great value is found in being alone. For some, I'm sure a monastic Druid tradition would be a most agreeable way to live, but for most they prefer to work *in* the world rather than *separate* from it, because they understand that separation is merely an illusion. Most non-gregarious Druids would prefer the path of the mystic rather than the monastic for that very reason. The mystic seeks integration, the monastic separation.

Yet both have many other similarities. Both seek to release the vice-like grip we have on our sense of self, the ego that we try to protect at all costs. The dissolution of the ego can be seen as at the heart of many Eastern traditions. Druidry teaches us integration, our ego perhaps not dissolving but blending in with that of our own environment. We don't think less of ourselves but rather think of ourselves less. The animism that is a large part of Druidry for many helps us to see the sacredness of all existence, and in doing so we are not seeking annihilation, but integration. We can perhaps dissolve the notions and outdated perceptions that we have, both about the world and about ourselves, leaving the self to find its own edges and then blending in to the world around us, truly becoming part of an ecosystem where selflessness is not altruistic, but necessary for the survival of the system.

The flowing inspiration (otherwise known as the awen) where soul touches soul and the edges melt away into an integrated way of being has always been at the heart of Druidry. The three drops of inspiration or wisdom from the goddess Ceridwen's cauldron contain that connection; they contain the awen that, with enough practice, is accessible to all. We have to spend time brewing our own cauldron of inspiration, filling it with both knowledge and experience before we can taste the delicious awen upon our lips. Some prefer to do this with others; some prefer to do so alone.

It is easier to quiet the noise of humanity and of our own minds when we are alone without distraction. Notice I said "easier" and not "easy," because again it takes practice. But time spent alone, daily connecting and reweaving the threads that we have dropped, can help us create a wonderful, rich tapestry that inspires us to continue in our journey through life, whatever may happen along the way. Though the solitary path might not be for everyone, having these moments of solitude can be a great tool for deep learning, working on your own as well as working within a group, grove, or order. Sometimes we need to remove ourselves from the world in order to better understand it and then come back into the fold with a new awareness and integration filled with awen.

The Hedge Druid is not afraid to be alone, nor with others, but seeks deep and utter integration in the world. Being a Hedge Druid requires determination in seeking out the ancient and modern lore and finding what aspects resonate within our soul. Not everything ancient is valid today and not all modern aspects have integrity. We need to take a step back from declaring authenticity when there is doubt and instead search for validity in our spiritual path. The Hedge Druid learns to walk her path with integrity, with solid research and experiential wisdom. She does the work, in the physical as well as the academic. Our learning is our own personal responsibility, and I hope that this book helps you on your way. Throughout, we will glimpse little snapshots of a Hedge Druid as she goes about her path honouring the natural world around her, filled with wonder and enchantment.

She closes the book, her hand running down the front cover, feeling the energy of the words flowing through her mind. She thinks about the history, what the ancients may have seen, what they may have done. She takes in

a deep breath and knows that she will never stop learning, whether from books, friends, strangers, or personal experience. She looks out the window and sees a blackbird, the Druid dubh, alight upon the branches of the elder tree. It begins to sing its evening song as the village settles into quiet. She nods to herself and says a prayer of blessing on her work and research before heading into the kitchen to make some tea.

Chapter 2

The Awen

The awen symbol is based on an original design by the eighteenth- to nineteenth-century Druid revivalist, Iolo Morganwg. It consists of three lines falling to the right, centre, and left. Modern Druidry incorporates the original source point of three dots, which can either be seen as points of light or drops from the cauldron of the goddess Ceridwen. The awen symbol represents, among other things, the triple nature of the Druid path, incorporating the paths of Bard, Ovate, and Druid. It is not an ancient symbol, but a modern Druid symbol, used widely by Druids the world over, regardless of their opinion on Iolo and his work.

The first recorded reference to the awen occurs in Nennius's *Historia Brittonum*, a Latin text of circa 796 CE. "Talhearn Tad Awen won renown in poetry" is where we first see the word, and it tells us that Talhearn is the "father of awen" in this instance. Sadly, this source tells us nothing more about Talhearn as being the father of awen, but perhaps later research may discover more clues about this reference.

A common translation of the Welsh word *awen* is "flowing inspiration" or "flowing poetry/poetic insight." Awakening to our own energy and stretching out toward the energy of nature around us, we begin to see just what is the awen. It is an opening of one's self, of one's spirit or soul, in order to truly and very deeply see and connect to all life around us. When we are open, we can receive that divine gift, the inspiration that flows, whether it is from deity, nature, or whatever it is that you choose to focus on.

Awen

For awen to exist, there must be relationship. We cannot be inspired unless we are open, and we cannot be open unless we have established a relationship, whether that is with the thunder, the blackbird, or a god. It is cyclical in nature; we open and give of ourselves, and in doing so, we receive—and vice versa. Letting go, releasing into that flow of awen, allows it to flow ever more freely and we find ourselves inspired not only in fits and bursts of enlightenment or inspiration, but all the time, carrying that essence of connection and wonder with us. There is, of course, a line to be drawn, for we can't be off our heads in ecstatic relationship with everything all the time. As with all language, a literal translation can be far too limiting. It's good to have a context and some sort of description to relate the concept, but when confined to literalism, we get stuck and are unable to see the bigger picture. Awen does mean flowing inspiration, but what is inspiration?

A really good idea, a bolt from the blue, is one interpretation; however, there are many others. Inspiration is not just something that happens to us. It is something that we can cultivate—in true relationship. We are not subject to the whims of inspiration but rather can access that inspiration on a daily basis through deep relationship. Indeed, awen is all about relationship, more than it being "a really good idea." When we literally translate awen into inspiration, we can lose that context of relationship. With good relationship, we will have good ideas.

When soul touches soul, there is an energy, a source of inspiration. When we are aware of our soul interacting with other souls, we can harness that inspiration and see it in everything that we do. It doesn't just happen every now and then like a bolt out of the blue, but rather is in everything that we do. It requires a willingness for deep relationship and a desire to be mindful in all our relationships.

This may sound a lot like Eastern philosophy, being very mindful. Mindfulness is a large part of many Eastern philosophies, but I am sure that it has been around as long as human self-awareness has been around. Indeed, it may have been a large part of ancient Druidry, now lost to the mists of time. Taking inspiration from Eastern traditions with regards to our way of thinking is not much different from reading the works of Nietzsche or Plato. There is no monopoly on wisdom.

Mindfulness relates to awen in that when we are aware of our relationship to the world, when we see how we fit in the world, we can work in harmony with the world. We become an integral and integrated part of an ecosystem, where we know that everything that we do matters to the system in its entirety. The discipline gained from such mindfulness as practiced in the Eastern traditions and philosophies can be a great teacher in expanding our minds and helping us to learn more about ourselves. That also goes for other religions and philosophies as well. I'm sure the ancient Druids, just as much as Modern Druids today, loved reading about world religions and discussing philosophy.

There is a lot of talk about cultural appropriation in Modern Paganism, however, and it's something that needs to be carefully considered. We do have to be aware of when we are taking something from another culture without its proper context and permission. Nevertheless, with religions or traditions such as Buddhism, for example, the Buddha said that enlightenment was for anyone to achieve, available to all, regardless of where they came from, whatever their background. It's why we see so many different forms of Buddha being represented in sculpture. We have fat Buddhas from China, giant slim standing Buddhas in India, reclining Buddhas in Myanmar, sitting Buddhas carved straight out of the rock temples in Sri Lanka, elegant bronze-plated Buddhas in Japan, and so on. In each country the Buddha looks different, as Buddha is within each and every person as well as having been a person in his own right. There is even a female Buddha known as Tara in Vajrayana Buddhism.

You will find that Druidry has much in common with many other earth-based religions the world over, as well as many philosophies, both ancient and modern. We can be inspired by these and let them help us to change our perception, our way of seeing the world, from a self-centred point of view to a more holistic worldview, from a less human-centred perspective to one that is more integrated. In that, we are living the awen.

Awen is that spark set off by interaction, by integration. We do not exist in a bubble. We are surrounded by the world at all times, by the seen and the unseen. When we live integrated, we see the meaning that each relationship has and that inspires us to live our lives accordingly. That inspiration is the heart and soul of Druidry.

Inspiration: to inspire, from the Latin *inspirare*, the act of breathing.

Indeed, it has many connotations to breath and breathing. Awen can connect us to the world through the very act of breathing. All living things breathe in some form on this planet. The human species shares this breath, breathing in the oxygen created on this planet and exhaling it into the twilight. The air that we breathe has been recycled by plants and creatures for billions of years. The breath is the gateway to the ancestors and to a deep understanding of the nature of awen. Awen is also shared inspiration, for we share this planet with everything else on it. Everything that we do has an impact—every breath we take, every action that we make. Breath links us to everything else.

When we remember that deep connection to everything else, we cannot help but be inspired. And we hope to inspire in return, much as our own exhalation is valuable to trees and plants who take in the carbon dioxide, turning it to oxygen for our own breath. Inspiration and expiration, inhalation and exhalation are all words for the act of breathing. Remembering the shared breath of the world, we come home to ourselves and rediscover the wonder and awe of existence. Then, we are truly inspired.

So where does the flowing inspiration of Modern Druidry come from then? And what is the difference between awen and the energy that is in all life?

In Welsh, we can trace it back to the nineteenth century, where *aw* means "flowing" or "fluidity" and *wen* is "spirit" or a "being." We can more easily trace the concept and word back to medieval texts retelling the tale of Ceridwen and Taliesin.

The goddess Ceridwen was brewing a special potion for her son, Afagddu, tended by Gwion Bach. Some of the brew bubbled over and three drops scalded Gwion as he stirred the pot, so he put his thumb into his mouth to ease the soreness, taking in the magic of the brew meant for Afagddu. Ceridwen was enraged and chased him, eventually eating him and then giving birth to him again. After she gives birth to him, she sets him on a boat and he was discovered alive and well later and renamed Taliesin, for his radiant brow. He becomes the most famous Bard of Britain.

The awen can be seen as being achieved through a deep connection to every aspect of the land, in whatever shape or form. We can undergo a kind of initiation into the awen much as Gwion Bach did, through the goddess Ceridwen and her special brew. We can drink from the cauldron of inspiration, but with that come great trials and tribulations that go hand in hand with awareness and enlightenment.

The awen is also related to water and rivers and not just the liquid brewed in Ceridwen's cauldron. In the medieval poem "The Hostile Confederacy" from the *Book of Taliesin*, it states:

> *The Awen I sing,*
> *From the deep I bring it,*
> *A river while it flows,*
> *I know its extent;*
> *I know when it disappears;*
> *I know when it fills;*
> *I know when it overflows;*
> *I know when it shrinks;*

I know what base
There is beneath the sea.[1]

The awen relates to water on so many levels. The flowing spirit of water and the flowing spirit of awen share many similarities. Both are fluid, able to be contained, and yet have their own freedom in their inherent sense of being. They follow their own currents and can be beneficial when used with respect. When we follow the currents of life, the interconnectedness of all things, we share that flow of awen and then come to know the fathomless depths that it can bring.

We have the shamanic diviners in the Welsh tradition known as *Awenyddion*, and there is awen involved in divination and the quest for relationship with the divine. The awen is a vast subject that requires much study, but more to the point, it requires experience. We can research the similarities between awen and the Hindu aspects of *shakti*, for example, or the Dao in Chinese philosophy. But we must feel the awen with every atom of our being in order the truly understand it.

What is the difference between awen and the energy of life or the life force? I would say that awen is the thread that connects us to that life force. When we connect in good relationship to the world around us, those threads shimmer with awen, with inspiration. We know that we are a part of the web, wholly and utterly connected. When we feel that connection with other beings, soul to soul, and our sense of self lessens, we are inspired by that connection. We then think of ourselves less and our perception opens out to a wider perspective on the world—one that is more inclusive rather than just our own self-centred point of view. We become a thread in the web.

Awen helps us to see beyond ourselves and perhaps paradoxically to allow us to see ourselves in everything. When we see that we are a part of a whole, we are inspired. When we lessen the sense of self, we are able

1. Mary Jones, "The Hostile Confederacy," *Book of Taliesin VII*, The Celtic Literature Collective, accessed January 12, 2018, http://www.maryjones.us/ctexts/t07.html.

to perceive so much more. When we have expanded our worlds to include everything within it, we become the awen. The poet Amergin described this beautifully in what is now known as the "Song of Amergin."

I am the wind on the sea;
I am the wave of the sea;
I am the bull of seven battles;
I am the eagle on the rock;
I am a flash from the sun;
I am the most beautiful of plants;
I am a strong wild boar;
I am a salmon in the water;
I am a lake in the plain;
I am the word of knowledge;
I am the head of the spear in battle;
I am the god that puts fire in the head;
Who spreads light in the gathering on the hills?
Who can tell the ages of the moon?
Who can tell the place where the sun rests?[2]

Many Druid rituals begin or end with singing or chanting the awen. When doing so, the word is stretched to three syllables, sounding like *ah-oo-wen*. It is a lovely sound, which opens up the heart and soul. Sung or chanted together or in rounds, it simply flows, as its namesake determines. Our hearts can open if we let them when chanting or singing the awen.

Yet I am sure that the awen is different for each and every Druid. The connection and the resulting expression of that connection, the Druid's own creativity, can be so vast and diverse. It is what is so delicious about it; we inhale the awen and exhale our own creativity in song, in dance, in books, in protest marches. The possibilities are endless, as is the awen itself.

---

2. Lady Gregory, *The Essential Lady Gregory Collection*, Google Books, accessed January 13, 2018, https://books.google.co.uk/books?id=fx0tOGYDZXQC&dq.

We are never born and we can never die: we are simply manifest for a while in one form and then we manifest again in another when the conditions are right. For me, this represents reincarnation—the nitty gritty basics and the science behind it. The threads that bind all this together are the awen.

The Hedge Druid sits in the back garden, the soft spring sunlight upon her shoulders. The scent of the earth is rising, mingling with the sunny smell of the daffodils that beam out at her from beneath the beech tree. She can feel the energy rising, the energy of the land. It is both within and without, all around her and also deep inside her soul. She puts her hand upon the mossy ground and feels the connecting threads that run through this land, the threads of awen that bind everything together. She is at once in her back garden and in the stone circle of Avebury, as well as on Glastonbury Tor and in the field behind her parents' house. She rides the currents of awen, of connection, and in her soul she is inspired. She feels the flowing spirit of the universe and hums along to the tune.

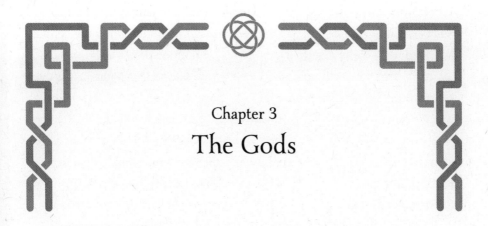

Chapter 3

The Gods

Who are the gods in Druidry? This is a vast question with many different levels of interpretation. I will offer my own view here, on what makes a god (when I use the term *god*, I am referring to deity of any gender, both and none), how we can honour the gods in our lives and create a relationship with deity that provides us with awen. If you are an atheist or prefer to not work with the gods, then please feel free to proceed to the next chapter. I will recount my own experiences with deity, in all shapes and forms, and encourage you to seek out your own should you so wish.

First let's define what is a god. In Druidry, we work with the ancestors and the spirits of place and these can often become interwoven with concepts of deity, their stories, and their form. As a Hedge Druid, I can make up my own mind about what constitutes deity and what does not, based on both research and experience. For me, deity can be several things. It can be a collective energy of a place in nature. It can also be a collective energy of human nature, such as love, anger, compassion, or time. I prefer to work with a less anthropocentric view toward deity, but when viewing concepts such as love or anger as deity, it can be very illuminating. Deity can also be the collective energy of ancestral stories, where we find named gods in the old tales, such as Brighid or Lugh, Taranis, or Nemetona.

Examples of the collective energy of a place in nature would be the god of the heath upon which I walk and work or the god of the North Sea that rolls up and down the coastline where I live. Some of these deities are named and some are not. The god of the heathland has no name or has not shared one with me. The god of the North Sea is sometimes known as Nehalennia, a female deity depicted on altars found in the Netherlands, just across the water from where I live on the Suffolk coast. Sometimes the North Sea is just the North Sea with all its murky waters and shallow depths, an ancient land bridge to the continent lying beneath its waves. When a deity is the collective energy of a place in nature, it is the sum total of all the parts. The parts may consist of the spirits of place (those who live there: animal, vegetable, mineral), the ancestors (again, animal, vegetable, or mineral), beings and Fair Folk from the Otherworld, and more. (More on these subjects in subsequent chapters.)

Some collective energies of human nature can be seen as deity in order to have a better relationship with that energy. Sometimes putting some specifications on an energy allows us to better relate to it. With nature, it's often easier to communicate to an anthropomorphised deity of the sun seen as a shining male god brandishing a spear of light than it is to honour a huge ball of gas. We can apply that as well to the collective energy of human nature and so we may see a version of "Father Time" when we work with the collective energy or the concept of time. There are anthropomorphised gods of love, war, fertility, and more, which help us to relate to these somewhat abstract concepts. For some, there is no need to humanise this energy and simply see it as a flow or current that runs through humanity accessing it, harnessing it, or working with it.

The named gods of mythology and folklore are, combined, the collective energy of ancestral stories, tales that have been passed down from generation to generation, shared among tribes and peoples. This energy might originally have started as a collective energy of nature or human nature and become something that now represents the concept—to be passed down along the lineage of human beings and encompassing a broad spectrum of associations. Brighid may have once started as a goddess of fire or of sacred springs or of healing and has since developed into an anthropomorphised goddess who shares all these attributes and more, with her own stories of how she came about with her powers and of bestowing them upon others. These tales are told, spread from tribe to tribe, eventually creating a deity that is recognised widely, but perhaps having different names. Brighid is also known as Brig, Brigantia, Brigit, Brighde, Bride, Braint, Ffraint, and more. They may have taken on many attributes; Brighid is the goddess of poets, healers, blacksmiths, the season of spring, sovereignty, fire, sacred wells, and more.

So why do we need or create gods of any specification?

As stated earlier, it is often easier to connect with an abstract energy or concept when we deify and anthropomorphise it. In doing so, we can talk to it, worship it, and work with the energy. It becomes personal. When we correlate a deity with a gender, we are expanding this notion even further and so the goddess Rhiannon might become an important deity for all women to consider—or Morrigan or Andraste. We might find a strong kinship with their stories, tales that resonate and reflect our own lives and experiences back to us, perhaps even providing us with guidance on how to get through the difficult times or how to receive the awen, how to live life fully, and how to die honourably.

There are many different forms of incorporating deity into Druid practice. Many Druids are pantheists, where the entirety of the universe is a connected manifestation of deity. We also have polytheism, which is the veneration of more than one deity or many deities, perhaps in a pantheon. Many Druids would advise working in a single pantheon, if one is to work with more than one deity, in order to keep the energy clear. Some deities from differing pantheons might not work very well together—then again, they just might. It worked for the Romans, who incorporated many British deities into their pantheon. When in Rome … or in Britain … or Gaul …

Most Druids also work with deities associated with Celtic religion and spirituality, although some have incorporated other deities. To each their own. Some examples of deity found in the Druid tradition are listed below:

Irish Deities

- Brighid—goddess of healing, poetry, smithcraft, fire, sacred wells, sovereignty
- Lugh—a many-skilled god, associated with the festival Lughnasadh, where he honours his mother, Tailtiu
- Danu—mother goddess of the Tuatha Dé Danann, associated with water
- Morrigan—The Great Queen, goddess of battle and regeneration
- Manannán mac Lir—god of the sea and guardian of the Otherworld
- Dagda—god of fertility, magic, renewal
- Tailtiu—goddess of agriculture, fertility, harvest

Welsh Deities

- Arianrhod—Lady of the Silver Wheel, of the starry heavens
- Llŷr—god of the sea
- Gwyn Ap Nudd—ruler of the Otherworld, Annwn, and King of the Faeries or the Tylwyth Teg
- Blodeuwedd—goddess of transformation, liberation
- Ceridwen—goddess of rebirth, initiation, and inspiration
- Gofannon—god of smithcraft

Gaulish and Brythonic Deities

- Belenus—god of the sun, light
- Cernnunos—lord of wild animals, the Underworld
- Andraste—goddess of victory, the indominatable one
- Coventina—goddess of wells and springs
- Taranis—god of thunder
- Nodens—god of healing, the sea, and hunting and dogs
- Epona—goddess of fertility and all equine
- Nemetona—goddess of the sacred grove

This is but a short list of the many deities that can be found in the Druid tradition. The descriptions are only a part of the whole of each deity; they are much more than their popular associations. Deity is something to be experienced and not merely called upon due to his or her aspects or associations. When we work with deity, we must first establish a relationship. No one likes to be called up out of the blue by strangers, asking for this or that. No one likes to be known as just having one or two skills and that's all they're good for. No one likes to be pigeon-holed. We must truly come to learn all that we can about a deity and then reach out in order to experience fully. If we're very lucky, a deity might choose to work with us, but it is still up to us to find out all about them, to do the work and not just know them in name only.

Later in this book, we will design a ritual to dedicate yourself to a particular deity, should you so wish, working with them for however long a period. We will also meet in inner journeys with certain gods such as Gwynn ap Nudd, Herne, and Arianrhod. It is important that you have a personal connection with deity before choosing to dedicate yourself to a particular god or goddess. Perhaps some of these gods may become part of your life, perhaps not. Deity is an extremely personal experience and though you may find many similarities between your experience and that of others, you will also find differences. Those differences must be respected in your experience and in that of others. Do not put down someone else's experience because it does not match yours, for who is to say who is right and who is wrong? Only the gods themselves can determine that, and it may be that they choose to present themselves differently to each individual.

She prays by the light of the moon to her goddess, Andraste, lady of the land upon which she lives. She feels her energy in the moonlight, feels her breath upon the cold winter's breeze. An owl hoots in the ash tree and a dog barks once in the darkness. She feels the energy of her goddess all around her, enchanting her soul, filling her with awen. She knows she has a duty to this land, to her goddess, and she recites a blessing chant upon the pool of water

before her, which at other times doubles as a bird bath. She gazes into the water and sees aspects of her goddess appear: the flames of a fire, the shoreline of the beach, the sandy heath and heather-laden countryside, the swift movement of the adder, the utter stillness of the hare. She calls in her mind to her goddess and connects to her deeply, allowing her to imbue her spirit and her work with her blessing. When she is done, the Hedge Druid bows deeply to the full moon, honouring her for all that she is.

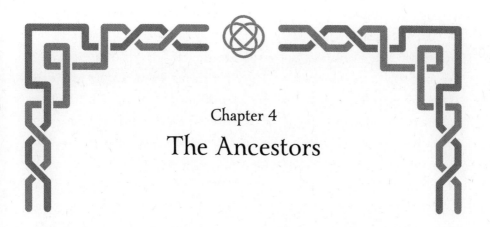

Chapter 4

The Ancestors

The ancestors are a very important part of Druidry. They have a lot to do with our moral and ethical framework. As we realise the interconnectedness of all things, we come to the point where we know that we are all related. We all came from the single-celled life forms that emerged from the oceans all those years ago. We have a shared ancestry. We also know that the world of the living is built upon the world of the dead. We cannot have life without death. The soil that we grow our food on is made of decomposed plant and animal matter, and so we honour the ancestors each and every day simply for the earth that we walk on, the food that we eat. We know that without the ancestors, without those who have gone before, we simply would not be.

However, most often when we are working with the ancestors, we think of our human ancestors. This might be because we can relate to our human ancestors, more easily than we can those single-celled organisms or, more recently, our ape ancestors. We still honour the fact that we would not exist were it not for *all* our ancestors, but for many, the focus lies on human ancestry and that is perfectly fine, as long as we remember our shared ancestry with all life forms.

In Druidry, with our human ancestors, we work with three different strands. We have ancestors of blood: those human ancestors with whom we are directly related. Yes, we are all related to each other if you go back far enough, but our blood ancestors help to narrow down the group a little bit in order to find a number that we can actually function with on a more intimate level. So we honour our parents and grandparents, our great grandparents, and so on, as far back as we can remember their names and their history. For their stories are also our stories, and their stories flow through our veins. If you are adopted, then you have two bloodlines from which you can work. You can honour your blood relatives, if you so choose. You can also honour the bloodline of your adoptive parents. You may want to work with both at the same time.

The second set of ancestors that we work with are the ancestors of place. These are the ancestors of our locality. As Druids, we need to learn the local history and geography of the place we call home. In doing so, we come to a deeper understanding of the place and of our place within that place, if you see what I mean. The ancestors of place are those who have gone before and who have lived upon this land. For example, in my home I have a large framed deed that came with the papers and other deeds to the land when we bought this house. This particular deed dates back to the reign of George III. Though this house is not that old, built as it was in the 1980s, the property has been owned by previous people for many hundreds of years. In framing the deed, I felt I was honouring the ancestors of place and could look at it every time I passed. I have other documents as well, which state that on this land where this very house was built were Victorian hovels set amidst apple orchards. It builds a very different picture from the view of the backyard today and yet is very much still a part of it. When I call to the ancestors of place, especially when I am outside at my altar, I can sometimes hear them, all these people who have lived here before. And I can smell the apple trees and hear laughter and tears, joy and sorrow. It brings back some of the past to live again on this land.

The third set of ancestors that we honour in Druidry are the ancestors of tradition, those spiritual ancestors whose faith, belief, work, or person has inspired us in our own journey. These could be modern-day Druids who do great work in the community or a teacher that we remember fondly who inspired us in our school years. It could be a religious figure or from any other tradition, such as Ghandi, Mother Teresa, or the Buddha. It could be an artist that inspires us. Some examples in my own work consist of honouring my Druid teachers in the tradition. I also honour brilliant artists, such as David Bowie. He taught me never to play to the gallery, to always do your art, to express your creativity, as something that is a part of you but also a part of the greater flow of inspiration, to not conform to ideas of normal. Another musical artist that I see as an ancestor of tradition is the Canadian musician and songwriter Loreena McKennitt. Yes, at the time of writing she is still alive, but she carries her own tradition forward and inspires others in much the same way as other artists from all different media can inspire. She leaves a legacy of inspiration and so ancestors of tradition can be those who are still living, those who inspire us right here, right now. For me, the way that Loreena McKennitt built her own business and how she worked to her own moral and ethical code and would not be swayed by what others in the music industry wanted her to be or told her to do was a great inspiration to me and still is today. It taught me to be my authentic self, to let that shine. To be practical as well as artistic. In a different vein, I also honour the Buddha's teachings. I honour a primary school grade teacher, a beautiful, warm, lovely woman from Barbados who taught me to simply be myself, who encouraged me to my strengths, who never had a harsh word for any student, and who always smelled of bananas and peanuts.

But what of the ancestors of blood or place or even tradition who were not lovely, inspiring people?

In our lives there are lovely people and not-so-lovely people. In our own families, we all have swindlers and con artists, murderers and rapists, thieves and scoundrels. We might not know them all, but we can be pretty sure that somewhere in our bloodline, there have been those who have lost their way. For some, the pain that it brings may be very recent. Some people might have had a parent, parents, or a step-parent who were abusive. In Druidry, we acknowledge the good and the bad in the world and seek to find a balance, a place where we can work to heal the wounds of the past and to make the world a better place for our descendants.

When dealing with issues of abuse or ancestors whose past is less than glowing, we can see our own faults and misgivings about ourselves within them. We can also work to release the energy created in the bloodline from these people, to heal ourselves, and to heal our bloodline. For example, I have a photo of a great-great-grandfather who sold his firstborn into indentured servitude in order to move back to Holland from the United States. Not exactly a shining example of fatherhood, in my opinion. My parents and my grandparents all have their faults, as do I. I can look at the history and learn from my bloodline. This brings compassion to the fore, as when we are working with our blood, we cannot divorce from them. We will always be related to them, no matter what. And so do we work with compassion, to heal the story, to tell the truth of the matter and then to work on making our own story one that will inspire others. We may need confrontation in order to change. Change, hurt, wounds, and confrontation are the stories of our struggles and our lives. But when we work with that, we can release the wounds created by them and find less and less of them in our lives as a whole.

If we look at the bigger picture, we can also bring a fourth strand of ancestors to the mix. These are the "ancestors" of the future, our descendants, those who will carry on after we have passed away and pass on their knowledge to their descendants. Descendants might be blood relatives or they might not be. These are the people who will inherit the world that we give them and in turn find their place alongside others. When we consider our descendants, as well as being guided by ancestors of blood, place, and tradition, then our Druidry is deeply rooted in time (however flexible we may consider the concept of time to be), in place, and in a deep sense of wakefulness.

I hope that I have shown just how important the ancestors are in the Druid tradition. Working with the ancestors can certainly change your life. The breath that we breathe is the same air that our ancestors breathed. It has passed through their lungs, and we can connect to them through our breath. It is wonderful, because it is a connection that we can take with us anywhere we are in the world. The breath is a wonderful tool of interconnectedness. Later in this book, we will do a ritual to connect with the ancestors.

We must know our own story in order to weave it into the wider story of all existence.

In the darkness before her altar, she breathes the air that her ancestors breathed all those years ago. She connects to her ancestors through her blood. She connects to the ancestors of this land through her dedication and commitment to it. She connects to the ancestors of tradition through her work. She knows that without them she is nothing; she would simply not be. Though she walks the path of her tradition alone, she knows that she will never be lonely, for the ancestors are always with her.

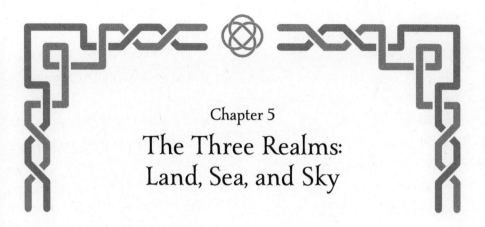

Chapter 5

The Three Realms:
Land, Sea, and Sky

The Celts loved triplicates. We see patterns of threes throughout Celtic religion and spirituality, and the three realms of land, sea, and sky are no exception. They are the foundation of everything, all that impacts our lives each and every second of each and every day. It is part of the cosmology of the Druid tradition that helps us to connect with the world around us, to quest the awen, and to find our place in the ecosystem, wherever we are.

The Realm of the Land

This is the first part of the Druidic triad. The land is the foundation, the stabilising aspect that grounds us, providing a firm foothold on reality. We begin with our feet placed firmly on the ground, allowing the earth to nourish us body and soul.

Druids have a deep and abiding affection for the land. They understand that it provides us with the nourishment we need to survive. We must acknowledge this in our own lives, opening our eyes to what sustains us physically, mentally, and spiritually. We look within ourselves and see what our inner cycles are telling us to do and whether or not they are in tune with the natural environment around us.

We explore our connection to the earth, learning about acceptance and integrity. This is what relationship is all about. The earth teaches us about acceptance when it absorbs the heat of the sun or the waters of the rain. The earth does not discriminate. It provides nourishment in a legion of ways. We learn how to work with the earth so that we too can begin to learn about acceptance. Acceptance does not mean passivity. It does not mean "Oh well, there is nothing I can do." Acceptance means seeing reality for what it really is and then working with it under no pretenses and no illusions. It is sifting through the threads of our story to find out what is relevant and necessary, opposed to what we tell ourselves to keep ourselves comfortable. It is accepting the light and the dark in equal measure. In acceptance, we find the deep learning of how to work in the world with integrity. For only when we truly connect to and accept reality are we able to truly work with integrity.

Integrity is working for the benefit of the land and not just for our own personal benefit. When we take into consideration all that we do and all of the repercussions of our actions, then we are living with integrity. Integrity stems from the word "integration," which is at the heart of the land's teaching. Integration is where we allow our small selves to fall away in order to truly connect to the land. The land is so much bigger than we are. If we allow our pride and prejudices to fall away, if we are silent for a while and simply work with acceptance and integrity, then integration will occur. We will begin to hear the songs of the land over our own songs, which often drown out everything else. We begin to learn the silence of integration in the depths of winter, that soft blending of edges and landscapes even as snow blankets the land and makes everything smooth. We actually become an active member of an ecosystem. We work in that ecosystem with intention and integrity. We learn about true relationship.

Working with the land we can explore ancestral roots, those of blood and those of the land. We see that the land is made up of the ancestors, from the earth in our gardens to the air that we breathe. These are not just human ancestors, but the manifestation of all things that have gone before us. Their bones, their decayed leaves, their tears and blood, are all in the soil that provides us with food, nourishment, plants, and more. The ancestors are in the land, right here. They are not some ethereal beings wandering like ghosts; they are in the apple that you eat, in the very air that you breathe.

When we work with the land, we explore our senses. We take the time to really feel what we touch, to see what our eyes behold, to hear what our world sings to us, to smell life and death in all its manifestation, to taste life to its truest potential, whether that is the rain, a salad, or an awakening of deeper senses to the world around us.

The earth hums beneath our feet. There is an energy present, which we can become aware of in each and every moment. It helps us to deepen our connection to the earth, to the land, to the ancestors, and to the spirits of place. Those who have walked this land before, whose bones and blood, leaves and wood, stones and pebbles, make up this land—their energy is contained within. So too are the energies of wind and rain, of sunlight, starlight and moonlight shining down on us. We are hurling through space at infinite speeds, spinning in an endless cycle of birth and death. In that cosmic dance, there is energy, the push and pull of the planets and our nearest star, the dance of orbiting moons. Open yourself to this energy, let it wash through your soul and awaken your heart to the wonder of the world.

The energy of the land may differ depending on where we are in the world. Each land has its own unique signature, yet always contains similarities as well, for we share this planet, and deep at its core around a strong iron centre is a heart of fire that is the spark of awen, which we can tap into wherever we go.

Later we will work with the energies of the land in ritual and awaken ourselves to the land within and without.

The Realm of the Sea

The realm of the sea surrounds the land, flowing around it in the deep patterns of the tides. It is a place that is often connected to the Celtic Otherworld and the realm of the ancestors. It is the place of emotion and healing.

We connect with the realm of the sea through the times and tides of our own lives. We see the experiences, joys, and sorrows ebbing and flowing like the sea. The blood that runs through our veins, the tears that we shed; all the water in our bodies is a reminder of that connection. We need water to live. Without water, there is no life. We learn to be responsible for our own lives and for the impact that we have upon others, for we are ever-flowing with everything around us, all the time. We live in a shared existence, and we must work with integrity and honour. Coming to terms with our own emotions, our thoughts and fears, the highs and the lows, helps us to connect to the overarching realm of the sea.

Taking time to become aware of the self is a large part of the modern Pagan movement. In many of the traditions over the last twenty years, exploring the psychological aspect has been as important as the metaphysical and the spiritual work. Many have done this as part of a training course or in their own deep learning, but perhaps subsequently allowing it to fall by the wayside; once it's been studied, that's it, let's move on. Being aware of your emotions and behaviour is a never-ending quest in self-awareness. In order to live and work in the Druid tradition, it should be a lifelong exercise —to ensure that we are living honourably and respectfully within nature and the natural cycle.

Indeed, it is our responsibility to be aware of what we put out into the world, emotionally and physically, as Druids. We know that we are a part of a greater web, therefore when one strand is tugged, the others shiver all the way down to the core. We need to be able to see when we have failed to act with honour, in our human relationships, in our relationships with the natural world, in our relationship with the gods and the ancestors. And in doing so, we can work to make amends, to reweave those threads that have been pulled apart.

Sometimes the damage is so great that we need to start again, especially in human relationships, and that is perfectly acceptable. When there is no possibility of working with another human without losing that sense of honour, when there is no respect, then we can walk away calmly and begin again, focusing our energy on creating the world we wish to live in that benefits the whole. We can still try to understand the situation, working with compassion, but we don't have to participate in it any longer, especially when the relationship becomes abusive.

We face many challenges in our modern world, some of which we shared with our ancestors, some not. Alienation, isolation, war, climate change, technology: all these we have shared previously with those who have gone before. How we respond to it makes all the difference. Former Head of the Druid Network, Emma Restall Orr remarks on the environmental crisis and how to respond gracefully as a Pagan:

> Primarily, allowing nature to be our teacher, we must be wakeful to our human nature: to the surges and floods of our emotions, their forces, drives and weight and to the beliefs that are hidden in the shadows of awareness. Only then can we learn how to ride the emotional energies, using their power positively instead of letting them batter and break us. Many traditions are slack in this teaching, even though playing in our own emotional mess is essentially selfish, often leading us to antagonize others and cause unnecessary harm. Yet the luxury of emotional indiscipline becomes less available as the reality of crisis increases.[3]

As Druids, we are gifted with the opportunity to explore our emotions and behaviour to really find some insight into the workings of our mind through connecting with the realm of the sea. I see it as our duty to be aware of how we are in the world, how we are able to respond, and our own personal responsibility in the world. Allowing our emotions to rule us, resulting in bad behaviour, war, genocide, and environmental obliteration (to name a few), will only hasten the process of our own self-destruction. We live at a time when perhaps things have gone too far, but we can still do damage control. It is our duty toward our descendants. If we allow fear,

---

3. Emma Restall Orr, "Honing Our Relationships with Our Gods: Emotional Discipline in a Time of Climate Crisis," Patheos.com, accessed September 29, 2017 http://www.patheos.com/topics/2014-religious-trends/pagan/honing-our-relationships-with-our-gods-emma-restall-orr-072314.

apathy, or other emotions to control us, we will never achieve what we want to achieve.

The realm of the sea surrounds and holds us. It is fluid and ever-changing, holding the firmness of rock and the stability of the land. Like the times and tides of life, emotion and ancestral experience form patterns that we can follow or alter in order to live with integrity. Flowing with the deep waters of emotional responsibility and working with compassion, we learn how best to work with the realm of the sea. Later we will perform a ritual to raft the currents of emotion and to connect with the energy of the realm of the sea.

The Realm of the Sky

The realm of the sky is very different from the realms of land and sea. Air is invisible, except when connecting with other elements such as water. As such, we take it for granted most of our lives. Yet without it we simply could not survive.

We only really notice air when the wind is blowing, sometimes blowing "a hoolie" (Scottish term for super windy) as it does often in the spring where I live. Though invisible, it is a powerful force that we often only recognise when it is creating damage. We also recognise the necessity and need for air when we are unable to breathe and a real visceral panic sets in. But what of all the other times? What of air right now?

Take a moment and simply sit, sensing the air around you. Open up your awareness to the air, feel it upon your face, upon your skin. Whether indoors or out, you can open up your awareness to air, be it still or breezy, cool or warm. It is something that is always surrounding you, something that defines you. Where you "end" is where air "begins" in a very basic material sense, though tiny molecules are passing through us all the time.

Take a moment and feel air; connect with it.

There is a Zen saying: *The material form of the vase is not what makes it functional; it is the emptiness within where we find its use.* In this regard, we see that the supposed emptiness is really all about potential. Working with air, working with the realm of the sky is just that: potential.

Let's begin by exploring the more physical aspects of air. We sense air and experience it through our breath. We experience air when we are standing in a stiff breeze, when a chill blows over our warm-blooded bodies. We need air to survive; we cannot take it in from any other source other than breath. Air is essential to our functioning. We are blessed to have a planet with an atmosphere that can support and sustain life. Yet, with our technological progress, we threaten the very things that sustain us, such as air. We pollute the skies with industry and with our very way of life: by our consumerism, by the flights we take to foreign lands, by the burning of petroleum-based candles in ritual. Some of the effects are unavoidable. Some of them are carbon-neutral. Some of them we can offset. However, the sheer numbers of human beings on this planet are what makes air so tenuous at this point in our history. We stand at the edge of a precipice, and if we don't act accordingly, we will plummet over the edge from where we cannot step back.

We must regard air as precious. We must not take it for granted; it is as precious as the land and sea. We see the land, we see the sea, we can connect with them on a more physical level because we can see them with our own eyes. But the air—the air we often forget. We are reminded with the flight of the buzzard keening overhead or when we sit in an airplane being thrown around by turbulence. We need to reconnect to this ethereal realm more deeply, to make it as substantial in our hearts and minds as the realms of sea and land.

What about the spiritual aspects of air? The realm of the sky can be a place where we confront our deepest fears. How many of us have a fear of heights or a fear of flying? Being away from the grounding, comforting, solid realm of earth and the supporting realm of water that holds us, when we step out into air, we are literally stepping out into nothing: or so it seems. When we connect on a soul level with the realm of the sky, we are facing our fears of lack of control. We are looking deeply at our desires to escape. We experience a complete lack of being held back when we allow ourselves to spread our wings, the breeze lifting us from the earth out into the vast realms of open spaces.

We can begin by acknowledging and affirming air as breath. The air that we breathe is the air our ancestors breathed. It is the mutual exchange with all life forms on this planet, from algae in the sea to trees in our backyards. We work in symbiosis, releasing carbon dioxide from our lungs and taking in the oxygen that plants breathe out into the world. Air is a great connecter, a great pathway to soul-deep relationships. Right now, in this very instant, all breathing creatures are breathing the same air, sharing the air, sharing in each other.

We then acknowledge the power of air through sound and vibrational energy. We are creatures of language. We communicate with words, with our vocal chords vibrating, creating sound due to the atmosphere that surrounds our planet. Without atmosphere, there is no sound. No one can hear you scream in space. Yes, we can communicate through body language. We can communicate with sign language, for instance. But for the most part, we are verbal creatures. The power of voice, the vibration of sound, can be a deep and meaningful way to connect with air. Words do have power. The old saying about "sticks and stones" is really not entirely true: words can hurt us. Yet we have the power to use words to heal, to reconnect us to the lost threads, the threads that we have dropped in the creation of our tapestry of life.

Sound can heal. Vibrations can heal. Explore the ways in which healing works with these techniques. Shamanic drumming often has the power through vibration to take us on journeys to other realms, to the Otherworld. Chanting is used in traditions all over the world to do the same. Mantras and prayers are sung with not only the power of words being expressed but the sounds themselves having a healing or connecting effect with the world, with divinity, with life itself.

With the realm of the sky we not only come across healing through vibration and sound, but also through facing some of our deepest fears. When we have nothing to hold on to, once we have let go and allowed our feet to leave the solid earth beneath us, then we are truly on a great adventure. Let the excitement of air and the adventure that awaits you fill you with enchantment and potential. The realm of the sky is the realm of potential.

Awaken to the energy of air. Awaken to the realm of the sky. Feel it upon your body, feel it within your heart. Allow the energy to take you on great adventures, to free you of fears and ride with the wind. Later in this book, we will find a ritual/meditation to connect with the realm of the sky.

The three realms of land, sea, and sky are often invoked in ritual, to bring our awareness of them into being, to bring them to the fore of physical manifestation. We honour them in ritual as realms that exist around us and also within us. Working with the three realms of land, sea, and sky helps us not only to understand the natural world around us, but also to understand our own inner workings. We see ourselves reflected in the world around us and carry the world around us within our own very being. We have the land within us, the sea and the sky, even as we reach out and connect with those realms in our practice. For the Hedge Druid, there is no one there to do it for us, so we must do it ourselves. We must take responsibility for our practice and for the work that we put into it. We may walk alongside others for a while, but ultimately the work is ours to do and the benefits, the highs and lows, are for us to experience. May we be the awen!

She stands at the shoreline on a small cliff-face that is slowly crumbling into the sea with every passing storm. Here the Hedge Druid stands between the realms of land, sea, and sky. Here is the liminal place where she works her potent magic, where she receives the awen in great abundance. The cold wind whips her hair across her face, tugging at her scarf and coat. She raises her arms toward the sea and calls out to the three realms for inspiration. After making her call, she sits down and meditates, waiting for an answer. The cries of the gulls pierce the clouds overhead, the waves crash upon the sandy beach below. She listens and watches in silence, listening to the land, sea, and sky, within and without. They will know what to do.

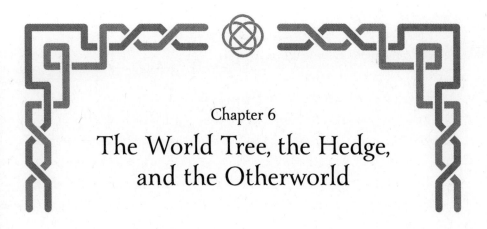

Chapter 6

The World Tree, the Hedge, and the Otherworld

Trees are magnificent teachers. They are so much larger than we are, both spiritually and physically. They remind us of what it means to live a life in service to the whole, to live a life filled with integration and harmony, sustainability, and peace. Trees teach us of communion and integration, both in the deep root levels of our soul and in reaching out toward the heavens of our soul's awakening. They teach us of symmetry and asymmetry, of cooperation and anarchy. They are a legion of souls across this land, swaying in the wind, living their intention, and benefiting all those around them by doing so. There is no sense of "I" with a tree; rather, it can instigate a better sense of "You" (or "yew").

Classical writers speak of Druids who worshipped in special groves of trees. These sacred places were called "nemetons," and here is where the Druids performed their rituals and sacrifices. I mentioned in chapter 1 the craft of hedge riding, and this term and practice can be particularly useful to the Hedge Druid. The German word *hagazissa*, which means "hedge sitter," and the Saxon term *haegtessa* apply to one who can walk between the worlds, riding the Hedge, and working with boundaries. The Otherworld is an important place for the Celts, its borders lying on and overlapping our world so that we can traverse these boundaries if we have the skill and vice versa. There are said to be special times when the veil between the worlds is thin, such as at the Celtic festival of Samhain (known to most North Americans as Halloween) and Beltane (otherwise known as May Day in the UK, a bank holiday weekend), where in both, beings from this world and the Otherworld can cross over.

Riding the World Tree, we find that all three worlds—the Lowerworld, the Middleworld, and the Upperworld—are connected, even as the Otherworld in its entirety is connected to this world. It may be called "Other," but it is more akin to a parallel dimension anchored into or layered over our own, rather than completely separate. Both worlds influence each other; both are interconnected. The World Tree, the Hedge, and the Otherworld are all deeply intrinsic to the practice of this Hedge Druid.

The World Tree

In my work as a Hedge Druid, connecting and having a good relationship to the Otherworld is central to my practice. The Irish *bíle*, otherwise known as the World Tree, is a motif that many Druids use in their tradition to connect to the Otherworld. Indeed, the World Tree is a motif used the world over in various religious and spiritual traditions. While not all Druids follow this format, in this work it is an important part of connecting to the Otherworld: to use the term "hedge" on multiple levels.

The bíle was a tree or long pole in an Iron Age Celtic settlement that usually stood in the middle of the dwellings. Tribes raiding other tribes would try to cut down the sacred bíle of an opposing settlement, thereby cutting their power and connection to Source. In one myth we see the king of Tara cutting down a bíle of oak in order to humiliate a rival. In the work *Settling the Manor of Tara*, each of the five ancient provinces or kingdoms had their old sacred tree or *Bíle Buadha*.[4]

For those of us in a Hedge Druid tradition, we may use the World Tree in a shamanic sense, to journey in the realms of the Otherworld (the Lowerworld, the Middleworld, and the Upperworld). There, we can quest the

---

4. Luke Eastwood, "Celtic Cosmology—An Introduction," Lukeeastwood.com, accessed October 21, 2017, http://www.lukeeastwood.com/cosmology.htm.

awen and seek inspiration and guidance from the ancestors, from totem animals, and from the divine. The hedge is the boundary between worlds: between civilisation and the wilderness, between the bottom of the garden and the farmer's field, between this world and the Otherworld. The hedge is made up of trees, which are sacred to the Druid and integral to her work. We establish a close bond to a tree, a specific type of tree, or a location of trees, if we can. When we do, we can begin to understand their wisdom, thereby fulfilling the name or label of *Druid*: one who holds the wisdom of the oak.

In the Welsh poem "The Battle of Trees," Gwydion secured three gifts for humankind from the army of trees: the dog, the deer, and the lapwing. The oak proved the toughest of all and defended all the other trees in that battle. Oak trees would have been enormous back then, and we only have a few remnants left now of old oaks that are hundreds of years old. They would have proved a great challenge to our Celtic ancestors in trying to clear land from these massive trees for farming as well as receiving great gifts from those that remained, such as acorns, which fed the pigs through-out the winter.[5] Kildare, in Ireland, is where the goddess Brigid's shrine is found and stems from *Cill-Dara*, which means "Church of the Oak."

In the Irish tales of Fionn McCumhaill's travels, he comes upon the Man in the Tree. This man has a blackbird on his right shoulder (the blackbird is also known as the Druid dubh, a creature of the Otherworld), while in his left hand he holds a bowl of water in which a trout (sometimes a salmon) was swimming. At the base of the tree stood a mighty stag. Cracking nuts, the man in the tree would give half to the blackbird while he ate the other half. From the bowl he took out an apple, half of which he shared with the stag and the other half he ate himself. He would drink from the bowl so that he, the trout, the stag, and the blackbird could all drink together. Here we see the magic of the three worlds coming together through the man and the

---

5. Courtney Weber, *Brigid: History, Mystery and Magick of the Celtic Goddess*, (Weiser Books 2015), 102.

tree, the blackbird of the Upperworld, the stag of the Middleworld, and the fish of the Lowerworld. This was, indeed, a very special tree.

The World Tree reaches deep into the earth, holds strong and fast in this world, and reaches high into the realms of potential and divinity. We can view it as a mighty oak tree, a tree that was and still is especially sacred to the Druids. An oak tree's roots reach as deep into the earth as its branches reach up and outward into the sky. It is a symbol of balance and unity, combining the roots, trunk, and branches into a single entity that we can connect with in our own work. We travel down through the roots into the Lowerworld to meet with the Fair Folk and the ancestors. We can travel through the trunk of the tree in this Middleworld, to meet with our spirit guides and/or totem animals. We can move upward into the branches of the World Tree to connect with the gods and our own inner potential. Do be aware that the above is only a generalisation of what we can find in the three worlds, for there are gods dwelling in the Lowerworld and Middleworld too. Ancestors can be found in all three worlds; spirit guides and totem animals can be found anywhere. For the purposes of this work, however, I will use each world as a motif to connect with a specific aspect for clarity and simplicity's sake later on in the text.

A Hedge Between the Worlds

In this work, we focus on the aspect of the World Tree in the form of the Hedge, a boundary that delineates one space from another. In doing so, we are able to travel from this world to the Otherworld and experience life on different levels through our connection to the Otherworld. Here in Britain, there are ancient hedges all across the landscape: wonderful corridors for wildlife to travel from one area to the next in relative safety, hidden from the eyes of the circling hawk and the hunter with his gun. They are a place of refuge for the night, where pheasants and deer can take their rest. They are also places of abundance, as in the autumn the many hedgerows of black-thorn and hawthorn are bursting with sloes and berries, interspersed with crab apple, elder, and other wonderful trees. In our modern gardens, the hedges separate our space from our neighbours, marking what is our territory and what is theirs. They are often of evergreen trees, such as cedar or laurel; I have even seen a rosemary hedge!

In the next section of this book, we will work with the Hedge in ritual, as a boundary between this world and the Otherworld, crossing over and meeting those who would cross over to our side, gaining wisdom and information that we can take into our lives to enrich them for the good of all, in balance and in harmony. The Hedge will become our sacred nemeton, our place where we can stand at the threshold and speak with the gods, the ancestors, the Fair Folk and more. It will be our place of magic, of intention and mystery. The Hedge is a special place of tree folk and other folk and can truly be an inspiration for our work.

When we develop a relationship with trees, we feel a shift in our perception and in our ego; we think about ourselves less, rather than think less of ourselves. We are reminded that we are a part of an ecosystem, that the ecology of our spirituality is all important to our everyday lives. Just as a tree is not alone and separate in a forest, so too do we see the interconnectedness of all things. This ecology is absolutely integral to who we are as a species, as part of a place and environment, as part of life on this planet. We cannot separate this ecology in any shape or form. It is in everything that we do.

The Fair Folk and the Otherworld

The Otherworld is the abode of the Fair Folk, the Sidhe, the Gentry, the Shining Ones, the Good Folk, or what we otherwise know as Faery or Fairy. It is the spiritual world connected and manifested in our world through the landscape which other beings can use to enter or leave, to travel between. It is also the place where ancestors and spirit guides dwell. We can also reach the divine through travelling from this world into the Otherworld, which shows us our true potential. Sometimes the three realms of land, sea, and sky are related to the Lower, Middle, and Upperworlds, but for this work we will keep them separate as they teach us different aspects of Celtic cosmology and understanding our own being.

The Fair Folk, Faeries, Sidhe (Irish), or Tylwyth Teg (Welsh) may have been derived from nature spirits from an ancient animistic worldview, culture, and religion in the British Isles. The Irish Sidhe are descended from the Tuatha Dé Danann (a race of beings/old gods who came from the north). When the Milesians (from which humanity is said to be descended) arrived in Ireland, the Tuatha Dé Danann were already there and eventually they came to an agreement to divide the land between them, with the Tuatha Dé Danann living below ground and the Milesians living above ground. The Irish word *Sidhe* can refer to a burial site or barrow as well as one of the Fair Folk, and so we see the connections forming. Faeries can also be viewed as working in conjunction with human ancestors. They may have lived alongside the spirits of the dead in the barrows and hollow hills. As we will see below, the Lowerworld of Annwn is a place of both the Fae and the dead.

Irish and Welsh mythology has the Otherworld as places below the ground or under the sea. The House of Donn or *Tech Duinn* is where souls go and gather, perhaps before moving on to other realms or being reincarnated. Tech Duinn is commonly identified today with Bull Rock, an islet off the western tip of the Beara Peninsula. Bull Rock has a natural tunnel through it, allowing the sea to pass under it as if through a portal: very befitting a realm of the dead or the Otherworld. There is also *Tír na nÓg* ("Land of the Young") or *Tír na hÓige* ("Land of Youth") which are both names for the Otherworld. There is also *Emain Ablach* (Irish) and *Ynys Afallon* or *Ynys Afallach* (Welsh), which are all mystical "islands of apples" that exist in the Otherworld where great healing and abundance can be found. Avalon, another legendary island of apples in the Arthurian lore, has connections today to the modern-day town of Glastonbury. On the "Isle of the Druids," Iona in Scotland, there is the *Sithean Mor*, the Great Fairy Mound of Iona, where it is said that Otherworldly music emanates from within the hill and that more than one person has met their fate in pursuit of it.

Christian lore has Faeries as fallen angels. The Victorians reinvented Faeries to suit their more modest temperament, and so the famous Flower Faeries were created. The author J. M. Barrie gave us Tinkerbell and solidified the Faeries as diminutive folk with wings. In Celtic lore, the Faeries or

Sidhe could be of any size, from a small child to a very tall human, and did not have wings. Many images and artwork portray the Faeries in a therian-thropic sense: part human, part animal. This may be the reason why today we view them for the most part as winged creatures. However, therian-thropes have existed in cultures for millennia, all over the world.

When working with the Fair Folk, as we will call the Sidhe or Faeries in this work, it is important to pay attention to the old lore that we have regarding our manners with them. The Fair Folk are like us and not like us. They have their own agenda and their own interests. They may seek us out, or they may dislike our intrusion. For instance, one should never say thank you to one of the Fair Folk, for in doing so it demonstrates that you are in their debt. When establishing a relationship with any of the Fair Folk, it is important to be on equal footing. Gratitude and good manners are a must, but this specific saying of thank you should (however) important in our world) not be used in dealing with Faery. The Fair Folk also don't like being talked about in the open, so euphemisms are often used. Many tra-ditions tell us specifically not to use the word "Faery." Another aspect of working with the Fair Folk is honesty: they will find you out if you are being dishonest, and like most people, they will not be best pleased. Some of the Fair Folk might try to trick you, when really they are testing your cleverness. At any rate, don't expect a Faery to act as you think they should. No one likes to be pigeon-holed. Another aspect in folklore that is very important is not eating or drinking anything whilst in the Otherworld, for then you may never be able to leave. Do not carry iron if you wish to commune with the Fair Folk, for it is said that they do not like it. However, other stories tell of how great some Faery smiths are in forging items with iron! Regardless, if you wish to protect yourself from them, then carrying iron, a cross made of rowan sticks bound with red thread, or having herbs such as St. John's Wort on your person can do the trick.

All relationships enjoy reciprocity. Therefore, it is important to leave of-ferings when working with the Fair Folk, to show gratitude (without saying thank you). A traditional offering found in Irish lore is the first milk from the daily milking of a cow. Honey and butter is also often used as an offering.

There are many Faery places, such as the burial mounds described above. Faery ringforts are often places to avoid, for the Faeries may come and take you away if you linger. Lone trees, especially hawthorn trees, are sacred to the Faeries and are often portal places to the Otherworld. Boulders and caves can also be Faery haunts, and to destroy or damage them can cause the trespasser terrible suffering and pain and may even result in death. It is said that there are many Faery paths that connect these sites to each other, and so we must tread lightly when walking in their domain. These Faery paths are most active at Beltane, Midsummer, and Samhain, when the Faeries are out in full force.

One of the most famous of the Faeries is the banshee or *bean sidhe* (or *ban side*—there are different spellings depending on the area of Ireland). Always a female Faery, her function was to warn a family of an impending death. The banshee was often connected to families or clans and followed them wherever they went. She was not the cause of death, but a warning of death to come. She wailed and keened (crying, weeping) into the night, with wild, loose hair. It is said that if you found a comb while out and about in the landscape, you should not pick it up, for it could be a banshee's comb and the death would be your own.

The modern-day view of Faeries and the Otherworld is that of superstition. To believe in these realms and beings in the modern-day mindset is to resort to a primitive worldview. This is often the case when modern-day materialism meets the more ancient animism. Scientific reductionism has claimed priority of place and is seen as the superior perspective in much of today's society. For the Druid, the wisdom received from an animistic worldview cannot be ignored.

When we seek to work with the Fair Folk, we also need to remember to word our intention clearly. When asking to work with them, we need to state why and in what manner of relationship. For example, it is important to ask, when calling to the Fair Folk, for those that are in tune with your intention. You would not approach just any strange person on the street and decide to talk to them, establishing a relationship with them. There needs to be a reason and a slow working of sharing trust and honesty with each other. You are, hopefully, trying to be friendly with those of the Fair Folk and so just as you would in any human relationship, you must proceed accordingly. If you upset the Fair Folk, they can return the favour with interest, causing you all manner of harm, from physical illness to madness. Therefore, it's important that you watch your manners when working with them, are polite but also that you safeguard your own being without offending them. It's interesting to note that historically, "normal" people avoid the Fair Folk at all costs and would not seek to establish any sort of relationship with them. This is reserved for the village wise woman or cunning man.

The Fair Folk teach us to treat the land with respect as well as other people, especially strangers, as they can often be a Faery in disguise. After a while, a good relationship is established and your work is guided by the forces from the Otherworld, giving you deeper insights into the way of the world. Faeries are still an important part of the landscape and stories in places such as Ireland, where the old tales are still known by most and even if you don't believe, you don't mess with them. Some Druid traditions don't work with the Fair Folk at all, and this omission is, I think, a very sad one. They are integral to the land of the British Isles and help us to better understand the wild and wily nature of nature.

The Three Worlds of the Otherworld

The three concepts of a Lowerworld, Middleworld, and Upperworld can be found in the more recent revivalist tradition of Welsh Druidry, as well as in more shamanic traditions. Several Druid organisations use these concepts as part of their tradition, and some don't incorporate it at all. Druidry is a wide and wild tradition that has no dogma, no liturgy. We are free to choose to learn our Druidry from a single point in time and relate that to our present moment, or we are free to learn from every period in history and apply that likewise to our tradition. The Order of Bards, Ovates and Druids explores these worlds in their approach to Druidry, for instance, but many other orders do not. Here I will discuss them briefly in a more shamanic sense, relating to them to the World Tree motif that spans religious and spiritual traditions the world over.

As Druids who seek the wisdom of the oak, using a tree motif can be wholly appropriate to the path. As we have seen, the Druids celebrated in groves, sacred nemetons, and trees were very important to their religious and spiritual tradition. Some Druids use this tree motif in connection with the three worlds; others see them as circles or spheres within spheres, interconnecting. These three worlds are sometimes referred to as Annwn (or *Ceugant* as Iolo Morganwg named it), Abred, and Gwynfed.

In our own tradition, the Hedge Druid can choose the method he or she will use in order to travel between the worlds—so use what you find applicable in this work to add to and/or create your own tradition.

The Lowerworld

This is the realm of the Sidhe, of the mound-dwellers, the Tylwyth Teg, those who live in the Hollow Hills: the Fair Folk. All of these are motifs in Celtic lore of the world of Faery, and when working with the Lowerworld we can know them through their king: Gwyn Ap Nudd (pronounced Gwin-Ap-Neeth). The Lowerworld, known as Annwn (An-oon) or Annwfn (An-oo-ven), is the Celtic Lowerworld accessed through travelling below the earth, into the ground, or into a mound or hill. Glastonbury Tor in Somerset, England, is often said to be the place where Gwyn Ap Nudd resides, deep within that legendary hollow hill. He rides out with the Wild Hunt every Samhain and traverses the sky throughout the winter months. The constellation Orion, the Hunter, is visible at this time, striding through the heavens, and the connection between the starry heavens and the myths cannot be ignored. Annwn is also accessed in Welsh mythology, by crossing bodies of water; and Glastonbury, which was once an island connected to the land by a very small causeway, comes into play yet again as here we not only have the hollow hill but also the water that surrounds the landscape.

Annwn means "the very deep place" or "the in-world." Annwn is also sometimes known as *Caer Sidi*, the fortress of the Sidhe or the Fair Folk. This can be translated as "Spiral Castle," and the winding spiral labyrinthine paths leading up Glastonbury Tor demonstrates this cosmology in its very landscape. It is also sometimes known as *Cair Wydyr* ("Castle of Glass"), which once again reflects the very name of Glastonbury.[6]

The realm of the Fair Folk and the abode of the ancestors are often seen as one and the same or at the very least closely connected in the Lowerworld. Annwn can be accessed through ancient burial tombs known as barrows, and as Gwyn Ap Nudd is seen to be the Lord of the Dead when he is out on the Wild Hunt, this dual sovereignty of the Fair Folk and the ancestors is apparent. In some tales the protagonist sees their dead relatives dining in the halls alongside the Fair Folk. It is sometimes seen as an in-between place, perhaps as a resting place for the soul, before it continues on in its travels. It is also the place where the cauldron of transformation can be found, warmed by the breath of nine maidens (from the mythological tale *Preiddeu Annwn: The Spoils of Annwn*). We can see Gwyn Ap Nudd as the guardian of the cauldron of Annwn, the protector of the Goddess deep within the earth. Her attendant priestesses keep her fire alive, serving her and the world. The Lowerworld or Annwn is not a dark and dreary place but a place of wonder, much like our own world. It is sometimes said that there is no sun or moon in the realms of the Otherworld, only an ethereal light that is neither daylight or moonlight. Later, we will work with Annwn/the Lowerworld in ritual as the abode of the Fair Folk and Gwyn Ap Nudd.

The Middleworld

This is the world where we spend most of our time, where the everyday happens. Yet this is not a world of the mundane; it is only our perception of it that makes it so. When we open our eyes to the beauty and sacredness of the Middleworld, we see all that it has to offer. The Middleworld is also sometimes known as *Abred* in the Welsh tradition.

---

6. Danu Forest, *Gwyn Ap Nudd: Wild God of Faery, Guardian of Annwfn*, (Moon Books, 2017).

The Middleworld is the mortal realm. That does not mean that immortal beings cannot enter, for those with the skill and courage can traverse all three of these realms, be they human, Fae, god, or otherwise. This Middleworld requires our attention just as much as the other worlds and just as much respect. Druidry is a tradition based in locality. Where we live is of utmost importance, for we are part of that ecosystem, amidst that of the wider world. We have to know and respect where we are, where we live first and foremost, for that is also the realm where we have the most influence. The Middleworld is also the world that influences us the most, so there is a reciprocity which is immediate in this relationship. We depend on the Middleworld for sustenance: food, shelter, and more. Our impact upon this world impacts our very being. We must look deeply into all our relationships, whether that is with the bird, the bee, the stag, or our next-door neighbour. We must work with honour and integrity if we wish to see that reflected back in the world around us.

Walking the landscape daily can help us to connect and see the beauty of the Middleworld. Learning about all the other creatures that share the same space is a brilliant way to come to know how everything fits together. Take the time to know the different species of birds, of insects, of all creatures that are in your locality. This will come in handy when we work further with the Middleworld in ritual, for there we will meet with the god Herne, the Lord of the Hunt and of wild animals.

The Upperworld

The Upperworld is the place of potential, our highest potential, as well as being associated with divinity. In Welsh it is known as *Gwynfed*, where form in its purest state exists. It is the place of the archetype, the greatest possibility. We can quest the awen in the Upperworld, seeking wisdom and guidance from all manner of being. This is the dwelling place of our soul's truth, of our sovereign self. When we work beyond our own shadow aspects, those parts of our ego that keep us rooted in our fears and soul wounds, we travel to the Upperworld in order to realise our fullest potential, fully in control and reigning supreme in our being.

When we regard the Upperworld in relation to the Lower- and Middle- worlds, we see how they all fit together holistically. The Lowerworld is where we can come face-to-face with our soul wounds, where the root of certain behaviours lie. We can connect to ancestral soul wounds as well and seek out the source of pain in order to work with it, to bring it to consciousness. When the unconscious is made conscious, we act with intention. No longer are we operating on a reactionary basis to everything, but instead we have a purpose and an honourable way to interact with the rest of the world, based on personal responsibility. Coming face-to-face with the hidden aspects of our soul, of our behaviour, and of the world around us, we can bring this knowledge with us back into the Middleworld, where we can work with it in our daily lives. We can then travel to the Upperworld to gain the inspiration to help us in our journeys through the shadow. This is not to say that the shadow is evil and that the light is good. It is being aware of *all* aspects of our very being. It is in the journey to understand ourselves that we come to understand the world. That journey does not stop with ourselves, for Druidry is not a self-centred tradition. We take that knowledge and integrate it with the world around us. It helps us to see *beyond* ourselves and work toward a wholeness with nature.

Later in this work we will travel to the Upperworld in ritual to meet with the goddess Arianrhod in her castle in the sky. Here we will gain inspiration into our own quest for the awen, for our greatest potential and inner sovereignty.

She knows in her work as a Hedge Druid that she walks between the worlds. She carries the information and knowledge across the Hedge, riding the World Tree to gain inspiration, awen. She works for her community, for the Fair Folk, and for herself. She knows where she can access the information that she needs; she knows the portals to the Otherworld that can be found in the landscape and in her mind. Here is the blessing of a walker between the worlds. Here is the real work of the Hedge Druid.

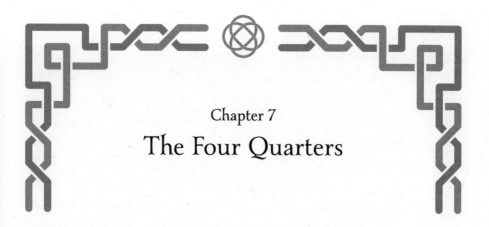

Chapter 7

The Four Quarters

It is thought that the introduction of the four quarters in Druidry is a modern invention, being hugely popular in Western Paganism, which in turn was influenced by many of the traditions found in ancient Greece. Though we cannot prove either way whether the ancient Druids honoured the four quarters, we know that some Druids do today and so it is presented here for you to incorporate into your own tradition, should you so wish. Many Druids find that working with the three realms satisfies their needs and gives it a more "Celtic" flavour. However, many others find it extremely beneficial to use a fourfold method, connecting it with the directions of the compass, the seasons, and more. In Celtic myths there are actually *five* directions: north, east, south, west, and centre. We will look at all of these in turn. In fact, Irish cosmology contains nine directions known as *Dúile*, which translate to be above, below, outside, inside, through, sky, sun, land, and sea. For the purposes of this work, we will work with the four quarters or directions, as well as the concept of centre.

The four quarters are north, east, south, and west. They can be viewed as four points on a circle, with north at the top of the circle, east at the furthest right-hand reach, south at the bottom, and west at the further left-hand reach. If we draw lines from north to south and from east to west, we find the symbol known as the Celtic Cross. There is some debate as to whether this ringed cross stems from the Bronze Age or is a later purport of Christianity.

Four cities are mentioned in the *Yellow Book of Lecan*, the ancestral home of the Tuatha Dé Danann (Irish race of gods). From these four cities, they brought with them treasures. The four cities and their corresponding treasures are: Falias and the Stone of Lia Fáil, Gorias and the Spear of Lugh, Murias and the Cauldron of Dagda, and Findias and the Sword of Nuada. We will explore these cities and treasures in relation to the direction in which they are attributed. Historically, there were five kingdoms in Ireland, which are now the four modern provinces, with the fifth historic kingdom (Mide or Meade) having been merged into another province (Leinster). The four provinces are Ulster in the north, Leinster in the east, Munster in the south, and Connacht in the west, which we'll look at below. In the poem *Ard Ruide* we see a vision of each of the four provinces and what can be found in each, described below. In the work *Settling the Manor of Tara*, we also come across the fifth city and ancient kingdom at the sacred centre: Uisneach in Mide.

The four quarters are often used in ritual in much the same way as the three realms of land, sea, and sky. They are to help us understand our world, our place in the world, and to honour it both within and without. They can also help us to set out a boundary when honouring the sacred in ritual. I was taught by my teacher that the four quarters help us to anchor in our sacred space, acting like guy ropes to keep us centred in ritual. In other Pagan traditions such as Wicca, the four quarters are invoked; however, in Druidry we see them as present all the time and work toward a constant awareness of them in our lives, both within and without. We're offering them our respect and seek to create a relationship with them to broaden our horizons, literally.

In much of Western Paganism, the four quarters have multiple associations. We will go over these each in turn and how they pertain to Druidry both ancient and modern. As Druidry is very much a tradition based on locality, the associations will vary depending upon where you are. For example, an Australian Druid would see south as the place of cold and north as the place of heat. A Druid living on the east coast of Canada would associate the direction of east with the Atlantic Ocean and water. Then again, some Druids prefer to use the more "ancestral" versions of the four directions, meaning as they relate to the United Kingdom. Even so, it can be difficult for a Druid like me, who lives on the east coast of England and sometimes calls to the powers of water in the west in group ritual, while the greatest body of water is, in fact, directly to the east. It is a personal choice whether you wish to honour your locality in the four directions, but be aware that in group ritual with many other Druids, you may be out of kilter with their perceptions of the four quarters! We'll look at honouring the four quarters later in part two of this book.

The wonderful part about being a Hedge Druid is that you are allowed to choose what suits you in your tradition. So long as it is based in good academic research and practical experience of the land where you live, who is to say what is right and what is not? You can allow your locality to inspire and inform you in your own tradition. You don't have to "follow the rules" set by other organisations, groups, or the collective "norm." You have only to look at nature, at how the world works around you, and at your own eco-system in order to find your place within it.

The North

In Modern Druidry the north is seen as the place of darkness. It is associated with the time of winter and midnight. It is a cold wind that blows from the north on these isles. It is stillness and silence. It is associated with the element of earth. It is the time of death, the quiet in the deep of the night. The north is the place of nocturnal creatures: the badger, the bat, the owl.

In ancient Celtic myth the north was the place of battle. It was also the place of fire, as opposed to the modern interpretation of fire being in the south. The north wind spoke of coming conflict. Warriors and gods were attributed to this direction. The city of Falias is connected to the north and is where the stone of Lia Fáil comes from. This stone is magical, of course; it sings with joy when the king of Ireland touches or puts his feet on it, as well as blessing him with long life. The north is connected to the element of earth and province of Ulster. In the poem *Arde Ruide*, Ulster in the north is known as the seat of battle, of boasting, and of valour. From here came the fiercest warriors of all Ireland, and its noble queens and goddesses are those of battle and death.

The East

Modern Druidry sees the east as the place of dawn and new beginnings. It is associated with the element of air and animals connected to it are the eagle, hawk, and the bee. It connected to the intellect and the birth of new ideas.

Ancient Celtic myth sees the east as the place of prosperity. An abundant harvest, material wealth, fine food and drink are associated with this direction. The city of Findias correlates to the east and from it came the Sword of Nuada, from which there was no escape in battle once it was drawn from its sheath and all would fall before its might. In the legend of "Nuada's Cainnel," it is said to glow with a bright light. The east connects to the ancient province of Leinster. The eastern kingdom of Leinster is where the most beautiful women and noble and eloquent men could be found. It is famed for its hospitality and rich finery from far-off lands.

The South

In Modern Druidry the south is the place of transformation, great heat, and the noon-day sun. It is the element of fire, passion, and action. Animals associated with it are the stag, the dragon, and the sow (ancient Druidry) or sometimes the boar (Modern Druidry).

Ancient Celtic mythology sees the south as the place of music, poetry, and the creative arts. Its city is Gorias, from which came the Spear of Lugh, famed for its ability in battle where none could last long against it and no man could hold out before it. Its associated province is Munster, the kingdom from which skilled harpers, horsemen, and ficheall players hailed (ficheall is a Celtic board game). It is said that Munster held the greatest fairs in all Ireland.

The West

The west is connected to the element of water in Modern Druidry. It is where the sun sets, the time of twilight. It is the realm of emotion and intuition. Associated animals are the salmon (Modern Druidry) and the stag (ancient Druidry). Other animals are herons, otters, and most aquatic creatures.

In ancient Celtic myth the west is the seat of ancestral knowledge, history, stories, genealogy and learning. It is the place of wisdom and mystery. It is connected to the city of Murias from which came the Cauldron of Dagda, which left no person unsatisfied. Connacht in the west is where the greatest and wisest Druids came from, as well as the most talented magicians. The men of Connacht are renowned for their good looks, speech, and ability to judge fair and true.

The Centre

As some Druids honour the centre alongside the four quarters, we will mention it here and incorporate it into ritual in the second part of this work. It is the fifth direction, the place of mastery and sovereignty. As such, it is an important place and can be viewed as the still and eternal centre from which everything revolves. The animal associated with it was the mare of sovereignty, as aspect of the Goddess of the land.[7] Here, in the middle of the four directions, we find the centre, which incorporates all four aspects to create a place of centredness and balance.

Ancient Irish mythology has Uisneach as the city of the centre, from the kingdom of Meath or Mide. This is associated with spirit and kingship, sovereignty of the soul and the land. At its heart we can find a sacred tree

---

7. Ellen Evert Hopman, "Two Seasons, Three Worlds, Four Treasures, Five Directions: the Pillars of Celtic Cosmology and Celtic Reconstructionist Druidism," Order of Bards, Ovates and Druids, accessed November 16, 2017, https://www.druidry.org/druid-way/other-paths/druidry-dharma/two-seasons-three-worlds-four-treasures-five-directions-pillars.

called *Craebh Uisnigh*, which stands at the centre. The centre is all seasons, all times, and all things.

Here is a table that incorporates some of the Modern Druid correspondences as well ancient ones found in Celtic lore. In your tradition, you can add as many as you like from your personal experience and research. You may add the centre to your work and even think of the centre as the World Tree itself, the *Craebh Uisnigh*, from the centre located in Uisneach.

	North	East	South	West	Centre
Element	Earth	Air	Fire	Water	All
Attributes	Stability, Fertility	Intellect, Freedom	Passion, Strength	Emotion, Fluidity	Sovereignty
Animal	Badger, Bat, Owl	Eagle, Hawk, Bee	Stag, Dragon, Sow	Salmon, Stag, Heron	All
Season	Winter	Spring	Summer	Autumn	All
Time of Day	Midnight	Dawn	Noon	Dusk	All
Stage in Life	Birth/Early Childhood	Young Adult	Mature Adult	Elder	All
Irish Kingdom	Ulster	Leinster	Munster	Connacht	Meath
Irish City	Falias	Findias	Gorias	Murias	Uisneach
Irish Treasure	Stone of Lia Fáil	Sword of Nuada	Spear of Lugh	Cauldron of Dagda	Craebh Uisnigh

On the path of the Hedge Druid, we find what sings to our soul, what resonates deeply within us. We work from a balanced place of integrity in our work, research, and practice. We don't know what ancient Druids really did, nor do we wish to emulate them in every aspect. We seek to find out as much as we can and to learn from it, thereby creating wisdom in our being.

She stands by the ancient burial mound, the sun setting in the distance. She calls to the ancient cities of Falias, Findias, Gorias, Murias, and Uisneach. She sees in her mind the totem animals associated with each and the World Tree at the centre. She recalls the associations that she has made through her research and experience and what she feels to be true in her own heart, asking each to bless her in her work. Strong and centred, she knows who she is, what she is here to do, and what part she has to play in the wider web of life.

Chapter 8

The Wheel of the Year

The Wheel of the Year is a motif known in Western Paganism as eight festivals that connect to the seasons or certain astronomical phenomenon. Some of these festivals have deep roots, going back to our Neolithic ancestors and possibly even further. We know that certain dates, such as the Summer and Winter Solstices and Spring and Autumn Equinoxes, were important to our Stone Age ancestors, who built many megalithic structures in accordance with sunrises and sunsets on these particular days. With the development of agriculture, more "seasonal" festivals were celebrated, such as at harvest time. The Celts had two seasons, summer and winter, and therefore two dates are important to remember which mark the start and end of the seasons: Beltane, the start of summer; and Samhain, the start of winter. The more seasonal/agricultural festivals of Imbolc in the early spring and Lughnasadh in the late summer reflect seasonal changes that occur in the livestock and in the land.

It cannot be said that all eight of these festivals were celebrated by the Celts. We know that the four seasonal/agricultural festivals, known as the fire festivals, were important and celebrated; however, the solstices and equinoxes may or may not have been. Some Druids today only celebrate the four fire festivals; others celebrate all eight.

The eightfold system was created by Gerald Gardner and Ross Nichols, who were mentioned in the first chapter. They brought together folklore and traditions to create a system that had a festival around every six to eight weeks. In doing so, they found a way to connect to the natural world around them more fully. In our modern-day society, we may not notice as we make our way to work that the snowdrops (often the first flower to appear in Britain) are out; however, when we have a festival that reminds us that this is happening, we begin to look and become more aware, integrating the natural world into our human-centric lives. It also connects us to our ancestors, for when we honour a festival that was important to them, such as Imbolc when the ewes began lactating after giving birth, we are also honouring our ancestors and their way of life. We remember or try to imagine how life was for them: the difficulty and the hardship of a long winter and the joy at the return of fresh milk to the dairy.

The eight festivals ground and centre us in our world. It reminds us that we are not separate and helps us to keep in tune with what is going on around us. You may or may not choose to use all eight festivals, keeping only to the fire festivals, and that is fine. You may decide to use all eight. The choice is yours in your Hedge Druidry. Here we will look at all eight festivals, and later in part two of this book we will have rituals for each that you can use, adapt, or be inspired by for your own tradition.

Samhain

The Celtic year was divided into two halves: the light half and the dark half. The light half began at the beginning of May, which marked the start of summer. The dark half began at Samhain (Irish) or Calan Gaeaf (Welsh), which marked the start of winter. The word "Samhain" is thought to be derived from "summer's end," being a linguistic inversion of *sam-fuin*.[8] Samhain is a time that lies between times and is a time that is not a time. It is the end of summer and marks the time just before we enter the dark half of the year, often referred to as the Celtic New Year. It is a liminal time and begins at dusk on October 31 on the calendrical year. (All Celtic holidays begin at

---

8. Dr. Jenny Butler, "The Festival of Samhain & Halloween in Ireland," Crypt Radio Station Interview, YouTube, accessed October 29, 2017, https://youtu.be/apzRcvlaufQ.

dusk the day before the calendrical date, i.e., the holy days run from sunset to sunset.) Some Druids follow a more agricultural or seasonal calendar and celebrate Samhain when the first frosts appear.

Samhain is known popularly today as Halloween. This stems from the Christian *Hallowmass*. What is interesting to note is that the Feast of All Saints, which follows the day after Hallowmass, used to take place in May. It was moved in the year 834 to November 1, presumably to compete with the more Pagan traditions and attempt to move the common folk away from such beliefs and practices.[9]

Samhain is a time to remember the dead and to welcome them. The dead are never far from us, and the Celtic worldview comprised a sort of ancestor veneration found the world over in Pagan traditions. Deceased relatives could come and visit the home and doors were often left unlocked so that they could enter. Some use the tradition of a "Dumb Supper," where food and places are laid out for the dead alongside the family's fare and the meal is eaten in silence. These plates were then taken outside as offerings to the spirits and the Fair Folk. Hollowing out turnips or sugar beets and later pumpkins (which were/are much easier to carve) and placing a candle inside could provide a lantern by which the dead could find their way. Candles may have been left in windows as well to help guide the way. Apples also have a place at this festival; one of the traditions was for a maiden to peel an apple and throw the peel over her shoulder: the letter that it formed was the initial of the name of the man she would marry. The custom of bobbing for apples is also thought to derive from Samhain traditions, with the lucky (and wet) winners receiving good fortune for the rest of the year. Brushing your hair and eating an apple while looking in a mirror at Samhain was said to reveal in the reflection the face of your true love. Modern-day trick-or-treating is said to come from the ancient *buachaillí tuí*, disguised people who characterised the dead and led a white mare (hobby horse) called *Láir Bhán*. This horse was symbolic of the Goddess of the land. In Scotland, a shoe

9. Des Baker, "Spiora na Samhna," Underground Short Film Festival, YouTube, accessed October 23, 2017 https://youtu.be/_nAYHHTz0Go.

was thrown over the house and the way it landed provided an insight into the thrower's luck; and a young lad who dipped his shirtsleeve in a well to the south would see his sweetheart entering sometime during the night turning the shirt by the fire (if he did not fall asleep first!).[10]

Samhain, when we arrive at summer's end, is a liminal time. The veils between this world and the Otherworld are thin, and so we see the custom of dressing up or guising to protect the living from any "unhappy dead." It could also be seen as an acknowledgement of the dead returning and as a sort of celebration of the fact.

Samhain was celebrated by the Druids in Ireland high on the hilltops with fire, from an ancient ritual on Tlachtga or the Hill of Ward in Meath (the ancient central kingdom). Tlachtga was sacred to the Druids, whereas Tara was the place of the high king. Tlachtga could be viewed from Tara and a fire on Tara may have been lit in response, allowing the Druids to light their fire first in their role as advisors. The Feast of Tara took place three days before and three days after Samhain.

At Glastonbury in Somerset, England, the Wild Hunt is said to ride out of the hill of Glastonbury Tor with Gwyn ap Nudd, the Lord of Annwn, at its head. He collects the souls of those who have died over the past year and acts in the role of psychopomp, leading the souls to their rightful place in the Otherworld or afterlife. Fire rituals may well have been a part of ancient ceremony on the Tor, being a hill that could be seen for many miles in the surrounding flat countryside. Recently, a Samhain fire festival honouring the Wild Hunt has been resurrected and now takes place at Glastonbury Tor every year, being hugely popular with modern-day Druids officiating the ceremonies.

The ancient Celts moved their cattle to the winter quarters, as mentioned previously, and those cattle that they could not feed over winter were

---

10. Ronald Black, *The Gaelic Otherworld: John Gregorson Campbell's Superstitions of the Highlands and Islands of Scotland and Witchcraft and Second Sight in the Highlands and Islands*, (Birlinn Limited, 2014), 561.

slaughtered and made part of a great feast.[11] Rents, debts, and accounts were settled on this day, and hired workers were paid their wages. This time represented a reckoning, an end to things, and a settling of accounts.

Samhain is also sometimes known as the third harvest in Modern Paganism. Where I live in Suffolk, the last of the apples are gathered, the hedgerows have been foraged, and the turnips, carrots, and onions that grow in the sandy soil have been collected. It is exceedingly bad luck to harvest anything more from the hedgerows after Samhain, for the *puca* (or in Christian mythology, the devil) "pisses on it." The winter crops are planted between the Autumn Equinox and Samhain and many of the fields now lie brown, seeds hidden beneath the soil, or have grass seed grown on it during the winter months, to be ploughed back into the soil in the spring, bringing much-needed nitrogen back into the earth. Samhain is a time of endings, to stop and reflect on the past year and prepare for the year to come.

Winter Solstice

The Winter Solstice is the shortest day of the year. It literally means that the sun stands still: from the Latin *sol* (sun) and *sistere* (to stand still). The midwinter sun rises at its furthest point in the southeast and sets in its nearest point in the southwest, thus making the shortest and lowest circuit in the sky. For three days (the day before, the day of, and the day after the solstice) the sun rises and sets on the same points of the horizon, until it begins to rise further east and set further west with each and every day. This phenomenon occurs between December 20 and 22 each year. The Welsh name for this time is *Alban Arthan*, a term coined by the nineteenth-century poet and writer of forgeries, Iolo Morganwg. This translates as "light of winter" or "light of the bear," although it is also known as *Alban Arthuan*, which means "light of Arthur." The "light of the bear" is an interesting translation, which may have roots going back thirteen thousand years and connect to the circumpolar constellation or Ursa

---

11. Jhenah Telyndru, *Avalon Within: A Sacred Journey of Myth, Mystery and Inner Wisdom*, (Llewellyn 2005), 88.

Major, which would be very visible and very bright in the British Isles at this time of year, during the greatest darkness.[12]

Here in Britain, the sun doesn't travel very high in the sky at all during this time and is always casting long shadows across the wintry landscape. The daylight doesn't really start much before 9:00 a.m. at the darkest point and the darkness creeps back in around 3:30 p.m. It can be a real challenge for people living in northerly latitudes at this time of year and the reverse in southern latitudes when they experience their winter months. The effects of seasonal affective disorder are now well known, as the brain produces less serotonin and melatonin during the winter months due to lack of sunlight, and the body's circadian rhythms are also affected.

In Britain and Europe, it is also known as the Midwinter Solstice, for indeed at this point it is the middle part of winter. For the Celts, winter began around Samhain and its effects diminished around Imbolc, when the first signs of spring began to show. There are even songs describing this time of year, such as "In the Bleak Midwinter" based on a poem by the English poet Christina Rossetti in 1872. Though the rest of the poem (put to music by Gustav Holst in 1906) is very Christian, it has a rather nature-based beginning:

In the bleak mid-winter
Frosty wind made moan;
Earth stood hard as iron,
Water like a stone;
Snow had fallen, snow on snow,
Snow on snow,
In the bleak mid-winter
Long ago.

---

12. Bradley E. Schaefer, "The Origin of the Greek Constellations: Was the Great Bear constellation named before hunter nomads first reached the Americas more than 13,000 years ago?" Scientific American, accessed November 1, 2017 https://www.scientificamerican.com/article/the-origin-of-the-greek-c/.

Pagan traces of another traditional British carol popular at this time of the year can be found in "The Holly and the Ivy," an amalgamation of Pagan and Christian influences:

The holly and the ivy,
When they are both full grown,
Of all the trees that are in the wood,
The holly bears the crown.
The rising of the sun
And the running of the deer,
The playing of the merry organ,
Sweet singing in the choir.

The tradition of wassailing happens during this time (found in another incarnation as carolling) and usually occurs during Twelfth Night (January 5–6). People could either go door-to-door in the form of house wassailing or in the orchards, as is a common practice in the western counties of England: Devon, Somerset, Dorset, Gloucestershire, and Herefordshire. Songs would be sung, toast dipped in cider and hung on branches, and shotguns fired into the branches of the trees to drive away evil spirits (or as a lazy form of pruning). This is the traditional chant/song, followed by banging on pots and pans and generally creating a ruckus:

Here's to thee, old apple tree,
That blooms well, bears well.
Hats full, caps full,
Three bushel bags full,
An' all under one tree.
Hurrah! Hurrah![13]

---

13. "The Diary of Samuel Pepys," accessed June 6, 2017, https://www.pepysdiary.com /encyclopedia/5948/.

There are many traditions related to the Winter Solstice, such as the creation of the Kissing Bough, which may be an remnant from Celtic times, when mistletoe, an herb sacred to the Druids, was honoured. It is at this time of year when mistletoe is the most obvious, not being hidden by any leaves and showing clearly among the bare branches of the trees in midwinter. Kissing under the mistletoe is a common custom, but the Kissing Bough is a more elaborate piece, created from two hoops entwined and covered with greenery, with mistletoe at the base. Inside are hung a male and female figure, and after every kiss, a berry is taken from the mistletoe until all the berries are gone.[14]

Bringing evergreens into the home is traditional and stems back from Pagan origins in Europe. Holly wreaths and spruce or fir trees are honoured at this time of year and signify the continuity of life even in the darkest depths of winter. We know that trees were very important to the Druids and the Celts, as well as for many other forms of Paganism found throughout Western Europe and, indeed, the rest of the world. The yule log is possibly a descendant of an ancient Pagan custom, where this year's log had to be lit from a remnant of the previous year. It is often said that the log is of either oak or ash, both considered to be symbolic of the World Tree, or axis mundi.

There are many ancient megalithic sites in Britain that are aligned to the Winter Solstice. The most famous of all, Stonehenge, is often known for its Summer Solstice sunrise, but rather more significant is the midwinter sunset, where every nineteen years the setting crescent of the new moon could be seen in the upper half of the Great Trilithon even as the sun set in the lower half. What a spectacle that would have been! Sadly, those stones have now fallen and this phenomenon is no longer visible.

The Christian holiday of Christmas seems to have been deliberately placed on December 25 to compete with the Pagan celebrations of the Winter Solstice, for at this time, usually around three days after the solstice, we

---

14. Karen Cater, *The Shortest Day: A Little Book of the Winter Solstice,* (Hedingham Fair, 2014), 38.

can begin to see the sun's change of direction when rising and setting on the horizon and the resulting lengthening days. It was recorded by a Christian writer, the scriptor Syrus in the late fourth century, why indeed this date was chosen by the Christians, when in the Bible no actual date for the birth of Christ can be found:

> It was a custom of the pagans to celebrate on the same 25 December the birthday of the Sun, at which they kindled lights in token of festivity. In these solemnities and revelries the Christians also took part. Accordingly, when the doctors of the Church perceived that the Christians had a leaning to this festival, they took counsel and resolved that the true Nativity should be solemnized on that day.[15]

Modern Druidry sees this as the time when the sun's strength returns and is celebrated. I can personally attest to the great joy in seeing the sun's return in lengthening days here in the UK after a long and dark winter, and each precious few minutes of extra sunlight are indeed something to be celebrated! It is a time to gather around the hearth and be with friends and family through the long winter nights.

Imbolc

The word Imbolc stems from the older *Oimelc*, which means "of milk" or "in the belly." Traditionally it was a time when the ewes from the sheep flocks began lactating, having just given birth. This was an incredibly important time for our ancestors, as the winter's stores would be running low and the fresh milk available would provide nourishment and sustenance to get people through until the first crops began to appear. Fresh butter, cream, and cheeses could be made to supplement the restrictive winter diet. Imbolc occurs around the beginning of February, if we are working with the traditional gestation period of the ewes. Nowadays, farmers have the sheep give birth at times that are more convenient; for example, a few villages over

---

15. Ronald Hutton, *The Stations of the Sun*, (Oxford University Press, 1996), 1.

from where I live, one farmer has his lambing season during the Christmas holidays, as that's when he and the rest of his family are home and can help out.

If we are following the calendar, the dates for Imbolc are January 31 to February 1. As the Celtic day began at sunset, we start the night before. Imbolc is often confused with the Christian holy day of Candlemas, which occurs on February 2. No doubt this was intentional, in order to compete with the beloved Pagan celebration of the lambing season and spring.

Imbolc is a holiday that is dedicated to the goddess Brighid. She is so entwined with the season and the time that most traditions honour her in some way during this festival. She is the goddess of poetry, smithcraft, and healing and is also often seen as a goddess of spring. She is the sacred waters of the wells and springs and the sacred flame tended first by nineteen priestesses and then later by nineteen nuns dedicated to her in the guise of St. Brighid. In Wales, Brighid is known as Braint or Ffraint and is connected to the river Afon Braint, which floods around this time every year.[16] The name, Brighid, has been adapted all over Britain and Europe and indeed Britain is named after her, in the form of Briganti (Romanised to Brigantia). There are also myths that link the goddess Brig with the spring in the form of the maiden, who alternates with the winter goddess the Cailleach. At Imbolc, the Cailleach drinks from a sacred stream or makes her way to the seashore before dawn and there transforms into the young maiden, Brighid. Other myths tell of Brighid immersing a white wand into the mouth of winter, which awakens the earth and brings in the thaw. Brighid's name might also come from the Gaelic *Breo-Saighead*, which means "fiery arrow," and many modern-day devotees of Brighid see this as her aspect in the flow of awen, the fire in the head of the poet and artist as well as the returning light of spring. For those who celebrate Imbolc by the signs in the vegetation, it is when the first snowdrops appear, pale white and green against the stark greyness of winter.

---

16. Kristoffer Hughes, *The Book of Celtic Magic*, (Llewellyn Worldwide, 2016), 98.

There are many customs associated with Brighid and Imbolc. It is the time when Brighid walks the land, and so offerings of milk, bread, butter, cheese, and beer are left to sustain her and thank her for her gifts. The hearthfire is extinguished, the hearth swept clean, and a new one lit in honour of the lengthening days and the return of the light. As Brighid is said to visit every home, a piece of cloth or ribbon is left out all night, to be covered with dew and then brought inside just before the sun rises. This cloth can be used to bless and heal for the rest of the year and is known as the *brat Bhríde*, having been blessed by the goddess. A Bridie doll can also be made, a poppet that represents the goddess, which is laid down in a small bed made for her so that she may pass the night in comfort and peace. Sometimes this doll is made from the last sheaves of the previous harvest and prayers are said over it to bring abundance for the coming year. Brighid's crosses are woven at this time of year, and it is traditional to use rushes (also called bulrushes) that have been pulled from the water, not cut.

Around Imbolc is when the swans leave their winter grounds in Ireland and the ravens come back to nest. The North American Groundhog's Day is a version of another custom of Imbolc, because at Imbolc it is said that the snakes emerge from their winter hibernation to bask in the sun (apart from in Ireland, where there never were any snakes). In the *Carmina Gadelica*, a collection of charms and prayers collected by Alexander Carmichael to preserve the old folklore and history, we see an invocation for Imbolc that pertains to this phenomenon:

> *Early on Bride's morn*
> *The serpent shall come from the hole.*
> *I shall not molest the serpent,*
> *Nor shall the serpent molest me.*[17]

Imbolc was also a time for divination, many of them involving fire. On Imbolc eve, you could smoor the fire (cover it with ashes so that it would

---

17. Niall MacFhionnlaigh, "Ortha nan Gaidheal," Carmina Gadelica, accessed December 2, 2017, http://www.smo.uhi.ac.uk/gaidhlig/corpus/Carmina/M70.html.

burn long and slow until the morning) and in the morning if you saw Brighid's footprints in the ashes, it meant luck and blessing for the coming year. Another custom is to light a candle for each member of the family and the first one to go out will also be the first to die. It is also said that the first person to hear a lark at dawn will receive good luck for the rest of the day.

Imbolc is a gentle holy day, one of welcoming and rejoicing in the longer days and counting our blessings during the cold nights.

Spring Equinox

The Spring Equinox or vernal equinox occurs between March 20 and 22. The word *equinox* is Latin for "equal night." It is also known as Ostara, Eostre, or by its Welsh name, *Alban Eiler*, "the light on the earth." It is a time when day and night are of equal length and the sun rises and sets due east and west respectively. In secular society, the Spring Equinox marks the first days of spring, but as we've seen above, Imbolc is actually when the first signs appear, at least in Britain.

The Christian holy day of Easter sometimes falls near this time, though it is a moveable feast with rather Pagan overtones (at least in the timing of it), for it falls on the first Sunday after the full moon following the Spring Equinox. Many are already aware of the symbols of this time of year, the rabbits and bunnies and eggs that abound, mostly in chocolate or sweetie form. Eggs and hares are common symbols in much of Western Paganism and indeed our Celtic ancestors held hares in high regard, for it was unlawful to kill a hare, apart from at the Spring Equinox, when they could be killed and eaten to share in their blessings and fertility through sympathetic magic.[18] Hens might begin laying again at this time, after a period of dormancy over the winter. If there is insufficient light, many breeds lay less or not at all and also may stop in very cold weather. With the return of the longer days and warmth from the sun, an increase in egg production would naturally occur and would be celebrated. The Druid's Egg, attested to by the Roman

18. Danu Forest, *The Magical Year: Seasons Celebrations to Honour Nature's Ever-Turning Wheel*, (Watkins, 2016), 57.

writer Pliny, was said to be a ball of twisted snakes; however, many mod-ern Druids hold that it was more likely to be an egg-shaped stone talisman carried and used by the Druids for magic and ritual.[19] Eggs, fertility, and all animals that provided sustenance for our ancient ancestors were venerated.

There are many Neolithic sites connected to both the Spring and Au-tumn Equinoxes. Perhaps the most famous of all is West Kennett Longbar-row, near Avebury stone circle and considered part of the Avebury complex which also includes Silbury Hill. The sun illuminates an inner chamber dur-ing the equinoxes, similar to Newgrange in Ireland during the Winter Sol-stice. At Silbury Hill, from a certain vantage point the sun actually rolls up the side of the hill and grows in size when it rises on the Spring Equinox.

The constellation Orion, which strides boldly across the sky during the winter months, is now close to the horizon and will disappear for the sum-mer months to come. Instead of the Hunter, we have the Herdsman appear-ing from the constellation Boötes the Herdsman, which reflects the times and tides of our Celtic ancestors, when thoughts turned now to more ag-ricultural matters as the earth warms up and makes ready for the lush pas-tures needed for cattle grazing. The cattle would be moved at Beltane, the next festival, which signalled the start of the summer season.

One equinox tradition is to try to balance an egg on its end, said to only be achievable at this special time. (I've not managed this one yet.) Eggs are hard-boiled and painted and left to find on Easter egg hunts (now replaced with sugary treats instead). Sometimes raw eggs are pricked on both ends and the insides blown out through the opposite hole, hollowing out the egg before painting and then hung on tree branches. Boiling the eggshells in onion skins creates a lovely mottled yellow colour. Egg-rolling or pace-egging is another tradition at this time of year in the UK, where eggs are rolled down steep hills and then given to egg-pacers, brightly costumed individuals parading and singing traditional festival-related songs and performing mumming plays (a form of folk play where the characters usually die and are brought back to life, often with music). Many morris dancers (English folk dancers usually

---

19. Ibid.

with bells attached to their feet) come out of winter hibernation at this time and can be seen in villages all around the countryside, honouring the season through the summer months.

This is the month when all the yellow flowers seem to bloom at once. The daffodils are everywhere and the forsythia reflects the growing sunlight in gardens all across the country. Where Imbolc has many white flowers, now the yellow of crocuses, lesser celandine, primroses, and dandelions are appearing. It is also when nettles start to come back, which provide a very nutritious herb high in iron and vitamins that is absolutely delicious as a soup at this time of year.

The Spring Equinox is a time to celebrate the tide of spring, the balance point between day and night, both outside in nature and within our own souls.

Beltane

Beltane is the start of summer, at the opposite end of the Wheel of the Year to Samhain, summer's end. Cattle would be brought to the higher ground and summer pastures, tended by the women and children while the men would work the farms. In Irish Gaelic it is *Beltaine*, in Welsh it is *Calan Mai*, and in Scottish Gaelic *Bealtainn*. It is the other time when the veils between the worlds are thin and the Fair Folk can be seen wandering the land in abundance. By the calendar, Beltane begins at dusk on April 30 and runs to dusk on May 1. If celebrating by the local flora, it is when the hawthorn or may is out in flower. In the UK, the first weekend in May is still celebrated with a bank holiday, perhaps as a remnant of this very important Celtic festival.

Fire is an integral part of this festival, for Beltane is often translated as "the fires of Bel," who is a sun deity. All household fires were extinguished on the eve of Beltane and then fires were lit on hilltops at dawn, similar to but in reverse at Samhain, where fires were lit at sunset.[20] It was important to not give away any fire from your household at Beltane, for your luck

---

20. Ronald Hutton, *Stations of the Sun: A History of the Ritual Year in Britain*, (Oxford University Press, 2001), 219.

would soon run out. Beltane is a hinge for the world to open and change, as at Samhain.[21] In Scotland and Wales, the Beltane bonfires were made from nine woods collected and put together by nine men and called "needfires." Cattle were driven between two bonfires on this day before heading out to their summer pastures. They were said to pass close enough to the fires so that their hair might be singed. The heat and smoke of the bonfires might have been enough to cause any parasites to fall off the animals that may have taken up residence in the winter quarters. Fire is also an important part of the Beltane ceremonies today, like at Edinburgh with the Beltane Fire Society putting on a spectacular event every year.

The growing power of the sun, symbolised by earthly fires, is balanced out by the importance of water during this festival. The power of morning dew still carries through relatively recent times, where early in the morning on May Day women would bathe their faces with dew for beauty. It was said that going barefoot in the dew of a May morn stopped feet from becoming sore and men who washed their hands with dew were the most skilled at creating knots and nets for fishing.

Beltane is the season of the Faery tree: the hawthorn. It is warned not to approach a lone hawthorn in a wild place, for it is surely a Faery tree, a portal to the Otherworld. Thomas the Rhymer fell asleep under a hawthorn on May Day and was taken away (willingly) by the Queen of the Faeries. Garlands and wreaths of hawthorn can decorate the outside of homes and gardens, but you must never bring hawthorn into the house or it will bring bad luck. Rowan was often used to create charms for the home and for cattle, made into a cross which was supposed to deter the Faeries' interest. Creating a may bush seems to have been one of the many pastimes and associated with the Faeries:

> Youth's folks now flocken in everywhere
> To gather May baskets and smelling brere
> And home they hasten the posts to dight

21. Alexei Kondratiev, *Celtic Rituals: An Authentic Guide to Ancient Celtic Spirituality*, (The Collins Press, 1998), 156.

And all the Kirk pillars ere daylight,
With hawthorn buds and sweet eglantine
And garlands of roses and sops in wine …

Tho to the green wood thy speeden them all,
To fetchen home May with their musical;
And home they bringen in a royal throne,
Crowned as a king; and his queen attone
Was Lady Flora, on whom did attend
A fair flock of faeries and a fresh bend
Of lovely nymphs. (O that I were there,
To helpen the ladies their May-bush bear!)[22]

The maypole is a traditional site at this time of year throughout Britain. It might be a representation of the World Tree, the axis mundi, and the ribbons woven into it by the dancers below symbolising our earthly dance in this life and how we are all connected. Much is made of the phallic nature of the maypole; however, I think the axis mundi concept, especially when considered alongside the Celtic *bíle* and its importance, is far more likely.

Beltane is also said to be the time of lovers, an ancient Pagan time of fertility. The more contemporary Pagans and Druids see Beltane as the time when the Goddess and God unite in sexual intercourse, as evidenced by the fertility of the land awakening and blossoming all around at this time of year. Historian Ronald Hutton has humorously criticised this interpretation of Beltane and its associations with sexual intercourse which seems to be the focus on many modern-day Beltane celebrations:

The behaviour of young people on May Eve and May Day had thus become a cliché of scandal and titillation alike. It took until the late twentieth century and the patient labours of demographic historians,

22. Edmund Spenser, *The Poetical Works of Edmund Spenser: In Eight Volumes*, 1788, Google Books, accessed on September 13, 2017, https://books.google.co.uk/books?id=3Q4UAAAAQAAJ.

to reveal that there was in fact no rise in the number of pregnancies at this season, in or out of marriage. The boom in conceptions came later in the summer. In practice early modern people seem to have found the night of 30 April generally too chilly and the woods generally too damp.[23]

Beltane is a liminal time, a time between the worlds. Beware of walking out and about on Beltane, for you never know who you may meet. It may be a Faery in disguise, especially out in the wild places or near barrows or ancient tumuli. I have met with the Fair Folk during the full moon at Beltane, and it has been a transformative experience. These encounters are not to be taken likely, for the Fair Folk are not like us and yet similar to us in some ways. They live on a different level and have different concerns which may or may not run alongside our own agenda. The Irish tend to avoid contacting the Faeries, but as Hedge Druids we may seek them out, with respect and not a little caution. Beltane eve is the perfect time or the nearest full moon to Beltane. Be sure to not carry any iron on your person or you may find your quest unsuccessful! Research all that you can on Faery lore before undertaking such a quest and familiarise yourself with the etiquette involved. The Fair Folk can often be found dressed all in green, with green hair, skin, eyes—everything! One tale goes that the Green Woman of the Faery Knoll called all the women from the village to her on the eve of Beltane and some went and some did not. Those that went came home with the light of Faery in their eyes and were skilled weavers with strong children and cattle and became wise beyond their years.

Summer Solstice

This is the second time in the year when the sun appears to "stand still" on its journey across the horizon upon rising and setting. Here, the sun rises at its furthest northeastern point and sets in its most northwestern. It reaches

---

23. Ronald Hutton, *Stations of the Sun: A History of the Ritual Year in Britain*, (Oxford University Press, 2001), 229.

its highest nadir in the sky and here in the UK that means that the days are exceptionally long and we may not even see full darkness before the light of dawn begins to permeate the skies. This phenomenon of the sun rising and setting in the same place lasts for three days, just as at the Winter Solstice. The Summer Solstice is known as *Alban Hefin* (Welsh), meaning "the light of summer," *Medios-saminos* (Old Celtic), and *Meitheamh* (Irish), which both mean "midsummer." Welsh tradition places the Summer Solstice as one of "three spirit-nights" or *tair ysbrydnos*, times when the veils between the world were thin, the others being *Calan Mai* and *Calan Gaeaf* (Beltane and Samhain). This is the longest day, before we begin our descent back into the darkness of the coming winter. It is considered the peak of the power of light, yet a reminder that everything changes.

We have already seen how our Neolithic ancestors built monuments to track the sunrise and sunset of the Winter Solstice, and equally each monument would also work in reverse six months later for the Summer Solstice. Many monuments, such as the Callanish stone circle, also include the equinoxes and so act as a giant calendar, marking out the time and the season. Four rows or avenues of ancient processional stones meet in the circle at a central stone, much like a Celtic cross. Stonehenge's processional way from the River Avon was marked by the sun's path during the solstices and the Ring of Brodgar on Orkey is also aligned to the solstices and equinoxes.

Being one of the three "spirit-nights" (Beltane, Summer Solstice, and Samhain), the Summer Solstice has long been connected to the Otherworld and the Fair Folk or Faeries. This is the time of the Faery ride, the Faery hunt, when the hosts of Faery emerge from the Otherworld to travel across this world. William Sharp writing as Fiona Macleod in the nineteenth century conjures up such an image known across the Celtic world:

> *Where the water whispers 'mid the shadowy*
> *rowan-trees*
> *I have heard the Hidden People like the hum*
> *of swarming bees:*
> *And when the moon has risen and the brown*

burn glisters grey
I have seen the Green Host marching in
laughing disarray.

Dalua then must sure have blown a sudden
magic air
Or with the mystic dew sealed my eyes
from seeing fair:
For the great Lords of Shadow who tread the
deeps of night
Are no frail puny folk who move in dread of
mortal sight.

For sure Dalua laughed alow, Dalua the fairy
Fool,
When with his wildfire eyes he saw me 'neath
the rowan-shadowed pool:
His touch can make the chords of life a bitter
jangling tune,
The false glows true, the true glows false
beneath his moontide rune.

The laughter of the Hidden Host is terrible to
hear,
The Hounds of Death would harry me at
lifting of a spear:
Mayhap Dalua made for me the hum of
swarming bees
And sealed my eyes with dew beneath the
shadowy rowan-trees.[24]

24. Fiona Macleod, "The Lords of Shadow," Archive.org, accessed September 16, 2017, https://archive.org/stream/writingsoffionam07macl/writingsoffionam07macl_djvu.txt.

In the poem above, Dalua reminds me of Gwyn ap Nudd, the Welsh Faery King and Lord of the Underworld spoken of previously. Faery rides are known to ride out across the land at these liminal times, and so it is wise to try to avoid them at all costs. There is a tale of a young woman named Kathleen who sought out the Fair Folk in Knockmaa in Tuam, Western Ireland, having caught the eye of the king of the Connacht Faeries. On the eve of midsummer, she dressed and went out, dancing among them until the king appeared, whereupon he took her in his arms and she never returned home again. At least, not alive: she was found dead upon the hillside near the Faery fort, a smile upon her face.

Fire is another aspect of this festival, and fire or sun wheels were rolled down hillsides by young men of extreme dexterity who then chased after it. It is thought that the cheese-rolling competitions of Gloucester began around this time and were then moved to nearer the Spring Equinox. I know what I would rather chase down a hill! The hills of Knockainey and Cnoc Gréin in Ireland were thought to be twin beacon hills upon which fires were lit at this time of year.

Seek out the Fair Folk at this time of year—if you dare. Just be sure to wear some St. John's wort in your buttonhole to keep the nastier ones away. There are many herbs associated with the Summer Solstice and said to be best collected at this time, such as St. John's wort, mugwort, vervain, and yarrow.

Lughnasadh

Lughnasadh, or *Gwyl Awst* in the Welsh tradition, is often termed "the first harvest" in Modern Druidry; however, the hay meadows would have already been cut for fodder late June and early July and the first harvest would have technically been for animal consumption. However, this can be seen as the time just before the first agricultural harvest for humans, a time to celebrate while the corn was ripening in the fields (wheat and barley as it is known in the UK, not the yellow corn known as sweetcorn and in North America as simply corn). It can also be a celebration just after the fields have been harvested, though it may be weeks into August before the full reaping of the first harvest is completed in any given region, with it all depending on the weather. You cannot harvest wheat and barley in the rain: it must be dry. You could simply celebrate the reaping of the fields closest to you, if you wish, to narrow it down to a particular point and place in time.

Lughnasadh was said to have been celebrated for weeks on end, which might be due in part to the waiting game for the crops to be ready. Some berries and other wild fruits are now available, and this might also be part of the first harvest. It was a time of celebration, of skills and tests, of daring feats and just plain showing off, knowing that the hard work of reaping lay ahead. Nowadays, we celebrate the cutting of the first grain at Lughnasadh, for the crops are ready earlier and the corn is usually ready to harvest in England at the end of July/beginning of August. It is also a remnant and amalgamation of the Saxon *hloaf-mass* or loaf mass, now known as Lammas. We still have a few weeks of school holiday in Britain, which begins at the end of July/beginning of August and is perhaps a lingering tradition of the old Lughnasadh: a reminder of our agricultural past, when there was a few weeks' grace before the hard work of harvest arrived. Today, children cele- brate their time off from school and August is seen as the holiday month in Britain.

Lughnasadh translates to "the assembly of Lugh" in Ireland (*nasadh* means "gathering"). Lugh was one of the chief gods of the Tuatha Dé Danann. He was known as "the Many Skilled" and this is perhaps why there were previously many feats and contests held at this festival, to show off people's various skills in honour of Lugh. Horse racing was a particular fa- vourite, said to have been invented by Lugh himself. Even today, there are still horse fairs held in August such as at Ballycastle's "Auld Lammas Fair." The Gaulish Celtic calendar known as the Coligny calendar marks this time as Equos or Horse-Time. Horses were "raced" through water, men riding unclad across rivers and small lakes while their horses swam.

However, the real focus for this festival lay with Lugh's foster-mother, Tailtiu, who died clearing a vast tract of land (related to Meath in Ireland) and asked Lugh to hold a festival each year in her honour. If this festival was upheld each and every year, it was said that there would be "corn and milk in every house, peace and fair weather for the feast."

The name of Tailtiu comes from Old Celtic *Talantiu*, meaning "the great one of the earth." In Modern Druidry, we celebrate the abundance and gifts of the earth, whom many see as the Goddess.

As well as having games and competitions at Lughnasadh festivals and fairs, it was also a time for marriages. Teltown (a name derived from the goddess, Tailtiu) in Ireland was renowned for its "Teltown marriages" that took place at Lughnasadh every year, where couples would thrust their hands between a stone without seeing who was on the other side and then could undergo a trial marriage for a year and a day. If it worked, then they would be properly married the following year. If it didn't, they simply returned and ended the relationship. Lammas in Scotland was a day for old women to sain or bless the cattle, which would keep away evil for three months thereafter. Like at Beltane, tar was put behind their ears and tails and charms were said over their udders. It was a time when "no one left the table hungry."

As at Beltane, the Summer Solstice, and Samhain, many celebrations were held in high places, atop hills and mountains, liminal places between the earth and sky. The ending of one time and the beginning of another was an important part of the Celtic festivals, and Lughnasadh was no exception. Flower garlands worn to the high places for celebration were then buried in recognition that summer had ended and the season of harvest had begun. Here in these places, order and sovereignty were acknowledged and tribal bonds were renewed.

The Irish Pagan god of the harvest, Crom Dubh, is a mysterious character of whom little is known, yet what we know of him connects him to the festival of Lughnasadh. His name means "Dark, Bent One," and he was known as bringing the first wheat into Ireland. It might be a connection to a ripe sheaf of wheat or barley, which bends when full with seed. In Mount Brandon people climbed the mountain to celebrate in his name, and at the foot of the mountain in the village of Cloghane in County Kerry, there could be seen a stone image in his likeness that was preserved in the local church. There is still a festival in Cloghane village at the time of Lughnasadh called *Domhnach Chrium Dhuibh*, meaning "Crom Dubh's Sunday."

On Croagh Patrick in County Mayo, Ireland, it was said that St. Patrick banished Crom Dubh and this is celebrated on "Reek Sunday," where at this location over twenty-five thousand people visit and services are held in the modern chapel at the top of the mountain. Locals know this place as "the Reek," and it attracts over one million visitors throughout the year.

Lughnasadh is also said to be the time when Lugh himself defeated the god Crom Dubh, the light defeating the darkness, but that is at odds with what is happening seasonally at this time of year, when the days are becoming shorter and the nights longer. Perhaps it is another version of a new generation of gods taking over from an older set and Crom Dubh might be a very, very ancient god indeed. What will you celebrate this Lughnasadh: the festival in honour of Lugh or Lugh's foster-mother or an even older veneration of an ancient deity? Why not all three?

Autumn Equinox

Known as *Alban Elfed* in the Welsh tradition, the Autumn Equinox is the second balance point, when day and night are equal and that knife's edge that we balance upon holds but for a moment, before we plunge fully into the darkness of winter's night. It falls between September 20 and 22. It is often called "Mabon" in Western Paganism, and this is a reference to the Welsh myth of Maponus, *The Mabon*, who is the divine child that was stolen and then returned the land, bringing with him the fruitfulness and abundance that nature has to offer. It is considered the second harvest in Modern Paganism, when the last of the grains have been brought safely in. It is also the apple harvest in parts of North America, as well as many root vegetables in my part of the world—turnips and onions, with carrots at the end of September/beginning of October.

In the night sky, Ursa Major sinks lower in the northern horizon, and Orion (associated in Celtic star lore as Gwyn ap Nudd or Herne the Hunter in England) rises for a brief period preceding dawn, where he will soon rule the winter night's sky. The Pleiades or the Seven Sisters are often an indicator that autumn is well and truly underway, and there are several Neolithic monuments across Britain and Scotland that have alignments to this particular constellation's rising, including Avebury stone circle in Wiltshire and especially Callanish in Scotland, where the stones mark beautifully the rising of the Pleiades just as the sun sets.

In Scotland, it was said that if the deer went into rut with a wet head (i.e., it was raining), then it will be dry for the whole month and the harvest can continue with ease. There is an event in Abbot's Bromley in Staffordshire, England, that takes place on Wakes Monday, which is the first Sunday after September 4. Here, dancers perform wearing headdresses of reindeer antlers, some of which have been carbon-dated to the eleventh century and may be replacements for even older ones. There is some contention as to when reindeer became extinct in Britain; some say it was in the twelfth or thirteenth century based largely on the fact that an Orcadian saga (the *Orkneyinga*) mentions them being hunted on Caithness; others state it was around 6000 BCE. All we can be certain of is that they were reintroduced to the Cairngorms in Scotland in 1952. That being said, this folk dance may very well be a link to a very distant past! It may be from a very old Pagan tradition, honouring the deer rut and the hunt, although some believe it to date back to the Anglo-Saxons and a form of sympathetic magic for the royal deer hunt.

Harvest suppers were celebrated around the time of the equinox and still are in many rural parishes across Britain. Many churches are also decorated with flowers, greenery, and some of the produce from the harvest. My local parish church has a flower festival during the Autumn Equinox, and the whole church is decked out in instalments from various organisations such as the Women's Institute or the local primary school. It looks and smells wonderful! There is also a Harvest Home supper celebrated every year toward the end of September. Harvest Home is an English celebration on the last day of the harvest with song, dance, boughs of greenery, and feasting.

The cutting of the last sheaf from the grain crops is held in high importance across Celtic lands. Many traditions hold certain rituals around the cutting and the preservation of the sheaf. Usually it is made into a corn dolly, sometimes an animal such as the *penn-yar* or "hen's head" in Cornwall, a possible link to the goddess Ceridwen. In Wales the last sheaf was often transformed into the *caseg fedi*, the harvest mare, symbolising the goddess of the land and sovereignty. These dollies were usually ritually burned a year later or sometimes at Beltane or Imbolc.

Wherever you are, the Autumn Equinox is a time of transition, as are all the holy festival days. We honour what has come before, we are in tune with what is happening at the present moment, and we think about the future to come. All this is beautifully represented in the Wheel of the Year, whether you follow the four Celtic Fire Festivals or all eight special days.

The Hedge Druid holds a Harvest Supper for a few close friends. At a long wooden table in her back garden, local foods and drink are laid out, with each guest having brought something to share. There is laughter and friendship, merriment and camaraderie. The path of the Hedge Druid may be solitary, but she can also share with her friends whatever she chooses to share. At this time of the year, the coming together of friends seems natural, a celebration of the bounty of the harvest. The soft golden autumn light casts its glow upon those gathered, who each take a turn stating what they are grateful for in their lives before they all tuck in to a hearty meal. The Hedge Druid looks at the faces around her, her love for them swelling within her heart. This is what it means to be alive.

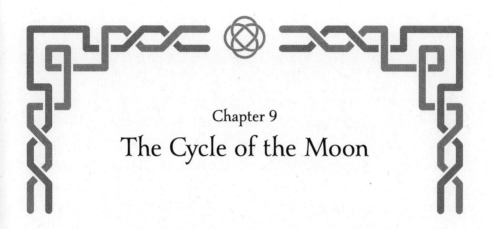

Chapter 9

The Cycle of the Moon

As we have previously seen, the cycle of the sun through the Wheel of the Year combined with the fire or agricultural festivals marks points throughout the yearly cycle. The moon is equally important in this yearly cycle, and based on the archaeological evidence from the Neolithic stone circles together with the recorded writings from Classical interpreters of Celtic culture, we can see that the moon's cycle was equally revered by the Druids and their predecessors.

Without the benefits of indoor lighting, streetlights, and so on, the moon's light was a very important factor to our ancestors. Have you ever tried walking outside at night at the time of the dark moon, without any light source? Today, too many suffer from light pollution, where the night sky is never as dark as it should be and the orange lights coming from towns and cities light up the night sky so that only the brightest stars can be seen and the true darkness of a moonless night is hitherto unknown. Walking out of doors at night was made much easier by the light of the moon, and calculating the cycles and eclipses were important to our ancestors on this very basic level.

The moon orbits the earth roughly once each month (once every 27.322 days to be precise), where the angle shared between the three objects of sun, earth, and moon affects how we perceive the moon, its shape, and its cycle. It also takes around twenty-seven days for the moon to rotate once on its axis, and this results in the phenomenon that the moon does not appear to be spinning but rather keeps almost perfectly still, which is known as synchronous rotation (hence the "dark side of the moon," which we never see). The moon is illuminated by the light of the sun off of its rocky and dusty surface. The new moon, or the first crescent with points facing left, reaches its first quarter and then afterward becomes a waxing gibbous moon, where the moon appears to get fatter and fatter and the points slowly diminish. The full moon occurs two weeks after the dark moon and then turns into the waning gibbous phase of its cycle until it reaches the third quarter of its cycle, whereupon it returns to the crescent shape again, this time with points facing to the right. Two weeks after the full moon, the moon appears to diminish in size until it "disappears" for three days. This occurs when the moon is in conjunction with the earth and the sun so that no sunlight can be visible upon its surface from the earth's perspective. A blue moon is technically when there are two full moons in the same astrological sign; however, nowadays people refer to the blue moon as the second full moon in a calendrical month.

The moon, like the sun, rises at a different point on the horizon each day. However, the moon's cycle is quicker and moves eastward roughly thirteen degrees every day, rising approximately fifty minutes later on each successive night. What is interesting to note is that the full moon rises where the sun will rise at the opposite time of year; so where the full moon rises on Samhain is where the sun rises at Beltane. Where the full moon rises at the Summer Solstice is where the sun rises at the Winter Solstice. The length of days and nights are swapped, and so during the summer months, the moon's journey appears shorter and the sun's longer—and vice versa in the winter months.

Eclipses and being able to predict them were important to our ancestors, hence the building of circles to mark out the cycles of the moon and sun. A solar eclipse is when the earth moves through the shadow cast by the moon, the moon itself blocking out the light of the sun. This can only occur when the moon is at its dark moon stage. In contrast, a partial or total lunar eclipse is when the moon passes through the earth's shadow, which can only occur when the moon is full. A full cycle of an eclipse, where the same eclipse appears in the same place in the sky, occurs approximately once every eighteen years. As well, eclipses are phenomena that occur together in twos or threes; a solar eclipse usually is preceded or followed by a lunar eclipse.

The moon also affects the tides, and where I live on the coast of the North Sea, this is something to be taken very seriously, especially in the autumn during hurricane season, as storms are swept across the Atlantic to hit our shores or cold winters surge down from the Arctic. If this is timed with a full or dark moon, we have spring tides, which can cause storm surges that flood the beaches, marshes, creeks, and rivers as the higher levels of water rush in at high tide. We take storm surge warnings very seriously, and any person living on the coast knows (or should know!) what phase the moon is in at any given time during this season. The moon's gravitational pull on Earth causes the part of Earth that is closest to the moon to bulge outward, toward the moon. In the fluidity of the seas and oceans, this pull is markedly higher, and so we see the real difference in high tide and low tide. There are two high tides and low tides each day, every six hours. Knowing the tides is important, not only for storm surges, but also to reach islands that are connected by land bridges, such as St. Michael's Mount in Cornwall or the holy island of Lindisfarne off the coast of Northumberland.

For the Celts, the cycle of the moon was used to determine important events and for declaring when sacred rituals should take place. The new moon, when the first crescent appears in the sky, was of importance to the Druids. In his Classical account of the Druids harvesting mistletoe, Pliny states that this was done during the sixth day of the moon, during the waxing crescent, which will have been newly visible after the dark of the moon. Lunar eclipses were also important. In 218 BCE, a Galatian army (Celts living in modern-day Turkey) was brought to a halt by a lunar eclipse, suggesting an apprehension of moving at this time, which would allude to a deep acknowledgement and perhaps veneration of the lunar cycle. Strabo records the Celtiberians worshipping an unnamed god at the full moon. In the *Dindschenchas* an oath is sworn to natural phenomena, including the sun, moon, and sea. The mysterious item known as "The Druid's Egg," which may have been a stone used for magical and/or ceremonial purposes, could only be collected at a certain time of the moon. Mistletoe was harvested at a certain moon phase, popularly recorded by Pliny the Elder in his work, *Natural History*:

> We should not omit to mention the great admiration that the Gauls have for it as well. The druids—that is what they call their magicians—hold nothing more sacred than the mistletoe and a tree on which it is growing, provided it is a hard-timbered oak [robur].... Mistletoe is rare and when found it is gathered with great ceremony and particularly on the sixth day of the moon.... Hailing the moon in a native word that means "healing all things," they prepare a ritual sacrifice and banquet beneath a tree and bring up two white bulls, whose horns are bound for the first time on this occasion. A priest arrayed in white vestments climbs the tree and, with a golden sickle, cuts down the mistletoe, which is caught in a white cloak. Then finally they kill the victims, praying to a god to render his gift propitious to those on whom he has bestowed it. They believe that mistletoe given in drink will impart fertility to any animal that is barren and that it is an antidote to all poisons.[25]

Some Druid groups today celebrate and hold ritual on the sixth day of the moon in accordance with this bit of information on the ancient Druids. However, drinking mistletoe is to be avoided—it is poisonous! Others hold ritual at the full and dark moon. As a new day in Celtic terminology begins at sunset, so does the importance of night time, darkness, and the moon hold an equal resonance to the sun and its yearly cycle. We can see that the Celts estimated time by the different moons throughout the year in addition to the sun, from what we know of the famous Coligny calendar dating back to the second century in Gaul. This calendar is known as a lunisolar calendar that

25. Pliny, *Natural History*, Celtic Literature Collective, accessed November 3, 2017, http://www.maryjones.us/ctexts/classical_pliny.html#16.

contains intercalary months. The word "month" is directly correlated to the word "moon" (Old English *mona*), which stems from the Indo-European word *mé*, from which the words "measure" and "month" can also be derived. The Coligny calendar attempts to bring together the cycles of the moon and sun. The phases of the moon are important to the Coligny calendar, where each month always begins with the same moon phase, the sixth night of the waxing moon. The calendar employs a mathematical system to keep a normal twelve-month calendar synchronised with the moon and keep the entire system in sync by adding an intercalary month every two and a half years. The Coligny calendar records a five-year cycle of sixty-two lunar months, divided into a "bright" or "light" and a "dark" fortnight (or half a moon, two-week cycle) respectively.

Month Name	Length of Days	Etymology	Time Period
Samonios	30	Seed Fall	October/November
Dumannios	29	Darkest Depths	November/December
Riuros	30	Cold Time	December/January
Anagantios	29	Stay At Home Time	January/February
Ogronios	30	Time of Ice	February/March
Cutios	30	Time of Winds	March/April
Giamonios	29	Shoots Show	April/May
Simivisionios	30	Time of Light/ Brightness	May/June
Equos	29/30	Horse Time	June/July
Elembiuos	29	Claim Time	July/August
Edrinios	30	Arbitration Time	August/September
Cantios	29	Song Time	September/October
Sonnocingos	30	Sun's March	Intercalary*

* Reese, Coligny Calendar, Ancient Origins, accessed November 30, 2017, http://www.ancient-origins.net/artifacts-other-artifacts/coligny-calendar-1800-year-old-lunisolar-calendar-banned-romans-002429.

The Welsh goddess Arianrhod is also known as "The Lady of the Silver Wheel." This might refer to her dwelling, *Caer Arianrhod*, which is also known as star constellation the Corona Borealis. It is interesting to note that this constellation forms a semi-circle, similar in shape to a crescent moon or the horns of a bull. However, as the constellation is not so much of a circle but rather a crescent, it is my opinion that the epithet of Lady of the Silver Wheel refers to the moon and not the stars that are commonly associated with this goddess. There are others who share this opinion, and it is certainly divided. For me personally, one look up in the sky at the full moon confirms this beautiful silver wheel, making its rounds through the heavens. As an aside, there is another Caer Arianrhod located in a reef off the coast of Gwynedd in Wales, said to be the goddess's castle and is only visible at low tide, which might reflect once again the connection between the moon and the sea.

Around the world there are different names for the full moons and their cycles. Popular ones today mostly stem from Native North American names for these moons; however, there are still some Celtic names (based on the Coligny calendar) and medieval ones to be found:

Celtic Moon Names

January	Quiet Moon	July	Claim Moon
February	Ice Moon	August	Dispute Moon
March	Wind Moon	September	Singing Moon
April	Growing Moon	October	Harvest Moon
May	Bright Moon	November	Dark Moon
June	Horse Moon	December	Cold Moon [†]

[†] "Full Moon Names," Moon Facts, accessed December 12, 2017, http://www.moonfacts.net/moon-name-meanings.

Algonquin Moon Names

January	Wolf Moon	July	Buck Moon
Febraury	Snow Moon	August	Sturgeon Moon
March	Worm Moon	September	Harvest Moon
April	Pink Moon	October	Hunter's Moon
May	Flower Moon	November	Beaver Moon
June	Strawberry Moon	December	Cold Moon [‡]

[‡] "Full Moon Names" The Old Farmer's Almanac, accessed December 12, 2017, https://www.almanac.com/content/full-moon-names.

English Medieval Moon Names

January	Wolf Moon	July	Mead Moon
February	Storm Moon	August	Corn Moon
March	Chaste Moon	September	Barley Moon
April	Seed Moon	October	Blood Moon
May	Hare Moon	November	Snow Moon
June	Dyan Moon	December	Oak Moon [§]

§ "Full Moon Names," Moon Facts, accessed December 12, 2017, http://www. moonfacts.net/moon-name-meanings.

In a Hedge Druid tradition, it would be encouraged to find your own names for each moon's cycle, if you do not live in a land that has already found and preserved its own names for the moons or if you are simply unable to find out what these names used to be, lost to the mists of time. Cycles change as well and the old names may no longer hold resonance with what is happening in your environment, and so new names might be required. Naming the moons helps to provide a deeper insight into the cycles within cycles, the phases of the moon throughout the longer cycles of the earth's path around the sun.

There is a lingering tradition of honouring the moon in Celtic countries still to be found today—in folkloric wisdom. In Scotland, in the historic work *Carmina Gadelica*, which records old folk traditions, we see several examples of the moon influencing behaviour and what one should do upon viewing it:

When I see the New Moon
It is fitting for me to lift my eye
It is fitting for me to bend my knee
It is fitting for me to bow my head.
I praise you, Moon of Guidance
Now that I have seen you again
Now that I have seen the new moon
Beauteous guide on the Pathway [26]

26. *Carmina Gadelica*, accessed December 13, 2017, http://www.smo.uhi.ac.uk/gaidhlig/ corpus/Carmina.

In the county of Cork, Ireland, women blessed themselves upon viewing the new moon, offering a short prayer: "May she leave us in good health." [27] Turning money in the pockets, especially silver coins when viewing the new moon for the first time was said to bring wealth. Other traditions state that when the moon is viewed for the first time, a garment should be turned inside out in order to receive gifts. In Cornwall, it was unlucky to view the new moon through glass and one should always see it outside first and foremost. "See the new moon through glass: you'll have trouble while it lasts." As well, there is the saying "two full moons in the month of May are neither good for corn nor hay." Scotland had an abundance of lore pertaining to sowing and harvesting by the moon, as well as cutting peat during the waning of the moon. In the Orkneys, marriages were conducted during the time of the waxing moon. In Wales, a child born during the new moon would be gifted with eloquent speech and those born in the third quarter had exceptional powers of reasoning.

Some Druid and Pagan groups work through the festivals according to the cycle of the moon in relation to the zodiac—celebrating Samhain at the first full moon when the Sun is in Scorpio, for instance. For the purposes of this work, we will work to the Modern Druid/Neopagan calendar (the Wheel of the Year) in part two, as well as offering rites and rituals dedicated to the dark moon and the full moon.

It is the Wind Moon, which is living up to its name. For three days storms have raged and the snows have fallen. Though it is the month of March and the snows are late, still the Hedge Druid struggles outside to catch a glimpse of the full moon through the tattered clouds. She wraps a blanket around her shoulders and stands on the patio overlooking the garden. The glow of the moon can be seen from behind the clouds, brightening the eastern part of the sky. Patiently she waits, the cold wind caressing her with icy fin-

27. Sharynne MacLeod NicMhacha, *Queen of the Night: Rediscovering the Celtic Moon Goddess*, (Weiser, 2005), 199–205.

gers. Then the moon appears, bright yellow and shining upon the garden. The Hedge Druid smiles, feeling the moonlight upon her face. Then, as quickly as it appeared, the moon is hidden once more and the snow begins to fall again, sideways in the biting wind. Shivering, the Hedge Druid bows to the moon and goes back into the warmth.

Chapter 10

Meditation

Meditation can be done for many different reasons. Some use it to find inner peace, others to help find a focus in their lives and their work, and still others to increase compassion in the lives of themselves and those around them. But for the most part, I think an aspect of meditation that is often overlooked is the simple fact that it's nice to just stop every once in a while, sit down, and enjoy the moment.

I use meditation for all the reasons given above and more. But the simple pleasure of stopping is when, perhaps, it is of most use. Taking the time to light some candles and incense, get some cushions out, and just simply be is a great gift that I can give to myself at the end of a busy day or week. As I sit in front of my altar, I allow all the thoughts that are running through my head to make themselves known to me, rather than just being background stress and noise. Eventually, the thoughts slow down and quieten, and then comes that exquisite moment when *all is still*. No more mental gymnastics. No more body twitches, itches, or squirming trying to find a comfortable, relaxed position. Everything settles. Even if this feeling lasts for just ten seconds, it is good. Better than good. The heart opens; the mind and body are one. There is nothing but myself and the world, here and now, sitting, breathing, peaceful.

Having even ten seconds to still the mind, to allow it to take a break from all thoughts, has an enormous effect on the mind and body for days

afterward. Taking the time to allow yourself to set aside the cares and worries, the reminiscing and the to-do lists, the work and the family issues has
a profound effect on all aspects of your life. Have you ever sat on the couch
after a busy day, flopped onto the sofa, and just stopped for a minute or two
in stillness and silence? Meditation is the same thing—allowing your mind
and body a moment of rest.

In that deep silence when that moment is achieved, we can have some
profound realisations. When we stop the mental chatter, we allow ourselves
to refocus on what really matters in our lives. Just a few seconds of that
blissful silent state can alter our perception and allow us to put things into
perspective. What really matters? Not what the guy said to you in that social media group. Not the office gossip or your infuriating work colleague.
Spending a little time in the quiet of our homes or meditation space,
whether inside or outside, allows us to see that it's in the joy of being alive
right now and the people whom we physically share our lives with and care
about that really matter: our family and friends, our home, our gardens;,our
religion or spirituality, the earth. Our perspective can get so skewed by what
is happening in the world around us. Allowing ourselves to stop and refocus
changes everything.

It's amazing what ten little seconds can achieve.

That sense of peace will then permeate all aspects of our Hedge Druidry, and we will find that the work we do is more focused and our perspective more integrated with the rest of the world. We may also find that
we can enter altered states with more ease, which we will cover in a later
section of this work.

Basics of Meditation

There are many different kinds of meditation, from simple mindfulness
meditation—where one focuses on the breath and body—to transcendental
meditation, journeying, guided meditation, walking meditation, yoga, and
more. Meditation is an important aspect of religious and spiritual traditions
the world over, simply because it allows a focus and perspective for a clarity
we might not otherwise achieve in our everyday patterns and behaviour. It

can even help us change those patterns and behaviour so that the spiritual becomes part of everyday life. The mundane and the sacred are not polar opposites but simply part of a large spectrum of existence. We could even say that after doing meditation for years, it allows us to see that there is no separation, no spectrum at all, and that everything is sacred.

Meditation allows us to connect with ourselves and with the world. Today's society seems focused on doing anything but connecting us with our minds and bodies and with "real" people, what with social media and mobile phones distracting people from even the simplest of tasks, such as walking down the street or going out for a meal with a loved one. Our modern world seems to be leaning toward isolation and virtual reality as opposed to being in the here and now, however dull, wet, uncomfortable, pleasurable, or lovely that may be. Why? Well, there are a lot of people making money from it, for starters.

In meditation, we learn to be with ourselves, in all our glory and all our failings. It provides us with emotional and psychological resilience. We learn to be with ourselves, whether we are in pain or are exceedingly happy. We learn about acceptance in the here and now and what we can and cannot control. We are not seeking any diversions from reality, but instead engaging with it to allow it to influence our lives on a profound level. We are not running away from anything; we are not "away with the Faeries." We are focused on the task at hand, the meditation, and engaging with our bodies and our worlds in a calm and peaceful manner. Hopefully, that engagement will spill out into the rest of our lives and we will find that calm and peace begin to permeate all aspects of what we do and how we live our lives.

Acceptance is a big part of meditation. We accept that our minds are a little bit crazy. We accept that we have created lives that may have taken us away from our goals or what really matters in life and that meditation helps us to refocus. We accept our bodies too, whether we can sit in full lotus position for hours or whether we need a chair and lots of cushions in order to achieve that peace. We accept the noises around us, the itches and the thoughts going round and round in our brains. And we stick with it, knowing that eventually—

eventually—it will all settle and we will find that peace we seek. We can only find this peace through acceptance, not striving or forcing it. You might as well force the wind to move in a different direction, for peace *is* acceptance.

Many people will say that they tried to meditate but just couldn't find the stillness. Everyone is different, but it is my belief that indeed everyone *can* meditate in some form or other; they simply have to find the right method for them and want to work hard toward it. That may sound a bit contradictory to what I just said about acceptance, but the peace achieved in meditation often doesn't happen in the first attempt—or second, third, or thirtieth. If someone has never meditated before, it can take a long time for the mind and body to settle. Our personality and disposition has a lot to say in the matter as well, whether we are natural fidgets or can find comfort relatively easily. We have to truly want to meditate and not just "give it a go." Meditation is a core element of many religious and spiritual traditions, and therefore it's not there just to play around with, but is a vital component in working toward your potential and your path's true potential.

So to begin with, it makes it easier if we are comfortable and without too many distractions. For most people, meditation is often easiest when performed indoors, as we can control the environment in which we are working. After we are able to hold that focus in a controlled environment, we can take it outside and meditate anytime, anywhere, with enough practice and commitment. So here we will begin indoors. Aim for around fifteen to thirty minutes per day for meditation. You can break this down into smaller chunks if you need to; say two ten-minute sessions, morning and evening. Choose wisely the time that you are going to meditate; if you are tired at the end of the day and will probably fall asleep, then meditate in the morning. If you are too busy getting the children ready for school or have a very early commute, then perhaps try meditating at lunchtime or as soon as you get home. I used to meditate in a nearby small church when I worked in a skyscraper building in downtown Montreal many years ago. There, they had a small chapel filled with carved wood and an image of Mary. It was rarely used and often I had it all to myself. I simply sat and meditated in that quiet space for half an hour every day, smelling the wood polish and the scent that all churches seem to have. It was a haven and a sanctuary in the middle of a bustling city and also nice and cool in the summer. Find a space and time that works for you.

Sitting Meditation

Find a room or a space within a room where you won't be disturbed. If you like, you can create an altar if you haven't one already (we will look more closely at altar creation in part two of this book). A simple altar consisting of a candle and some incense can go a long way to creating the atmosphere that many enjoy in their meditation practice. If you don't like incense and are not able to burn candles, then you can simply have a potted plant as a symbol of the natural world and your connection with it. I find that having something to look at and focus on helps greatly when beginning on the meditative path, and candles, incense smoke, plants, mandalas, or pictures of gods, goddesses, or other things that inspire us can help. Don't have too many things when first starting out, however, as this can again be distracting. Simple and easy is always the best when starting on this endeavour.

If you are able to comfortably be in a seated position on the floor, then please go ahead and do so. I find it very grounding, and you can take this posture anywhere you choose to go once you have mastered the basics of meditation (i.e., you can use this outside, where you might not be able to take a chair, in the middle of the woods). Some people may not be comfortable on the floor for various reasons, and so using a chair is perfectly acceptable, though that may limit the places you are able to perform meditation. If you are sitting on the floor, try not to sit cross-legged if you can, because this can cut off the circulation in your legs. I find that the "easy pose" in Zen Buddhist meditation is the most comfortable. In this pose, you bring in one leg toward the body and then have the other pulled in after it without overlapping. This pose is also demonstrated on the Gundestrup cauldron, often considered a masterpiece of early Celtic art. I sit raised up on a couple of cushions, so that the knees are in line with the hips. If they are still raised, you can experiment with adding cushions until you have developed the flexibility that allows them to fall in line with the hips. This provides a stable platform to sit in for any period of time. You may be able to do this without any cushions at all or you may need several. As the years have trundled on and my knees and hips have suffered injuries, I find I need more cushions to raise me up than I used to require, say, twenty years ago.

If you prefer to use the half lotus (one foot resting on the opposite thigh) or full lotus (both feet resting on opposite thighs), then please feel free to use these positions. This requires a high level of flexibility in the hips, knees, and ankles, and if you've suffered any injuries to these areas, these postures may not be for you. I sprained my ankle badly years ago and it won't move into that position easily. My knees are now not able to take the strain of that position either. Forcing your body into any posture is simply *not* a good idea, and you could do yourself great injury in the attempt. *Never* force a meditation posture if it is painful or uncomfortable or if your circulation is being cut off.

Sit with your back straight and allow your shoulders to relax. Keep the neck long and "float" the head toward the ceiling. You can tuck the chin slightly to elongate the back of the neck and keep the shoulders from hunching forward. Tuck your tongue to the upper palate of your mouth, which will stop the "double chin" effect as well as decrease salivation in the mouth. Have the mouth relaxed, however, and do not clench the teeth together. Allow the tongue to be soft, but suctioned to the roof of the mouth. Place your hands upon your thighs, palms up or down, whichever you find most comfortable. If you find yourself hunching forward, bring your hands higher up on your thighs until your elbows are at your sides: this keeps your back straighter. You can also place your hands in your lap and sometimes I like to hold one hand cradled within the other. Keep the face and body relaxed, but not so relaxed you fall over, of course! Shift your weight from side to side and front to back and then find that spot in the middle where you feel centred. Then, keeping your eyes and focus soft, you can begin.

If you are sitting in a chair, then you can do much the same as on the floor. Ensure that your feet are placed flat on the floor, that the chair's height does not raise or lower you too much, and that your knees are more or less level with your hips. Sit forward on the chair if you are able so that you do not have to use the back support. If you need the back support for any reason, you can put a cushion behind you to keep you forward and stop you from slouching in your seat. When my back goes out and I am in the process of recovery, I find that I need this back support for a few sessions before I can go without. Do what is comfortable for you. Place your hands on your thighs, palms up or down or sit with them in your lap. Ensure that the shoulders are down and relaxed and have the head, chin, and mouth in the same position as previously described. Keep the eyes soft.

If you are unable to sit in any position, you can also meditate lying down. I myself am unable to lie flat on my back on the floor due to back problems, but if you find this is the easiest pose, then do please feel free to use it, as long as you don't fall asleep too often in your meditation. In any pose, you may fall asleep, and I have done so for a few minutes in a seated pose just resting my eyes. This can be as beneficial as meditation if your body requires the rest, and so don't beat yourself up about not staying awake should you fall asleep. However, if this is a regular occurrence, you may want to change the time you are meditating and do this when you are less tired. Relax the body and keep the tongue up on the upper palate of the mouth to reduce salivation. If you are familiar with yoga, many sessions end with the corpse pose or *savasana*, which is lying on your back, feet slightly apart and allowed to fall outward, arms slightly away from your sides. Relaxing the whole body in this pose can be extremely restful. People with back issues can raise their knees up slightly if they need to, with blankets or cushions beneath their knees.

Now to meditate!

Allow your thoughts to do what they will, but be aware of the thoughts. The trick to simple mindfulness meditation is to allow the thoughts to arise without becoming lost in them. If we start to lose ourselves in our thoughts, we lose our focus and the thoughts simply won't settle because we're engaging with them. Think of it as whirlpool that we create that is stirring up the mud at the bottom of a body of water. If we engage and continue, helping the whirlpool in its spinning, the mud will never settle. If we stop engaging, if we stop stirring, the water will calm and the mud will settle to the bottom. Our thoughts are much the same. If we pay attention to the thoughts that are arising without engaging in them, say, becoming angry or sad or happy or lost in a memory, then the thoughts will eventually stop coming up. Our mind will lose interest in the thoughts if we stop paying them attention. And as we stop feeding the thoughts, they will settle and quiet down. So, we might say to ourselves, "That's a thought about that paper I need to write," and then disengage. Then we might say, "That's a thought about last night's event," and then disengage. Worries, memories, to-do lists—all these will pop up and we can just label them and disengage. Eventually, they will stop coming up. And when that happens, you get the stillness and silence that you seek, even if it is only for a few seconds. The world may seem to quiet down. It may seem that there is nothing but you and your body, maybe the candle in front of you. There is not a care in the world. You can just sit still, simply be in the moment, without thought, without worry, in full peace. Enjoy that moment.

You can always set aside a different time for pondering, thoughtful contemplation, and problem-solving. We need our thoughts in order to achieve many things in our lives. The difference lies in being in control of our thoughts rather than letting them be in control of us. You can think of them as a small child; they will require much of your time and need nurturing to reach their full potential. But you need to be in control of them, otherwise they might do things that are unwise or dangerous and harmful. We need to understand our minds. We need to be aware, because what we are not conscious of can control us.

Some use the breath as a tool to quiet down the mind. This can be done, but I prefer to pay attention to my thoughts, as described above, for this allows me to understand my mind better and helps to quiet the restless unproductive thoughts in between meditations as well. If I am focusing on counting, then I'm ignoring the thoughts, pushing them away, and then perhaps they will arise as I lie in bed, awake at two o'clock in the morning. However, this method does work for some people and so let's look at it here.

When we breathe in, we can focus on our breath and simply count "one." When we breathe out, we again focus on the breath and count "one." Our next inhale and exhale will be "two." Go up to five or ten and then start again. Some like to be even more mindful with the counting and say to themselves "one breath in, one breath out," "two breaths in, two breaths out." Taking the attention away from our thoughts can help us in the short term to achieve the stillness that is necessary and at the heart of meditation. It is a quick fix, however, and the long-term benefits will not, in my opinion, be the same as if we were mindful of our thoughts. Another version of this method doesn't involve counting at all and is simply saying to yourself "breathing in" followed by "breathing out." This pinpoints our focus on the breath, and after a few minutes of this, we might be able to stop focusing on the breath and simply enjoy a moment of peace.

Enjoy that moment, when the peace arrives. Savour just sitting there without worry, without fear, without extremes. Feel the solidity of your body, the timelessness of the soul. And know that you are grounded in the here and now, in reality, in peace and quiet, flowing through you and out into everything you do.

Walking Meditation

For the Hedge Druid, walking meditation allows us to connect to the land where we live as well as give us a good meditation practice to follow. I would advise beginning with sitting meditation first and foremost and then trying that outside before moving toward walking meditation. The distractions can be difficult to overcome when out of doors and especially when moving. However, for some people, engaging the body allows the mind to rest and we see this through many forms of yoga, for instance. Finding that moment of stillness in sitting meditation first, however, prepares us better for when our bodies are physically interacting with the natural world around us and can provide us with a better knowledge of what to expect and how to maintain that sense of peace and calm.

When performing walking meditation, we need to be aware of our surroundings. Indeed, that is the sole focus of the meditation. In paying attention to the world around us, we are not paying attention to our thoughts. We are simply putting one foot in front of the other and noticing the sights and sounds without becoming lost in them. Our bodies are moving, but our minds are empty of worry and doubt, distraction and fear, instead focused on the feel of the ground beneath our feet, the smell of wood smoke, the cry of the hawk overhead. We're allowing our minds to take a break from our thoughts and instead focus externally upon our environment. Walk as slowly or as quickly as you feel comfortable; there is no set pace. Simply be comfortable and be aware. Awareness is the key in walking meditation.

How often do you see people walking past, completely lost in thought? Their bodies are here, with you on the street, but their minds are not. In walking meditation, we aim to not become lost in our thoughts, but to be truly awake and aware of the world around us. At the very least, it will be safer that way, as we're paying attention to cars and cyclists, tripping hazards, and more!

Walking meditation works beautifully with a sitting meditation practice. With sitting meditation, we become aware of our thoughts and how our minds work. With walking meditation, we become aware of our environment and how the world around us works. Blending the two together provides a holistic view of the world that is utterly integrated. Do both, if you can. If you are unable to walk for any physical reason, then you can do a similar meditation simply looking out a window and focusing on what is happening outside the window without becoming lost in the action occurring outside. Notice the crow flying overhead. The light on the cloud. The child laughing. The sound of the lawnmower. Don't engage, just notice.

Simply by noticing what is going on through our feet, our eyes, our ears, and our sense of smell, we become a part of our environment. Walking meditation is not about walking *through* an environment, but *becoming* a part of it. If you can combine walking meditation to a spot where you can do sitting meditation, so much the better. You will be able to find that sense of peace, combined with a better awareness of the world around you, what is happening in nature, without the distraction of the myriad of thoughts whirling around in your head.

For this is the goal of the Hedge Druid. To be an active and contributing member of an environment, of an ecosystem. Not merely an observer, but a functioning part of the whole. In order to do so, we must become aware of ourselves, of how our minds and bodies work and in doing so better understand where we need to let go in order to allow the stories and songs of others to enter into our world. If we are constantly living inside our heads, with our thoughts in control, then we will never know the joy and beauty of the external world. We need to understand our minds in order to get outside of our heads. Then, we can find the peace necessary to begin to understand how the lives of others work, how they contribute, how we can work with them in harmony and in balance. Meditation is a great tool to help us on our journey, both sitting and walking meditation.

Journeying can be seen as another form of meditation, sometimes used for problem-solving. As opposed to guided meditation that involves the person following guidance from another in their mind, journeying travels deeper still with the soul, traversing the boundaries through to the Otherworld. The Irish form of this is called *immrama* and consists of a journey over water to start the quest. You can combine both guided meditation and journeying with drumming, chant, and song to create a truly unique experience for all the senses. You can also combine both guided meditation and journeying with various forms of sensory deprivation, such as the "sweat house" or *teach-an-alais* in Irish Gaelic. There is record of Druids performing *imbas forosna*, another form of sensory deprivation that involved utter darkness and then being brought out into light.[28]

In part two of this book, in ritual we will go through various meditations: guided meditations and journeys.

---

28. For more on these techniques, see my book *The Crane Bag: A Druid's Guide to Ritual Tools and Practices.*

She sits upon the heath, the warm sandy soil beneath her, the air shimmering in waves of heat before her. She breathes the dusty scent of the earth, the gorse, and heather. She hears the pigeons in the trees at the wood's edge and the cry of a hawk circling high overhead. She listens, fully aware of where she is, fully aware of her body, of her breath. She breathes in and out, breathing with the land. She feels beads of sweat from the hot summer sun roll down her hairline. She doesn't move, just feels and experiences the sensation. Breathing in and out, she simply is, living and breathing and being. There is only this moment. There is only now. There is only peace and integration ...

Chapter 11

Prayer

Prayer and meditation can go hand in hand in your practice. Indeed, prayer is sometimes seen as speaking with the divine and meditation as listening for the response. Prayer is a large form of my own practice and I pray several times every day.

So what is prayer? Prayer is simply communication with the divine. It can also be communication with the ancestors and the spirits of place. It is taking a moment to stop and connect with something that is both within and without. As Druidry believes that deity is also within, we are connecting with our own soul when we connect to the divine.

The simplest form of prayer is one of gratitude. This is a very important aspect of prayer, for it brings an awareness of the blessings in our lives and can also take us outside of our own thinking minds, outside of our sense of self, and instead focus on the wider world at hand. We can be thankful for our friends and family, but we can also be thankful for the beautiful sunset, the rising moon, the stream that we dip our toes in, the nourishing rain, or the lightning that brings electrical balance back to the earth. We can go within and we can also expand our connection to the world. It's a wonderful practice in that regard. Druidry is all about integration with the world, and prayer is perhaps the best trodden path toward integration that we can take in our daily lives.

How do we pray? Well, that is up to each individual. There is no dogma within the tradition, and so you may pray however you see fit. You can study and be inspired by other traditions, discover how they pray, and see if anything resonates within your own soul. We know very little about how our Celtic ancestors prayed, and so we need to piece together what little we know with what feels right in our hearts while being aware of the issue of cultural appropriation. We know that the Celts swore by their gods and the gods of their ancestors, so that can give us a small clue as to whom to pray to. We can then expand that and take into consideration our own locale, our own environment where we live. The gods of the heath, the forest, the mountain, or the seashore may be evident in the landscape around us and so we can seek out and find the gods of these places. Some of these gods may not have a name, some may share it with you, or some simply remain nameless. What matters most is that we reach out to connect with them through prayer, for they are always reaching out toward us, in whatever capacity. We have simply become far too good at ignoring them.

Prayer can also give your life more meaning and more intention. It can clarify your thoughts and direction and set the pace for the day ahead or provide a sense of security for yourself and those you love. We are setting an intention for the most part when we pray, whether it is to work with more compassion or be open to receiving messages from the divine. We are giving thanks and working with the present moment in an intentional way. We're taking the time to stop, listen, and be heard.

When I pray in the morning, I am in a sense rededicating myself to Brighid each and every day. I honour her with a set rote of prayers that I have written and light a candle at the shrine dedicated to her next to my fireplace. I anoint my forehead and lips with water and set the intention to honour her in all the work that I do today. I also ask a blessing on hearth and home, on kith and kin. I take a moment to honour various people in society, perhaps the less fortunate or the artists that inspire. I also use prayer as a form of magic.

Prayer and magic are intertwined. Magic is using the will to determine an outcome, and so is prayer to a large extent. With prayer, we might perhaps turn the power over to deity for the final result, but still work through our own efforts. We might do the same with magic, invoking deities in our magical work, and so it becomes more akin to prayer. The differentiation for me lies in that a magical working will more often than not also have physical tools, herbs, candles, stones, and feathers for magical use. It is prayer done in a "magical" way. Prayer and magic are two sides of the same coin.

To begin working with prayer, it's helpful to understand where it is coming from and to be in the correct mindset in order to pray with intent. The Benedictine monks believe that prayer should be short and concise, and this too feels right for me in my own practice. Others may prefer long, eloquent prayers, but the simpler ones are easier to perform alongside one's everyday routine in the modern world. Lengthy, flowery prayers might not work when we're dog-tired at the end of day, after working hard and taking care of a sick cat, for example. Short and to the point might be just what is needed to clarify the intention. It may also be all that we have the energy for.

Prayer needs to come from the heart. We may memorise and recite the same prayers every day, but they should never be spoken without due attention and diligence or without feeling. Otherwise, it's just theatrics and offers us nothing in return except, perhaps, a false sense of righteousness for having prayed that day, when really our prayers were careless and inattentive. I speak my opening prayers for the day, repeating the same words, day after day, focusing on them. I find that the meaning behind them may shift and change over time or a prayer that I have spoken for months suddenly adopts an entirely new meaning due to life experience. However the prayers are spoken, attentiveness is key for effectiveness. When I say effectiveness, I don't necessarily mean that we will be instantly gratified should we be petitioning the gods for something. Effectiveness is when communication between the divine and the self has occurred and a sense of communion and integration follows.

Some prayers will be spontaneous and/or dependent on a certain need. If our sick cat is in pain, we might pray to our matron deity to send her healing, to ease her pain, and to help us treat her as best we can. If we see an ambulance whizzing past us on the motorway, we might say a quick prayer for the person suffering and for their families. When our previously ill cat becomes much better and brings us a mouse, we might say a quick prayer as we bury the dead animal. When a loved one is in need, when we feel powerless and afraid, when we are joyous at the sight of an incredible moonrise: these are all spontaneous moments where prayer is applicable.

The effectiveness of our prayers is also helped by our attitude and sense of self when we are praying. As Pagan Druids, we do not necessarily prostrate ourselves before the gods, feeling unworthy in their presence. But we still need to maintain some semblance of respect and perhaps even be a bit more humble in our attitude than we would normally be. In doing so, we are setting aside our chattering minds and our egos and opening ourselves to something greater both within and out there. It's not just us involved in this situation, and so all due respect is required. We can adopt a more prayerful attitude in our daily lives, especially if we perform prayers throughout the day on regular basis. This instils within us a sense that the world is more than just us, that we are only one thread in the great web of life. There is a sense of humility in this and when I use the word "humility," I don't mean in the sense of humiliation, but of a humble attitude toward all existence. When we are in a prayerful attitude, the wonder of life itself fills our body and soul and creates a bridge between us and the divine.

This bridge is the essence of all prayer. It is also traditionally the role of the priest to be a bridge between self and the divine, between community and Source. In Druidry, as in much of Western Paganism, each individual can be that bridge that connects the individual to the divine. Each person can be said to be their own priest (or priestess, if you prefer that term). Prayer helps us to build that bridge, bit by bit, until we have a strong and firm connection. When working as a priest, we are also fostering that connection in others, showing them how it can be done so that they can achieve that connection on their own. Being a priest is being a guide, enabling people to help themselves. When we are working in a prayerful attitude, we can do the work without issues of ego and power getting in the way and simply be helpful and of good use in a given situation.

There are some famous examples of prayer in religions throughout the world. Many in Celtic traditions adopt a form of "The Deer's Cry" otherwise known as "The Breastplate of St. Patrick," which is an intriguing combination of what appears to be Pagan poetry and Christian condemnation of other religions. A part of the prayer goes thus:

> *I arise to-day*
> *Through the strength of heaven:*
> *Light of sun,*
> *Radiance of moon,*
> *Splendour of fire,*
> *Speed of lightning,*
> *Swiftness of wind,*
> *Depth of sea,*
> *Stability of earth,*
> *Firmness of rock.*[29]

However, the prayer then goes on to ask God's hosts to prevent the seduction of nature and counter the spells of women, smiths, and Druids. When researching prayers, it's important to acknowledge the entirety and context in which a prayer was recorded and to do the investigation to see whether or not it would work for you in your tradition. We can use aspects of "The Deer's Cry" to inspire us in writing our own prayers, for example, instead of reciting bits and pieces and cherry-picking the good parts while ignoring the fact that much of this prayer goes against Druid traditions. The awen can come in many forms, and when the inspiration strikes, use it wisely.

---

29. Mary Jones, "Lorica of St. Patrick," Celtic Literature Collective, accessed December 10, 2017, http://www.maryjones.us/ctexts/lorica-e.html.

Alexander Carmichael (1832–1912) recorded prayers, chants, blessings, and more in his work *Carmina Gadelica*. Though much of it is flavoured with Christianity, again we can see the Pagan roots of the prayers and be inspired by them in our own tradition. It is often acknowledged that these prayers are influenced by pre-Christian traditions.[30] Indeed, we see influences from all over the world in these recorded prayers and charms, such as in the "Ora nam Buadh / The Invocation of Graces":

> *Thine is the skill of the Fairy Woman,*
> *Thine is the virtue of Bride the calm,*
> *Thine is the faith of Mary the mild,*
> *Thine is the tact of the woman of Greece,*
> *Thine is the beauty of Emir the lovely,*
> *Thine is the tenderness of Darthula delightful,*
> *Thine is the courage of Maebh the strong,*
> *Thine is the charm of Binne-bheul.[31]*

Here we see Celtic mythology and the Faery Faith coming through, as well as the exotic from far-off Greece and the Virgin Mary of Christianity. The prayers, charms, chants, hymns, and more that are recorded in the *Carmina Gadelica* provide us with a snapshot to a point in history when faiths blended together, through an ever-expanding knowledge of the world and other cultures. It is a strong blend of Christian and Pagan imagery and thus can be easily adapted for use by either tradition. Some working in the Druid tradition have even written books of Pagan versions of these prayers, such as Morgan Daimler's *By Land, Sea, and Sky*.

We might want to build a stronger bridge between us and our ancestors, and by praying to the ancestors every day, we might be able to achieve a stronger connection. People all around the world do this on a regular basis, from many different faiths. We might want to create a shrine or altar to the

---

30. *Carmina Gadelica*, Vol. 1 online, accessed December 1, 2017, http://www.sacred-texts. com/neu/celt/cg1.

31. Ibid.

ancestors, research our genealogy, and find out about ancestors of place and of tradition that have an impact upon our lives. By praying to the ancestors, we become more aware of our own mortality, of our limits and potential. It can have a very grounding and rooting feel to the practice, as we come to an awareness that without the ancestors, we simply would not be here today.

A useful way to create effective prayer is to remember a simple format. By effective, I mean that the prayer should connect you with that which you are trying to communicate. So you could be praying to the gods, to the ancestors, or to the spirits of place. A simple format to create your own prayers is made up of three elements:

- Raising consciousness of that which we are praying to (invocation)
- Stating need or other communication (intention)
- Offering thanks and renewing dedication

Raising consciousness is reminding ourselves of the attributes of that which we are praying to. For example, if praying to a deity, we recall associations that we know of them and state them aloud or think them if we are praying quietly and internally. As Druidry accepts that deity is immanent, we are honouring the gods both outside of ourselves and within. We acknowledge the power of the gods and that spark of divinity that lies within everything. We might say something like:

Lady Brighid
Goddess of Poetry, Smithcraft, and Healing
Bountiful Lady of Grace
Of the sacred fire and the holy well
I call to you now

We might then state our need or the intention of the prayer. We might say something like:

Lady Brighid
Help me to heal myself

Grant me the inspiration and knowledge
Of how to deal with this illness
May I be healthy, happy, and whole

Wait for however long you need in order to be open to receiving an answer or inspiration. Remember, it is only when we are silent that we can truly listen. Then we offer thanks and renew our dedication. We might say something like:

Lady Brighid
Lady of the three strong fires
Fire in the head, in the heart, and in the belly
You who are my inspiration
I thank you for all that you are
With all that I am
May I be the awen

In this, we are thanking Brighid for her inspiration and all that she is, all that she provides us in relationship with her. We are also dedicating ourselves to our own path by being the inspiration or awen itself. This is a lovely way to end prayer.

By adopting a prayerful attitude and incorporating prayer into everyday life, we can re-enchant our souls, make us more aware of what we have to be grateful for, and also build a strong bridge, an everlasting connection to that which we are praying to: whether it be the ancestors, the divine, or simply acknowledging, with respect, the world around us. As Druids, we see the divine in nature, and in doing so, we come to know the nature of the divine.

Her cat is very ill. The Hedge Druid sits with her, having done all that she can. Many trips to the vet, different medications, and still there is no improvement. She calls upon her goddess, Brighid, to help heal her little one of

her ills. Bone to bone, flesh to flesh, sinew to sinew, as Brighid healed this, so may she heal that. She wipes the brat na bride over her cat three times and sits back, praying to the goddess of healing.

Two weeks later and the illness is almost gone. The Hedge Druid goes to her shrine that she keeps for Brighid next to the hearth and utters a prayer of gratitude, giving her utmost thanks for the help and inspiration needed to heal her little one.

Chapter 12

Magic

Magic in Modern Paganism is often seen as the ability to make changes through Will: the will of the mind combining with and focusing the energy of the universe. Druid magic is not that different and there are several ancient accounts of Druid magic that can be found throughout history. As well, there are the Celtic myths and legends to look to, with tales of the spells, feats, incantations, and more of certain characters. Indeed, the Tuatha Dé Danann, the gods and goddesses that travelled on the North Wind to make their home in Ireland, were also called the *Aes Dana*, or the Gifted People. They were known for their magical ability and the first Druid magic worked in Ireland was done by them. In Irish, *draíocht* translates as both "spells" and "magic" and shares its root with the word *draoi*, meaning "Druid." Druid magic is often known as *druidecht* today.

Druid magic was used for many different purposes: to curse, to bless, to transform, to repel, to create illusion, to provide healing, to divine, and to bring harmony. There are as many uses for magic as there are intentions of the individual, and so magic was and still is widely used in the Druid tradition. Magic can be empowering to the individual who has tried everything else and has no other recall in a given situation. Many in Modern Paganism adhere to the Wiccan view of the Threefold Law, which states that what you do comes back to you threefold, for good or ill. Druids don't believe in this law as such. But as those who are questing integration—to create balance and harmony within an environment—performing malicious magical acts isn't exactly suiting the purpose. Sometimes things will need to be removed, much like pruning a diseased tree. What is most important is that the whole is taken into consideration and not just the desires of the individual.

A special caste or group of magical workers in Celtic history were the poets, the *fili* in Ireland, who had the greatest ability to satirize, and in doing so, magically force others to obey their will. They could also praise and elevate an individual in form of blessing. The fili, alongside the Druids, also cast curses upon people, including the *glam dicin*, the curse of all curses. This is a "shout," so we can assume that it was a form of curse that was shouted upon someone, usually in threes. In an Irish tale, Druids were sent by Queen Medb to seize the hero Cuchulainn and to perform the *glam dicin*, the result of which would cause three pimples representing injury, shame, and fault upon his face. In another tale, the Welsh hero Culwech threatens a porter when he is denied entrance to a feast in Arthur's hall and tells him that he will give three mortal shouts, loud enough that they will be heard in Cornwall and Ireland. These shouts will cause miscarriages and infertility in all the women. The Roman writer Tacitus records black-robed women with wild hair running amongst the Druids on the shores of Anglesey, brandishing torches and shouting curses and screams causing fear in the opposing Roman soldiers. There were also curses to cause an unquenchable thirst as well as to prevent people from urinating and cause them extreme discomfort.

The power of the spoken word was evidently the most important factor in this and other kinds of magic in the Druid tradition. As a mainly oral tradition, this applied to magic as well. To write a magic spell on something would be akin to setting something in stone, most likely irreversible. Oaths were a very serious matter to the Celts and often included something along the lines of the land swallowing them, the sky falling upon them, and more should they break their oath. There is also something known as a *geis* from Ireland, which comes from the same root as the word *guth*, meaning "voice." This can be seen as a form of curse upon someone or a limitation upon one's life that, should they break it, has devastating results: often death. The *geis* or a *geisa* had repercussions in the material and the spiritual world, which to the Druids were interrelated. To adhere to a geis meant that order was maintained throughout the cosmos. It was the responsibility of the individual to adhere to or take on a geis and not simply the result of "fate" as normally viewed in other mythologies. Some heroes were tricked into breaking their geis, however, and this highlights the idea that we must be careful and mindful throughout our lives.

The power of words, of your word once given, was all important. These words could be hurled in satire or curses, sung or chanted for victory, and more. The voice, when used in a certain manner while saying certain words, could have very real and life-altering power. We will look at the voice later in part four of this book.

It was said that Druids could call up mists or create fog banks to hide themselves from their enemies. The art of illusion or misdirection was not unknown. In the Irish tale, the beautiful Deirdre was made invisible by the Druid fostering her so that no one could see or hear her. In a Welsh tale, Aonghus Og covers Diarmuid's lover, Grania, with his mantle, thereby making her invisible so that they could escape their pursuers. A mantle is a cloak and we can still see the use of the word "cloak" meaning "to conceal." What's more, "mantle" in ornithological terms also refers to the wings of a bird, and there are instances of Druids and even the Tuatha Dé Danann being described as wearing a cloak of feathers. Irish Druids could also provide protection to the nobility through a mantle of concealment called the *celtar*. Sometimes this mantle is also known as a *fe-fiada*. St. Patrick, though obviously not a Druid, is said to have been able to say the invisibility charm of *fe-fiada* over him and his followers, to render them in the appearance of a herd of deer to all who sought them harm and escape detection. This ability to render things invisible or shape-change is also known as *fith-fath*.

Divination was a form of magic often used by the Druids. The most popular methods were by determining auguries from the flight of birds or, more gruesomely, through the reading of entrails. Dreams were also important and, combined with sensory deprivation, had valuable results. The Irish *imbas forosna* is a form of sensory deprivation in which one excludes all light and the Druid might go into a trance or even a slumber while he sought wisdom, then to be revealed figuratively and literally in the light of day. The transition from darkness to light is what caused the illumination, if you'll pardon the pun. Speaking of illumination, there is also the *tenim laegda*, which means "illumination of song." An offering or sacrifice is made, a song is sung, and the querant is touched with a wand, while the spellcaster places a thumb in their mouth, similar to when Finn Ma Cumail gained wisdom from the salmon after he sucked the hot juices from the cooked fish that spattered on his thumb.

Shape-shifting is a regular occurrence in magical workings in Celtic mythology. *Fith* may be a derivative of the Irish word for *deer* and often we see people being turned into deer, swans, owls, hares, hawks, even a grain of wheat and more in the old tales. There are a lot of medieval accounts of witches being able to turn into hares, and so the magical working of shape-shifting continued. In relation to *fith fath*, the actual process itself might not be the physical transformation into a creature but a journeying of the mind and/or spirit in the shape of a creature. One can become a specific creature in order to see a challenge through when journeying, though this requires immense mental discipline and a large amount of practice. The more one practices, the better one becomes. However, it's not just the practical part of the exercise that is important; researching and learning all that you can about the animal in question is imperative in doing this correctly. Otherwise, what you will be doing is having a nice daydream of what it would be like to be this animal and not a spiritually transformative magical working. As Druids seek integration with the world, becoming another being in the world allows for a different perspective and enables us to forego our human-centric worldview. The Druid Robin Herne states in his work, *Old Gods, New Druids*:

Shape-shifting...and its importance cannot be emphasised enough. It forms the core of our approach to mysticism—transforming one's consciousness into something that will have a far greater effect later on … Far from rejecting the world, fith-fath seeks to embrace it in all its diversity, seeks to become the bird or beast or tree.[32]

We also have the *tarb-feis*, which involves a ritual sacrifice of an animal after which part of its flesh is eaten. In eating the flesh, the Druid can become one with the creature or absorb its magical or physical power. For those who are vegetarian or vegan, I personally don't see why this can't be done with herbs and other plants. (Note: Druids today do not sacrifice living animals, though they may rear animals for food just as they grow their own vegetables, as self-sufficiency is growing in the tradition.) We know that the Druids used mugwort in divination, both for ingesting and using the smoke to induce a trance-like state. Plants have just as much power and just as much to teach us, as animals do in their being.

There are various healing techniques in Celtic culture. Healing wells abound through Britain, Ireland, and Europe and are associated with Celtic deities. Other popular magical acts and items include the *brat na bríde*, which was a piece of cloth left out on the evening of Brighid's holy day of Imbolc and brought back into the house with the power to heal as well as to protect cattle, ensure abundance of milk, and aid in calving, lambing, and foaling. This cloth was not to be washed, otherwise its power would be drained. A brat na bríde that was seven years old was especially powerful. Herbs were also used in healing, and special charms were recited as the herbs were being collected, as demonstrated by many various charms found in Carmichael's *Carmina Gadelica*. We will look at herb lore in the part three of this book.

The Druid, author, and herbalist Ellen Evert Hopman describes two types of power to be found in the landscape: *búad* (power found in the land) and *cles* (power found in human activity in an area).[33] *Búad* can be found through ley lines as well as through shapes and phenomena found throughout the landscape. These energies can be connected with and used in Druid magic, flowing through and empowering the magic that she or he is enacting. *Cles*

---

32. Robin Herne, *Old Gods, New Druids*, (O Books, 2009), 192.

33. Ellen Evert Hopman, *A Druid's Herbal of Sacred Tree Medicine*, (Destiny Books, 2008), 150.

can be found in stone circles and ancient groves, in ancient tumuli, barrow mounds, and more. It can be viewed as human-directed energy, perhaps built up over time in an area and combined with búad energy. Cles energy can be harnessed and worked with, though much of this energy has been abused or ignored for many years, such as at Stonehenge, where the sanctity of the temple space is lost when all night parties are held at the Summer Solstice by those who care nothing for the temple space itself. One can work to restore the energy of cles in an area by visiting and reweaving the energy back to a point of balance and harmony with the landscape, reaffirming the intention of the space and clearing it of energies which are out of tune with that intention.

We have some ideas, a few tantalising morsels to help us understand what magic was to the ancients Celts. As well, we have our own understanding of how the world works, and can combine the two in order to achieve magical workings for our own day and age. Sacrificing something that is alive (such as a bull or a horse) is no longer suitable in our society, and the ethics of magical work is a hotly debated topic in the Pagan community. Some would say that to do any negative magic is very wrong indeed; others would say it's perfectly appropriate in certain situations like self-defence. Others would say there is no such distinction in magic between what is "good" and what is "bad," for what is good for one being may be bad for another. It is up to you to determine your own ethical code regarding the use of magic, and we will look at ethics in more details in part four of this book.

For my own path, the success and harmony of my own environment comes first and foremost, and so I try to work with that in my mind in all magical workings. I have to carefully consider what it is that I am trying to achieve and who will be affected by it. While ancient Celts may have brought down curses upon others, I personally am not completely comfortable with this idea. I would rather open dialogue in a given situation, and if that doesn't work, then avoidance is probably best. Much as I don't go rolling in a briar patch, I can avoid situations that would hurt me as much as I can. I have to take personal stock of my emotions and come to terms with the fact that vengeance and anger are a part of my being, just as they are for everyone. How I act upon these feelings determines who I am. It requires me to be in touch with my shadow aspects, acknowledge the things that aren't so nice, and work with these in order not to cause further suffering in the world; for indeed, there is enough of that already. I will protect my kith and kin, my environment, but there are ways to do that which cause the least amount of harm. Your own path may be different.

Some Druids don't practice any form of magic at all. For the longest time, I never used magic in my own path, thinking that it was more of a Wiccan/Witch tradition. After research I indeed found out more: that magic is in fact a large part of Celtic tradition and that it can also enrich our lives. We need to re-enchant our souls in modern society, and using magic is one of the best ways we can achieve this goal. Daily charms, chants, rites, and rituals are all forms of magic that we can use to awaken to our own power as well as that of the land, the gods, and the spirits of place. Some would say that magic should only be used when absolutely necessary, but when parking the car, I certainly know that I say a quick word or two in the hopes of finding one of the free twenty-minute parking spots that are like gold dust in the nearest town. I stir my soup in a certain direction when cooking, depending on the results I wish to achieve. I charge herbs and incense with my personal energy in ritual before using it, to bless it or to give it intention. These actions and a legion of other things that I do each and every day constitute magical acts.

So, essentially, what is magic? It is energy that we can harness and then use to our own purpose or that of others. The intention must be investigated clearly before any magical working is done, and divination is a great tool to use before any magical working to determine whether or not we should go ahead with the magic. We combine the energy that flows through the universe, the energy that is the bright spark of all life. In more modern Druid traditions such as OBOD, they see this energy as *nwyfre*, a term coined by Iolo Morganwg in the nineteenth century. Others might see it as awen; however, for me awen is that which connects everything to each other and so is not the energy of life itself but the loom upon which it is woven. That energy is what causes the seed to germinate, the amoeba to split, the sun and stars in the heavens to shine, the earth to turn its course. It is the energy behind the wind, in the lakes and oceans, the currents that run through the earth, the lava spilling down an erupting volcano. Everything is in constant motion, atoms bouncing off each other to create solidity and manifestation. Magic is the energy of motion, of movement, of life itself in all its myriad forms.

We can harness this energy in many different ways. Some use prayer to tap into this energy, as previously discussed. We may still call upon deity to aid us in our work, but it is *us* doing the work, perhaps with a little extra boost of blessing by the gods, but not some external being doing the work. We have a purpose in mind and not merely communion. We focus on intent for a certain situation and create the results we desire. We can use the energy of others in this endeavour, such as the energy of certain plants, stones, even animal allies. We use our own personal energy as well and blend these all together to create a source of power that, with practice, can be directed toward a certain outcome.

Magic requires focus and concentration. It also requires a good deal of visualisation. There are many different ways to foster these within our lives and meditation is one of the best. We can practice visualising certain things during meditation, to hold our focus and concentration on certain objects, extending this over periods of time until we can hold the intention deep within our mind and souls for a half hour to an hour. Once we can achieve this, we are ready to do spellwork.

For myself, I find that the use of herbs, candles, and natural objects are the best way to perform magic workings. For instance, I can create a poppet out of cotton fabric and stuff it with charged herbs, chant while embroidering symbols that came to me during meditation and trancework, and charge the whole finished poppet with my intention. I can keep charging the poppet for an entire cycle of the moon and then release it into the fire at the next full moon, with focus and intention, directing the energy toward a certain goal.

Using the fire and flames as a vehicle for transformation, I might also call upon the gods and beings of the Otherworld to aid me. These are beings that I have worked with for a while and are not beings that are at my command. Much as I would call on a family member to help me in a certain situation, they might refuse or be unable to help. We don't command the gods, the ancestors, or the spirits of place. That's just bad form. At best, you will be ignored by those you are commanding, in my opinion, for they have a different purpose in life that must be respected. At worst, you'll fall flat on your face at some point or another. We don't command in Druid magic but seek aid in that which might be attuned to our work. That aid has a choice whether or not to come to the fore—much as we would like the same in return. (We will look more at magical workings and spellcraft in part two of this book.)

A Druid studies the natural world around her, coming to a deep sense of place, her place, and the place of other beings in the environment. She knows how the ecosystem works, and in that knowledge she can work toward helping maintain that balance necessary for all beings to thrive. She also understands the importance of darkness, decay, and death as necessary parts of the whole. Knowing your place is essential. By this, I don't mean to bow, scrape, and feel subservient or sub-par, but rather knowing our place in our environment through self-knowledge that is so very necessary in today's world. Magic can help the Hedge Druid to re-enchant her life and work to be a functioning member of an ecosystem.

A match is struck in the darkness. With a soft incantation, the Hedge Druid lights the wick of the candle. She has prepared the beeswax taper with scented oils and scattered charged herbs around its base. She holds the intention of her spell within her mind and casts her eye over the symbols that she has carved upon the soft wax. She watches the flame, seeing it burn slowly down, holding the intention for as long as she can. When the candle has burned all the way down, the spell is fully done. She knows the energies have been released into the wider world and knows that her magic will work.

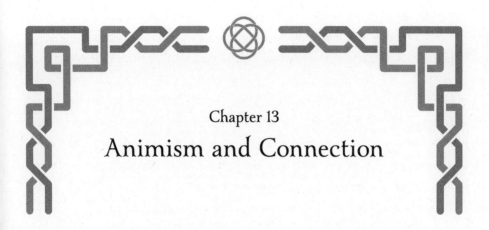

Chapter 13

Animism and Connection

Seeing the divine in nature, and thereby the nature of the divine, is a gateway to understanding animism. Many Druids are animists and the term "animist" means very different things to very different people. Some would say that being an animist means acknowledging that everything has a spirit or soul, from a rock to a cow, a human to a tree. Others would define animism as sensing an inherent value in all things. Others still would argue that there is no such thing as inanimate matter and that all matter is energy manifested and in constant motion, atoms bouncing off of each other, therefore animate, and therefore animism. All of these are valid.

We often apply a human-centric perspective to life. Many of us humans of whatever faith believe that we have a soul that is eternal. However, many do not believe that other species share a similar state of being. Why humans are different from the rest is often a result of a tradition that contains hierarchy, where humans are at the top and everything forms a chain below them. Within animism, this notion is utterly incomprehensible. Humans developed and evolved alongside everything else on this planet and as such are interwoven with all life—not in charge of it or controlling it or at the top of some imagined "food chain." To keep us humble, we must never forget we're soft, squishy, rather tasty to many creatures, and—without tools— pretty much helpless against them.

An animist can believe that everything is "ensouled," but for me and many others, this applies too narrow a human viewpoint on life itself. Perhaps souls are different depending on species, perhaps not. All that we can say is that it is unknowable and should be respected as such. No one's views are entirely right or entirely wrong, but simply offering a perspective. The perspective that offers each thing as having an inherent value sits closer to where many animists feel today. This perspective can include different views upon what makes each thing special or even what makes each thing a thing in itself. For example, to use a poetic term, the soul song of a rock is what differentiates it from that of a bird or a tree. It is difficult to apply scientific terms to such a concept and our language often fails in that regard, returning to poetry to fill in the gaps. The most important thing to remember in this concept is that of honour and respecting each thing for what it is, by knowing and acknowledging its soul song. When we do so, we can no longer cut down the tree without communion, swat and kill the wasp interested in our drink, or ignore the homeless person lying in the doorway. Animism is deeply concerned with ethics and how we act in the world; it's not just what we think but what we do.

When we work with an animistic perspective, we are connected to the world around us. Jhenah Telyndru, the founder of the Sisterhood of Avalon, once said that "we cannot be apart from the world, but are a part of the world." [34] We are never separate from the world, even though our modern-day lives may make us feel isolated and lonely. Gadgets galore intended to make social connections further distance us from real-world connections, and many people lack a community to call their own in their own locale. Whether you are living in a city or in a small rural village, that sense of community that previously connected people together, for better or for worse, is fast falling by the wayside. When we expand the idea of community beyond the boundaries of humanity, we see an even greater failing in many who are unable or unwilling to connect with the environment that they live in. Ecosystems within eco-

34. Jhenah Telyndru, "Journey to Avalon: Walking the Path of the Priestess," accessed January 12, 2017, http://www.jhenahtelyndru.com/online-courses/journeytoavalon.

systems, we are all a part of something, and animism allows us to bear that in the front of our minds in everything that we do. It can be a balm to the soul in times of loneliness, for the simple act of going out of doors and remembering that we are a part of an ecosystem can help us to re-member our being in our environment, reconstruct our sense of self, and bring a wider perspective to our humanity and our place in the world.

The Celts honoured the world for what it was, venerating sources of clean, fresh water, high hilltops where the earth meets the sky, and deep trackless forests. Some of these were given names and (after Roman influence) human qualities and features. This anthropomorphism of the natural landscape is a part of animism, allowing the human to connect to the spirit or sense the power and value of that which inspires. It might be something that keeps us alive, such as sunlight or rain or a source of food. It might be the powers of birth and death. Everything had its place, including humans, and in honouring the world around them, enabled one to deal honourably with the land, sea, and sky and perhaps make life a little easier for the individual and one's community. We've already discussed how trees were venerated by the Celts, the sacred bíles that contained the energies of the land such as the five sacred bíles of Ireland (according to the *Dindsenchas*, the "lore of Irish places"), which were the Ash of Tortu, the Bole of Rossa (a yew), the Oak of Mughna, the Ash of Daithe, and the Ash of Uisneach. This is a form of animism that allows one to connect not only to the energies of the trees themselves and respect them for what they are, but also creates a bridge using the spirits of these trees to embody the energy of the land and all that inhabits it. It is a vast concept, but one which works beautifully within any earth-centred Pagan tradition. Just as humans are both material and spiritual, so is the rest of existence, each with their own inherent value and ability to bridge the sacred and the profane, to allow those boundaries to fall away and lose the duality so prevalent in our culture today.

Animism is a key part of Druidry, both to the ancient Celts and to modern-day Druids. It allows us a mindset that enables us to work with our landscape in honour and with respect. It reminds us that we are a part of the whole and that everything that we do has consequences in the spiritual and the material sense, for the two cannot be separated. Animism bridges the gap that has been created in the last five hundred years between the material and spiritual, the sacred and the profane, and allows us to move freely, fluidly, and honourably between perspectives.

She watches the herd of deer running from the wood, across the path before her, and out onto the heath. Her heart runs with the deer and she knows that they are her brothers and sisters. Wild and free, so is she, untamed and a daughter of Cernunnos. She smiles at "civilisation" and exults in the freedom of the wild, picking up her skirts and running through the trees, laughing.

Part Two
PRACTICE

We have studied the theory; now let's do the work! In this section, we look at how the Druid constructs a ritual practice and then we get down to business. Included in this section are sample rituals to use or adapt to your own liking in addition to meditations, prayers, and more.

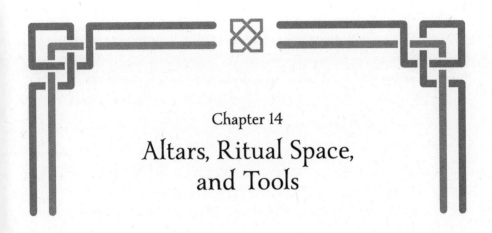

Chapter 14

Altars, Ritual Space, and Tools

Every spiritual tradition has its own practices that define it from others, whether it is the simple silence of a Quaker meeting, an elaborate Catholic mass, the raucous celebration of Krampus/*Krampuslauf*, or the magical Druid ritual. The tools and places of gathering, the costume, and the intention all vary depending on the tradition. In this chapter we will explore Druid tools and ritual before we move into the practical work itself. For a further description of Druid ritual tools and practices, see my book *The Crane Bag: A Druid's Guide to Ritual Tools and Practices*.

Altars and Ritual Space

We begin with the altar. An altar is that which creates a focal point for the ritual. Altars can be almost anything, from a sacred tree or stone, or a copse of trees in a meadow, to an indoor table set up with candles, incense, and the trappings of the tradition. It is a place where we can work, where we can return to repeatedly to build a rapport with a place and thereby establish a connection to the world around us through that particular focal point. It helps us to narrow down the wide diversity of nature and brings it to a point of attention where we can do our work: whether it is daily, monthly, or during the seasonal festivals. Some Druids might have more than one altar. I have an indoor one that I use daily as well as a shrine next to the hearth. But

I also have an outdoor altar where I leave offerings to the spirits of place and the Fair Folk. There are places out and about in the landscape where I live that I return to time and again and which have become special to me in my working with the land. Though there is no visible altar there, the place itself is a focal point for the work that I do and the energy of the land.

Altars can be of any shape and size and made from whatever is available. My indoor altar is an old pine chest upon which I have candles, incense, a censer, the tools of my tradition, various fetishes (human-made or natural items such as bones, feathers, stones, and the like that have power), and images of the gods that I work with. My outdoor altar is nothing more than a flat stone laid atop another stone and has next to it a statue of the guardian goddess who protects the space. Nothing else adorns this altar and it is left free for offerings. Near to it is a shrine to the Fair Folk, and the two are deeply connected.

Your altar may be in whatever form you wish. As a Hedge Druid, the choice is yours, whether to have it indoors or out, made of wood, stone, metal, or even a square of fabric placed upon the ground. As a focal point that one returns to, the energy of the place can be affected, and so if outside of the home, it is best to ask the spirits of place whether an altar would be acceptable in that area. Wait to hear for an answer or to receive a feeling of acceptance before creating your altar. If it is in a place that you will return to repeatedly and have stated your intention as such, you may not need to do this each and every time, though perhaps once a year it is good manners to see if your presence and energy is still acceptable. Some places will not wish to be altered too much (pardon the pun) in their energy flow, and should your work begin to change this against the wish of those who inhabit it, then it is your responsibility to either commune with these beings or to move to another site. If this is ignored, you might find that your rituals become cumbersome or you feel unwell or that things begin to happen in the ritual or on the site that are disruptive. There must be a clear respect between all parties as to the nature and intention of the space.

So when constructing your altar and choosing your ritual space, bear all this in mind. As you are not separate from the rest of the world, you have to take that into consideration. Your work is your own; true, but that work happens in the world that is cohabited with others. You will need to be respectful of where you do your work and how you go about doing it. When using a public space and public altars, temples, and sacred sites, you will also need to bear in mind the energy of all those who have used it before and all those who will use it after you. It might, in my opinion, be better to find a space near your home where you can work in peace and quiet and is just as important as the better-known focal points for Pagan worship. Just because a place has been regarded as sacred for thousands of years doesn't mean that your private little spot in the forest is any less sacred or special. As long as you are mindful of the energies that you are working in and of the place itself, you cannot go far wrong. Druidry is all about locality.

Coming back to altars—they can have a very significant role in daily practice and worship, providing a focal point in establishing relationship. I try to highlight this importance with my apprentices, explaining the benefits of having a focus within an area in which to open up communication with the spirits of place (or the realms of land, sea, and sky), the ancestors, and the gods. Communication is essential to good relationship, and finding a spot to come back to again and again helps us to not only strengthen the bond between the person and the place but also give it a ritual context within which to commune. Often this ritual context is held within a temple, whether it is a building or creation of stone and/or timber or a sacred circle cast with energy around the practitioner. The importance of the altar and the temple should not be taken for granted, though neither are exactly essential.

I leave offerings of food and drink upon both my indoor and outdoor altar, sometimes making offerings/sacrifices to the water in our pond instead. The indoor altar is held within the temple that is home: my own sanctuary delineated from the rest of the world, where safety and nourishment is found inside its walls. My outdoor altar is set within the temple of stones and the boundaries of the garden itself, though the energy flows freely through either altar, not confined to the spaces of the temples, just as energy is not confined to the temple that is the physical body.

Working at my altar indoors, it is a space where I can commune with the spirits of hearth and home, as well as my goddess Brighid in her more anthropomorphic state. I feel the ancestors of blood deeply in my soul at this particular altar, as well as the ancestors of tradition. Surrounded by my collection of books, these wisdom keepers have their energy flowing into that sacred little room where I meditate daily, lighting candles and incense and communing. I also perform some magic and spellcrafting rituals there, should the need arise, as well as journeying meditations. At the outdoor altar, I connect with Brighid in her serpent energy form, the white dragon energy that runs throughout the British Isles, connecting each part to the other in a vast network of flowing energy. I also find a deep resonance with the ancestors of place there, those who have lived upon this land before me, who tended the apple orchards and lived in hovels. I also connect to all the ancestors of the flora and fauna around me: the birds, badgers, beetles, trees, and other plants whose bodies make up the soil. Outside, I realise that we walk upon the bodies of our ancestors with every step, that they are an essential part of our life, for out of the soil comes the food that nourishes us. I am closely connected to the realm of the land. I feel the realms of sea and sky more fully too, for living near the coast, the air is often tinged with the scents of the North Sea and I can see the weather patterns happening all around me.

As I spend time at these altars, I establish a relationship that grows and grows with each visit. Instead of scattering the energy here there and everywhere, it becomes focused into a place. There are several other places nearby that I visit regularly that have the same effect, places where I spend time getting to know the spirits of place, and they in turn get to know me. In coming back to these places time and again, there is a familiarity that develops, as with old friends, that helps us in our work, whatever is it that we are doing. Altars really can alter our perception and our relationship with the world around us by providing that focal point to which we can return repeatedly. Spending time at a designated place allows us to get to know it intimately, rather than having a passing conversation with an acquaintance of a place. As my teacher before me always said: "It's all about relationship."

A place has a very real impact upon a person, as we come to realise that we are not separate from the rest of the natural world. When we find our place within a place, we are able to communicate openly, sharing freely that wonderful dose of awen, the hum of energy where souls meet.

The nemeton is the temple space that we create in which to hold our ritual. It is also our own personal space, the "aura" around our bodies in which we don't allow entry to anyone but those who we are intimate with or very familiar. We can work with our nemeton and use it to delineate a space in which we would like to hold ritual, work our magic, or pray. We honour the nemeton of others as well and in ritual blend our own with that of the natural world around us, sometimes layering them to create a sanctuary and a haven in which to do our Druid work.

Some Druids see no need to create or delineate a sacred space, as they feel it unnecessary in their work to connect with all of nature. Others find it useful, providing a microcosm of the world to work with, which might be more easily approached and amenable than dealing with the macrocosm. Finding sacred space can, like the altar, help us in our focus when doing the work. The choice is yours: whether you feel you wish to delineate an area and bless and/or consecrate it for your work or whether you see this as completely irrelevant to your path. We will look at creating sacred space/ the nemeton in the next section.

Tools

There is very little that we know about ancient Druid tools from what was recorded by the Romans. We are told that they cut mistletoe with a golden sickle and caught it in a blanket so that it did not touch the ground. There is a mention of a Druid's Egg, but in a confused description. Apart from this, there isn't much that we have to go on and so we look deeper into the myths to find sacred items, as well as what is practical and relevant for use today.

Let's begin with the sickle. Pliny recorded its use in Druid ritual in his work *Natural History* and it has become a popular tool today, for its links back to these ancient times. It was reported to cut mistletoe during a specific phase of the moon (sixth night after the new/dark moon). Though there is dispute as to whether or not this singular account is indeed correct in stating that all the ancient Druids used a sickle in similar or other rituals, there are many Druids today, myself included, who use one and who find it beneficial in their work. Though our sickles are not made of gold, as in Pliny's account (gold is too soft a metal to hold any workable cutting blade), they are widely available if one knows where to look. Car boot sales (flea markets) and antique shops are the perfect places to find these, and they are often lumped together in a box with other tools that someone's grandfather owned. I found mine for less than ten pounds in an antique shop. The blade is dull, but I don't use it for cutting and so I have never sharpened it. The handle is made of oak, which is very appropriate to me as a Druid. It feels lovely in my hand and connects me to a time and people who worked at a slower pace, honouring agricultural ties. The handle is smooth and polished from use and has a wonderful patina. I use it for circle casting and delineating sacred space, which we will discuss later.

The staff is a tool that many of think of when they envision a Druid. Think of an old, bearded man with a long staff holding magical powers (not unlike Tolkein's Gandalf). This image has been popular since Victorian times. We can view the staff today as representing the World Tree, the *bíle* or microcosm of the universe and that which connects this world and the Otherworld. The staff can be used to take us between the worlds and act as a doorway. It's also useful when out and about walking the countryside! Smaller versions of the staff are wands, which can also be used in the Druid tradition. There are tales of wands being used by the Celtic magician Gwydion, who used one to turn the magical woman Blodeuwedd into an owl after he created her to marry his nephew and she betrayed him with a man of her own choosing. (I know I'd rather be an owl than be in that situation!) Staffs and wands can be made of any wood of your choosing, but do choose wisely. Research the tree from which it comes and ensure that it is in tune with your work. As well, when harvesting the wood, if you are using live wood you *must* first ask permission from the tree as to whether it is willing to offer a part of itself to your work. If not, you may find that something you took from an unwilling being will just not work and may even turn against you. If permission is given, then cut the branch cleanly and do so during the winter months when the sap isn't rising. Cut as close to the trunk as possible so that the bark from the trunk can quickly cover up the cut and the tree won't "bleed out" come the spring. If you are using fallen wood, ensure that it is fairly fresh and not rotten, diseased, or full of insects. The last thing you want to do is bring wood worm into your home! Going out after a wind storm is an excellent time to harvest wood for wands and staffs, allowing nature to do the hard work for you. Always leave an offering, no matter how the item was collected.

The silver branch is an item that is used to signal working between the worlds. It is a branch from a tree, usually apple, that has silver or gold bells upon it. In various Celtic myths, a silver branch is used, such as in the *Voyage of Bran* or Cormac's tale in the *Cup of Wonder*, where the arrival of an Otherworldly and beautiful woman was heralded by the shaking of a silver branch. You can use it to call Otherworldly beings to your aid or to signal that a working between the worlds is about to begin. I use it at the start of most rituals, as I find that in ritual I am often working between the worlds, with the Fair Folk aiding me and guiding me. It's not a tool to be careless or reckless with, for it has a deep mythology and connection to the Otherworld. You can make a silver branch from any wood, but apple is traditional today, as it is a tree often connected to the Otherworld, sacred isles such as Avalon, and places that are "in between." You won't find many silver branches for sale in shops, but making your own is fairly simple; finding a good branch and bells from any craft shop will do, tying them to the piece of wood with leather cord or cotton string. I like to use nine bells on my silver branch for the Celts' love of threes.

The cauldron is found in many Celtic myths and is a symbol of regeneration and inspiration. As opposed to other traditions such as Wicca, it is not solely a feminine symbol in the Druid tradition, as the great god Dagda has his own cauldron, which satiates all who come to it. There is also a cauldron deep in the realm of Annwn, ruled by the Faery King Gwyn ap Nudd, warmed by the breath of nine maidens. Though there are many legends of women and cauldrons, such as Ceridwen and Gwion Bach's tale, to assign a gender to any of the Druid tools isn't quite fitting in with Celtic tradition and is more suited to modern Wicca and Witchcraft. The cauldron was later replaced in mythology by the cup or grail, as we see from the legends of King Arthur and the quest for the holy grail. Here the vessel is indeed linked with the divine feminine, sought by Arthur and his knights, but is a much later version of the previous cauldron. The cauldron or cup is used in ritual in various ways: items can be burned within it or it can hold liquids to be used in ritual. It can hold water used in ritual, for saining (blessing) an area, or for scrying (a form of divination). It can also represent the three cauldrons within the human body, which we will look at later in this section.

Ephemera such as candles, incense, and herbs are also tools of many in the Druid tradition. If your Hedge Druidry takes you out into the wilds of your landscape, you may not have much use for them; however, for indoor spaces many prefer to use these to "set the mood." It can help with meditation and scrying work, clearing the energy of an indoor space, and as part of magical spellwork. If used out of doors, lanterns to protect and keep candles alight will be necessary and waterproof matches are advised.

Fetishes found in the natural world are often a part of Druid ritual, whether on the altar or on the person. Feathers, stones, bones, pieces of bark, flowers, and berries can all be part of the Druid's tradition. You can keep these on your indoor altar, to connect you to the natural world outside, or you can create a pouch or bag to carry these with you or wear on your person, either every day or for magical workings or seasonal celebrations. A bag to hold your Druid tools is called a crane bag, after the myths in

Celtic lore where heroes are gifted a bag of items to help them succeed on their journey, made from the skin of a crane.

Some Druids wear robes for ritual; some do not. As a Hedge Druid, it is entirely your choice as to whether or not you decide to wear robes in your practice. There are beautiful robes that can be made or bought from shops online or in person that can put you in the right mood and frame of mind, connecting you to what inspires and makes you feel at home in your tradition. You might, at the other end of the spectrum, feel much more comfortable in plain street clothes, and if working out of doors in wild and wet weather, having technical clothing to keep you fairly warm and dry will make the experience all the more enjoyable (and allow you to avoid hypothermia). I personally do both, depending on the circumstance. I have a small group that I work with in my back garden, and for these rituals I dress in ritual clothing of blue and black. If I am going out into the forest or on the heath, I ensure that I wear appropriate street/technical clothing. Good boots are a necessity, as there are adders on the heath and long, flowing robes would not work very well out in that landscape, where they would constantly catch on the brambles and gorse that line the paths and thrive in that environment. If you're in Britain or in a similar wet and windy climate, waterproof clothing may also be a good idea. If you don't want to attract too much notice either, it's wisest to not go fully cloaked with all your ritual gear out into a public space.

There are many in the Druid tradition who associate with Bardic paths and who are gifted storytellers, musicians, and poets. For them, the voice and instruments form a large part of their tradition, and if you are so blessed, then do incorporate that into your own path. I often use song and drumming in ritual to help me express what is deep in my soul and also to help me work on new levels of consciousness. Drumming can be a great tool to altering consciousness and there are studies that show 180–210 beats per minute (around 3–4 beats per second) can send one into a trance state.[35]

---

35. "Brain Frequencies and States of Consciousness," Whale Medical, accessed February 3, 2018, whalemedical.com/brain-frequencies-states-of-consciousness.

These tools mentioned form the majority found in the Druid tradition today. Herbs and plants are sometimes used in ritual, but we will look at these in a part three. Some people may use more tools; some may use none at all. Some are influenced by other traditions and have found a way to incorporate them into their own. As one who walks the path of the Hedge Druid, the choice is yours and yours alone.

She looks out at the tools of her craft lying on the altar before her. These things have been well-loved and often used, but she knows that she has no deep need of them; she simply enjoys using them sometimes. She could equally do her work with nothing at hand, out in the depths of the forest. She picks up the sickle, its oak handle worn smooth by many hands over the years, and she feels the connection to the ancestors. The blade hums with its own energy, and she turns to face north to begin her rite.

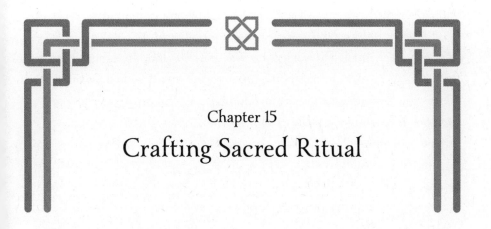

Chapter 15
Crafting Sacred Ritual

Ritual is taking time out of your day to perform certain tasks that connect you with your spiritual tradition. Each tradition has different ways of going about this act, and even within Druidry there are so many variations on a theme that one can follow or create on their own. It is important to study Druidry, to learn the history, in order to ensure that what you are doing, the ritual that you are creating, fits with the tradition itself—otherwise you are simply creating an entirely new spiritual tradition. (If that is your wish, then please go ahead, but it might not be Druidry!) We can use what we know of Druidry from the past, learn from modern-day Druids, and carry the tradition forward into the future, evolving with the times to ensure that it is a spiritual path that is relevant for the day and age.

What, Where, How, Why, and When?

We already have daily rituals in our lives, actions that we do each and every day in order to affect a certain change. We might have a morning ritual where we get up, splash some water on our face, and make a cup of coffee. If we do this each and every day, we have established a sort of ritual action to prepare us for the day. Likewise, when doing Druid ritual, we are preparing ourselves to receive inspiration, awen, insight, connection, and communion with the gods, the ancestors, the spirits of place or the Otherworld. We can incorporate our small daily rituals into a daily practice, which helps us maintain a conscious awareness of our integration with the natural world. (See part four for more on this subject.)

There are rituals in Druidry that celebrate the four or eight festivals in the Wheel of the Year, depending upon which format you choose to work with. You can also perform a ritual during certain phases of the moon, for special occasions such as birthdays, weddings/handfastings, naming ceremonies, or simply to connect and commune with deity, nature, or the elements. Rituals can be as simple or as elaborate as you wish them to be. As Hedge Druids, it is our choice as to how we would like to do these workings, which resources we wish to use, and how it will affect our practice. What is most important is that we do them and not just think about them. Druidry is what you do, not what you think.

So ritual in Druidry consists of a set of actions and words used to create a shift of consciousness and/or energy, usually in order to deepen our connection to the natural world. We might write up a list of actions to use in our rituals that we perform over and over again until they become second nature. Or, we might familiarise ourselves with ritual forms that speak to our soul and improvise on the spot according to what feels most suitable at that moment. My own ritual practice consists of both; I follow a set pattern of certain ritual elements and then speak spontaneously from the heart during certain sections, to allow the moment in time to be truly recognised and spoken about and which includes all that is happening around me in that point in time.

Where we perform our ritual depends largely on what is available to us at the time. We may have vast swathes of forest nearby in which to work or we might find a quiet corner in a city park. We might not be able to perform outdoor ritual for various reasons such as mobility issues or safety. If it is possible and you are able, do perform as many of your rituals out of doors, to truly connect you to the environment, what is happening right now, and to allow the energy to flow through you, nourishing you. If outdoor ritual is simply not possible, you can always open a window to allow fresh air into a room or pull back the curtain to allow the sunlight or moonlight into your ritual space. If we are using an outdoor space, it is important to remember that other beings also inhabit this space and that what we do may alter the energy of an area. (This also applies to indoor spaces that other people might use, to a certain extent.) So, it is always wise to ask permission of the spirits of place first and foremost before choosing a ritual area. Be conscious and aware that ritual is not just about you, but about the entirety of the world around you in which you coexist with myriad other beings.

How we perform our rituals is largely dependent on what we have studied, people we may have previously trained with, and what we feel is relevant to both our needs and those of the environment around us. We may be flamboyant in full ritual robes with our cauldron and staff, standing on the shore of the sea and intoning ancient chants in Celtic languages and invoking the gods to our awareness. Or we might simply find a quiet space in our back garden, where we have a small altar to leave offerings, our only tools are that of the mind, and the ritual is done in silence. I personally think that the spoken word is important in Druid ritual, for it was important to the Celts. Your word was your bond, and as an oral tradition, we cannot underestimate the importance that words had on individuals and society. Whether rehearsed or spoken on the spur of the moment, choose your words carefully and speak clearly out loud if possible. If performed in the mind, again be very conscious of what you are saying—even if not spoken aloud.

Why do we perform ritual? Well, as already discussed, it can deepen our awareness of the natural world and remind us of our connection. It also helps us to establish a tradition, a sense of being part of something, perhaps a tribal feeling of belonging. When we know that what we are doing is in accordance with others, it can bring a feeling of cohesiveness. Alternatively, it can also be stifling to some who prefer to sing their soul song regardless of what others are doing. I would say that it is important to ensure that what you are doing is, indeed, Druidry as much as you are able and also to maintain that wild sense of freedom within your soul. To some, this may sound like a paradox, but I believe it is achievable if approached with an open mind and a willing attitude. My ritual outline may be similar to many other Druids, but my words and the results may be very different from the group that

I know living in the next town. We perform ritual to achieve something, whether it is simple celebration or deep communion. We don't usually just perform ritual for the fun of it, for there is always a reason behind it. It might be a daily practice or a seasonal celebration or a shortened form of ritual while travelling and away from home. But whatever you do ritually, it should always have an intention.

This leads us to the "when" of ritual. Essentially, if you have an intention in mind, then you can perform ritual. You may wish to welcome the swifts, swallows, and house martins back to your area in the early summer, acknowledging this sign of the season with ritual. You may wish to honour the cycle of the moon and perform ritual at the dark and full moon or on the sixth night of the waxing moon. You may wish to celebrate Beltane, Lammas, or the Winter Solstice. You may have achieved something remarkable in your life and wish to commemorate that with a special ritual. Whatever your intention, as long as there is an intention and a focus, then the work can flow smoothly. It's like driving your car: if you have a destination in mind and know where you are going, you will get there quicker and easier. If you do not know your destination, you may be driving around in circles and get completely lost. (I will admit that sometimes this is a great way to discover new places, but for this analogy I'm sticking to intention!)

Ritual should also be performed when you have the time to do so. Rushed ritual is never truly satisfying, though it may be better than no ritual at all. Planning ahead can make all the difference. If you know that a holiday or festival is coming up, plan to ensure that you will have time to celebrate it, whether you choose to do so on the calendrical date, the nearest full moon, when the stars align, the nearest weekend, etcetera. Be consistent with your approach, and you should not forget the important ritual days/nights. You can even plan them out a year in advance, marking them on a calendar and if you need to, ensuring that you have time off work either on the day or the day after to allow the energy of the ritual to move through you. If you need to organise babysitting, planning ahead can make all the difference. If you choose to work with another person or several other people at certain times, then planning ahead is necessary. I currently work with two others during the full moons and the seasonal festivals, and all other rituals are done as a solitary. This means that I need to check schedules with the others to ensure that we can celebrate together when it is most appropriate and I can be more flexible for other ritual times.

Elements of Druid Ritual

Below is a list of ritual actions found in most modern Druid practice, although some may or may not use certain elements in their own work. This is a broad view of ritual elements, and the order in which I present them below may also change depending on the tradition one follows. As a Hedge Druid, you can choose which elements you wish to use and in what order, but please do be aware that what is listed below is largely agreed upon by many in the Druid tradition today, often in the order that it appears here.

- Asking permission for ritual to occur in a particular place
- Call for peace
- Delineating/creating sacred space (preparing the nemeton)
- Honouring the spirits of place
- Honouring ancestors
- Honouring the three realms of land, sea, and sky
- Honouring the four quarters and centre
- Honouring the deities
- Declaration of ritual intention
- Performing ritual action
- Prayers, magic
- Offerings and eisteddfod (sharing of poetry, song, creativity)
- Feast
- Closing

Permission

We begin with simple manners. If working outdoors, it is good practice to ask the spirits of place whether or not they agree to the ritual you would like to perform in that area. Otherwise, it might be like barging into someone's living room and doing ritual there and then, regardless of what they might think. When we are looking for ritual places, we can spend some time communing with the spirits of place beforehand, the flora and fauna around us to see whether or not our energy and intention will work well in that place. Really take some time to ask and even more to wait for an answer. You may get a feeling of openness and welcome or you may get a definitive "go away." You may be unclear and so it is good to restate your intention, perhaps in a slightly different way and await an answer. If one isn't forthcoming, then move on to another location. You may not have to ask permission each and every time you wish to perform a ritual. It entirely depends on your relationship with the place and whether you feel welcome. If performing ritual indoors, you may not need to ask specific permission, but you may need to ensure that you won't be interrupted by others during that time. So, either indoors or out, all beings have to agree to some extent.

Call for Peace

Many within Druidry begin with the Call for Peace. The Welsh poet (and literary forger) Iolo Morganwg is accredited with this practice, and whether authentic or not, it resonates with many in Druidry today. In doing the Call for Peace, we are establishing that there is peace within and without, in our hearts and minds and in all who are a part of this ritual, including all that inhabit the space we are doing ritual in. It is a petition: almost a prayer that there *be* peace. Sometimes the Call for Peace is performed by half-drawing a sword or knife and asking if there is peace; however, for me personally this isn't very conducive to establishing peace, as it almost seems a threat that if there isn't peace, you'll "make some peace" by force. I do understand that sheathing a weapon is an action of peace, but I'd prefer to not use any weapons at all, to really demonstrate peace. In your Druid tradition, you can Call for Peace in whatever form you wish. You can use whatever words or actions you feel are appropriate, but below are the words that are common to many Druid traditions:

May there be peace in the north
May there be peace in the east
May there be peace in the south
May there be peace in the west
May there be peace in our hearts and minds and toward all fellow beings.

Delineating/Creating Sacred Space (Preparing the Nemeton)

Not all Druids feel the need to delineate/create sacred space (otherwise known as preparing the nemeton) as described previously. Especially when working out of doors, some do not cast a circle as is popular in other traditions, feeling that there is no need as they are out there to connect and commune with the world around them and that all is sacred; therefore we cannot "create" sacred space in any sense. This is why it is sometimes referred to as delineating sacred space, which in effect means to delineate the area that we are working in, to narrow the focus down to a specific point. However, this again can be too confining for some Druids and so they forego the practice altogether. In Wicca, a circle is cast mostly to contain the energies raised within ritual, and some Druids today use a similar reason for their creation/delineation of ritual space. However, others see this as irrelevant to Druid practice and so do not incorporate it at all. In my practice, I delineate sacred space or prepare the nemeton when working with others so that we are all on the same page. What this means is that we are working with the energies of a delineated space, to narrow the focus; so for example, we would raise a boundary of energy around the entirety of the back garden so that we can focus on what is happening in that area, as sometimes widening the focus can be too distracting, what with everything going on all around us at any given time. This way, we can really concentrate on using a smaller area, the microcosm of the macrocosm. However, when working alone I don't always feel the need to delineate the space as my personal nemeton is sufficient. Much of it depends on my mood, where I am, and what feels most appropriate to the ritual. In magic and spellcrafting, I will usually delineate sacred space—or for rituals where I aim to go deep into the intention, on an inner journey of the mind, or when working between the worlds. When casting the circle or delineating sacred space, we can push out energy from our own bodies or expand our own nemeton (some would use the analogy of the auric or one's own energy field) and say something similar to the following:

I now cast/create this sacred space, a nemeton of inspiration wherein to do my work.

Visualise a stream of energy flowing from your outstretched hand or ritual tool as you walk in a circle around your designated space. When you have arrived back at the beginning, see the circle of energy around you in your mind. If you like, you can expand this circle of energy into a sphere that envelops you above and also below. Another way to create the sacred space is to envision your own aura as glowing energy around your body and then expand that energy around you until you have a sphere of your own space to work within.

If we wish, we can use a tool such as a staff, wand, or blade to direct the energy that we are pushing out of ourselves and delineate the sacred space. I use my sickle in this action.

We can then ask the spirits of place and/or the realms of land, sea, and sky to overlay the nemeton:

Spirits of place, lend your energy to my nemeton, that it may be strong.
Guide, guard, and bless my work.
May the realm of the land provide this nemeton with stability,
May the realm of the sea provide it with love,
And may the realm of the sky provide it with inspiration.

When overlaying it in this manner, you can create a space that has been encircled three times, defining a temple space and strengthening it with this triplicity, something which I'm sure our ancient Celtic ancestors would have appreciated.

We can then consecrate the space, should we feel the need. I carry burning incense to represent earth, air, and fire, as well as carry a bowl of water around the circle to consecrate it. Sometimes I simply smudge the area with mugwort. If I have nothing at hand, for instance, when I'm doing impromptu ritual out in the wilds, I might simply ask for a blessing on the space in lieu of consecration. You may say something like:

I now consecrate this area through the powers of earth, fire, air, and water.

Or

I now consecrate this area through the powers of land, sea, and sky.

Or

I ask a blessing on this sacred space, from the spirits of place, the gods, and the ancestors.

Honouring the Spirits of Place

Here we take a moment to honour and connect with the spirits of place, those of our immediate environment. This is a good opportunity to really settle into the space, to listen and become aware of our body in a particular place and time. We really open ourselves to an awareness of the area, if we haven't already. We might say something like:

Spirits of place, I honour you for all that you are, with all that I am. Spirit of beech and birch, of the grass growing beneath my feet, of the blackbirds and robins singing in the hedge, of the clouds above and the breeze playing through the leaves: know that you are honoured.

Honouring the Ancestors

Now we turn our attention to the ancestors, invoking our awareness of them, remembering that they are all around us, all the time. We can honour the three strands of ancestors: those of blood, of place, and of tradition. We might call to them and honour them like this:

I honour the ancestors of blood, of place, and of tradition. To ancestors of blood, whose stories flow through my veins; to ancestors of place, whose stories flow through this land; and to ancestors of tradition, whose wisdom flows through the teachings: know that you are honoured.

Honouring the Three Realms

We previously called on the realms of land, sea, and sky to create our nemeton, and here we are simply honouring them, both within and without. Some Druids would combine this with honouring the spirits of place; however, I like to separate the two as it helps me to focus more on my immediate area with the spirits of place and then extend my awareness to the larger three realms of land, sea, and sky. To do this, I envision and honour each realm within me and also surrounding me and my nemeton, layering one upon the other, beginning with the realm of the land. We feel the land, sea, and sky both within us and around us, as we are all part of each other.

I honour the realm of the land, of foundation and stability, of abundance and fertility. I honour the realm of the sea, of flowing and change, of emotion and release. I honour the realm of the sky, of inspiration and higher consciousness, of vision and attainment of desire.

We can use gestures to accompany our words in whatever manner feels comfortable for you. When calling to the realms of land, sea, and sky, I hold my hands palm down in front of me for land, then make small waving motions for sea, and then raise them up with fingers spread for sky. Don't feel that you have to stand stock-still in solemnity when speaking or thinking the words in your mind if you are unable or unwilling to speak out loud. You are allowed to move, to dance, and to use gesture and your body in ritual!

Honouring the Four Quarters and Centre

Many Druids do not include this in their rites, seeing it as an influence of other Western Mystery traditions. However, we do know that in Irish mythology, as we have previously seen, the four directions (which here we call quarters) as well as the centre are noted as distinct, with different attributes. As such, we can include them in our rituals, should we so wish. We might say something like:

> I call to the north, ancient city of Falias and the Stone of Lia Fáil. I call upon fertility and stability and bring these attributes into my rite.
>
> I call to the east, ancient city of Findias and the Sword of Nuada. I call upon intellect and freedom and bring these attributes into my rite.
>
> I call to the south, ancient city of Gorias and the Spear of Lugh. I call upon passion and strength and bring these attributes into my rite.
>
> I call to the west, ancient city of Murias and the Cauldron of Dagda. I call upon emotion and fluidity and bring these attributes into my rite.
>
> I call to the centre, ancient city of Uisneach and the great tree, the Craebh Uisnigh. I call upon the sovereignty of the land and my own soul and bring these attributes into my rite.

Honouring the Deities

This is where we call upon the deities that we wish to honour in our particular path or tradition. As a devotee of Brighid, I would say something like:

> Bright Lady Brighid! Lady of the sacred flame, lady of the holy well, white serpent energy of Albion. Lady of poetry, smithcraft, and healing, I honour you for all that you are with all that I am. I kindle my soul at your hearth-fire; may the awen be upon my lips and may your bright arrow guide me in my work. Blessed be Brighid, lady of brightness, of the Tuatha Dé Danaan.

I also honour the wild god Cernunnos and so might say something like:

> Cernunnos, Wild Hunter, of forests and mountains, I honour you. May my soul sing with the spirit of the woods and hills, of the wild creatures, and of the green and growing things. Guardian, protector, and friend, blessed be the Lord of the Wildwood.

Declaration of Ritual Intention

Now we come to the main portion of the ritual, the reason why we are here in the first place. We reaffirm our intention and let all those with whom we have opened our awareness to hear what it is that we wish to achieve in this ritual space. We can also ask for their blessing on our intention.

Spirits of place; of land, sea, and sky; ancestors and gods, I come here today to celebrate the festival of Imbolc, of the growing light and the coming of spring. Bless this rite with your love, may it be done in peace and with love to honour the season of renewal, of new life and light.

Performing Ritual Action

Here is the main body of the ritual. This is where we do what we have come to do. We have stated our intention. Now we put it into manifestation physically. Ritual consists of physical action for the most part, a blending of the body, mind, and spirit to create a change in consciousness and to honour a specific place and time. So, we might say words in celebration of a festival and perform ritual actions. Using the example of Imbolc, we might say:

This is the season of growing light, of snowdrops and sunshine and the warming of the earth. The lambs are in the fields and the presence of Brighid is deeply felt. I light this candle in this lantern to welcome Brighid's flame back to the land and I anoint myself with this water from a sacred spring. (These actions are performed.) Welcome Brighid! Brighid, blessed lady, I call you in! (A doll for Brighid might be carried around the circle in a basket and welcomed.) Bless my work, bless my life with your love. (Place wand/staff in or near the basket and ask for blessing.) May the work that I do in the coming year be filled with inspiration and guided by your light, blessed by your sacred waters. Hail to the Lady Brighid!

Prayers and Magic

This section may take place under the Performing Ritual Action section we just covered, or it may be done separately afterward, if you wish to do so. After we have done the ritual action, we might take a moment to quietly pray. If, for instance, we are doing a ritual to honour the full moon, we might take a moment to pray and then work some magic to harness the natural energy of the place and time. So the ritual action would be to stand in the moonlight, feel the cool light wash over us, and perhaps dance under the light of the moon. After that, we might pray and then perform a magical working.

Offerings and Eisteddfod

This is a good way to begin to close down the energy of ritual, to give back and to allow your own creativity to flourish. You may simply give an offering such as food or drink in return for the blessings that you have received, for gratitude is one of the best ways in which to commune with nature and the constant abundance around us. When giving an offering, you might say something like:

> *I give my thanks for the blessings that I have received. As I have received, so shall I give back. May the cycle of awen flow evermore.*

You may also wish to dedicate the offering to the gods, the ancestors, or to the Fair Folk. You might say something like:

> *I offer this gift of food and drink to the Fair Folk. May there always be friendship between us.*

Offerings should be something natural and preferably biodegradable that you can leave at a site and will quickly decompose or be eaten by wildlife. Please note that not all food is safe for wildlife, and care must be taken with regards to nuts and seeds when used as offerings. You don't want to alter the natural balance of flora and fauna in a location. When giving an offering, simply walk to where you would like to leave the item or items and, with a feeling of reverence and gratitude, place it upon the ground, bury it, or give it to the water or whatever feels appropriate and is ecologically responsible. Take a moment to pause and reflect upon the cycle of give and take and then continue with the rest of your ritual actions. If you have created sacred space, stay within the boundaries and speak of your intention with the offering, placing it at its designated spot after the ritual has finished.

To take this even further, you may have an eisteddfod, which is a Welsh term originally used for a sort of poetry competition, but which in Modern Druidry also now denotes the part of the ritual where you offer aspects of your own creativity, such as a poem, song, or story. It doesn't matter whether you are alone or with others in your ritual; you can still do either offering or eisteddfod or both. If you think of awen as inspiration, then this part of the ritual is the giving back of the inspiration received in the form of creativity; the exhalation to the inspiration (from the Latin word *inspirere*, meaning "to inhale"). It completes the cycle.

Feast

You may or may not choose to perform this part of ritual; however, it can be a good way to ground the energy of a ritual and bring yourself back to an awareness of the sacred integrated with the mundane. (Although this concept provides a duality, which isn't quite what Druidry seeks to accomplish: rather, the mundane and the sacred are parts of each other and when we see through the Druid's perspective, we realise that everything is sacred and that the sacred is also the mundane.) If you have performed a magical act in ritual, this can help bring you back to earth or be a form of grounding for any extraneous energies that may still be around. It may also be a form of communion, of ingesting the gifts of nature in a manner that truly honours the relationship between you and the world. It may be as simple as taking a sip of water or as elaborate as hosting a real feast for you and your friends. As a Hedge Druid, you will find that most of your rituals will probably be solo, but you may occasionally wish to invite other like-minded people around for a celebration, such as the first harvest, and this is the perfect time to incorporate a real feast. To make things simpler, you can even do a potluck, where everyone brings something to the table!

Closing

The ritual has finally come to an end and now it is time to close it down in a respectful manner. You may wish to do the closing in the opposite order to which you opened the ritual, which is everything that came before the declaration of ritual intention. So you may thank the gods, the three worlds, the ancestors, and the spirits of place.

> I give my utmost thanks to my Lady Brighid and my Lord Cernunnos for being with me in my sacred rite. May you walk with me always, may I be guided by Brighid's light through the darkest depths of the Wildwood. I give my thanks to the ancestors, without whom I would not be here, without whom this land would not be here, and without whom the awen would not flow. I give thanks and honour the realms of land, sea, and sky and the four ancient cities and their treasures. I also give thanks to the spirits of place for being with me in my sacred rite. Know that you are honoured.

You then will take down the nemeton, if you have created one, in a similar fashion to its creation, but perhaps in reverse order. If you created it in a triple manner as in the example above, you might walk the circumference more than once to take it down, drawing the energy back into yourself or into the tool with which you may have cast the circle, perhaps walking in the opposite direction to which you created the sacred space:

> I now release this sacred space, the nemeton of inspiration wherein my work/ritual/celebration was done.

I use my sickle to "cut" the circle and draw the energy back through the blade and into my body. Then, if it's a triple-cast circle, I also honour the spirits of place and the three realms for their part in the designation/delineation of sacred space and envision them releasing their layers of the nemeton.

> Spirits of place, thank you for bringing your energies to my nemeton; I ask that it be released into the world for positive change and transformation.

May the realms of the land, sea, and sky release the energy of this circle, to flow throughout the worlds in respect and in harmony.

With that, the ritual is almost done; however, it is good practice to formally end the rite. If you used the call for peace at the start of the rite, you may say:

May there be peace in our hearts and minds and toward all fellow beings.

Or, if you prefer, you might simply end the rite with a few words about what has happened, such as:

May what has been done and witnessed here go out into the wider world, to nourish, strengthen, and sustain us in balance and in service to the whole.

Your Druid ritual has ended!

She has spent many days crafting her ritual and now she stands at her outdoor altar during the time of Lughnasadh. She has prepared, meditated, and fasted since yesterday, and now under the strength of the mid-afternoon sun, she performs her rite. The bees buzz in the flowers around her and the sound of the combine harvesters grumble softly in the distance. She knows what to say and when to say it; she has memorised and chosen the specific time and tide to perform her ritual. In this, she knows that the gods and the ancestors will approve. She feels the energy of Lughnasadh flowing through her and within her soul.

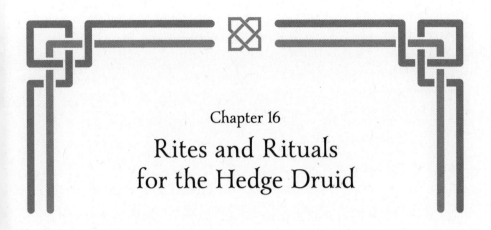

Chapter 16

Rites and Rituals
for the Hedge Druid

Now we come to the exciting part of this work—actually doing the work itself! Here I will present some examples of rituals that you can use or can inspire you to create your own in your own tradition and on your own path as a Hedge Druid.

Rite of Dedication

When starting out on a new path, it's nice to be able to dedicate yourself to it, to set up an intention to do the work, to actually walk the walk and not just enjoy the scenery. A rite of dedication can do just that; it can set our intention to walk the path of the Hedge Druid, confirm to ourselves that this is indeed what we want to do, and be a poignant starting point from where it all began. Like a Wiccan or other Western Paganism form of initiation, it marks the beginning of the journey (from the Latin *initiat*: "begun"). It doesn't mean that this intention will be the one we will follow for the rest of our lives. We can rededicate ourselves as our journey continues and as we have new goals and aspirations in mind. Much like renewing a wedding vow, as we progress in our relationship with the world, our perspectives change and we can bring all that experience forward in anticipation and in relation to what is yet to come. It goes without saying that this is not something to do be done every week or every month, but it is certainly something you can do every year, perhaps on the anniversary of when you began. Good times to perform this ritual might be Samhain or Imbolc.

For this ritual, you will need:
A bowl of water
A candle (in a lantern if outside)
Matches
A biodegradable offering
Any other tools you wish to have / use in your tradition

Try to find a liminal place to perform this Rite of Dedication, whether it is by a forest edge, the seashore, or an actual hedge or a tree that you wish to use in further ritual for "riding between the worlds." Begin by laying out your ritual space and tools, if using any, as you normally would or as you would like to if this is the first time you are performing ritual of any sort. Take some time in the ritual space and remember to ask permission of the spirits of place. You might like to meditate in the space beforehand in order to attune yourself to the environment. Then, you can do the following as previously described:

- Make the call for peace
- Delineate / create sacred space (prepare and create the nemeton)
- Honour the spirits of place
- Honour the ancestors
- Honour the three realms of land, sea, and sky
- Honour the four quarters and centre
- Honour the deities

Declaration of Intention:
I come here to dedicate myself to the path of the Hedge Druid. I seek to follow the flow of awen and to allow my love for nature to inspire me in my life and to live my life accordingly. With the spirits of place, the ancestors, the three worlds, the four quarters, and the deities as witness, I make my pledge

to walk my path as a Hedge Druid to the best of my ability: to seek balance, harmony, and integration with the natural world. May I be guided by the ancestors and the gods in my work, may my work be blessed by the spirits of place and the three realms, and may the powers of the four quarters grant me strength and guard me in my work.

Take a moment and really reflect on being guided by the ancestors and the gods and reach out to them heart and soul. Visualise in your mind the World Tree and the realms connected to them: the Lowerworld, the Middleworld, and the Upperworld. Then, look and listen to the environment in which you are working and seek out the blessing of the spirits of place and the three realms of land, sea, and sky. You might hear a blackbird, for instance, or an owl. A breeze might pick up or it might start to rain. Know that these are the blessings from the world around you that you seek. Then, feel the power of the four quarters flowing through you, strengthening your resolve and your intention.

Take the bowl of water and hold it up to the sky, then bring it to your heart, then bring it to the ground, blessing it by the powers of land, sea, and sky. Dip your finger into the bowl and draw the symbol of the awen upon your brow (page 18). Then bring the bowl to your lips, taking a small sip. Drink in the water, symbolic of the awen. Drink in the awen and allow it to fill your being. Remember this feeling. Pour the remainder of the water onto the ground. You may wish to say a few words from the heart or perform this part in silence, intent upon the feeling rather than the words.

Then take the candle and light the wick. Hold it high, then bring it to your heart and then to the ground, blessing it by the powers of land, sea, and sky. Hold the flame before you and feel the spark of awen, the flame and fire in the head. Allow your being to merge with the flame and feel a similar flame grow within you, perhaps on your brow marked by the awen symbol or maybe in your heart. Connect with the flame and know that its bright and shining energy will guide your path. After a few moments, place the candle in a safe place and then continue with the rite. As above, you may wish to say a few words from the heart or perform this part in silence, intent upon the feeling rather than the words.

Take a few moments and allow what has just happened to settle within your soul. When you feel settled, say something like:

I now walk the path of the Hedge Druid. I walk the path with honour and intention. So may it be.

If you would like to dedicate yourself to a particular deity, now is the time to do so. You might say something like:

Andraste, lady of victory, goddess of the heath and forest, field and meadow, of bright sunlit dunes and crashing shorelines, I dedicate myself to you. May I come to know you deeply, may I feel your guidance in my life. May the work that I do reflect your power in the world and may I honour you in all that I achieve. Lady of the moon, may I be swift and clever like the hare, resourceful and intelligent as the seal, purposeful and powerful as the adder, and wise as the owl.

Take as long as you wish to commune with the energy of the deity that you are incorporating into your dedication, should you so wish to do so. Allow the energy to flow through you and bless you.

Meditate, pray, or do whatever else you would like afterward, perhaps offering a song or poem if you're so inclined. Then, make the offering, dedicating it to whomever you see fit: you might dedicate it to the spirits of place, to the deities, to the ancestors, or to the Fair Folk as they watch and guide you on your path. You might say something like:

I offer this as a gift for a gift. As I have received, so do I give back. The cycle ever turns and the balance is kept. May there always be friendship between us.

The ritual is now nearing its end. Spend as long as you wish in your ritual area, and when the time feels right, you can begin to close down the ritual as previously described. When you have closed everything down, stand for a moment with your face turned toward the vastness of the sky, feeling the powers of nature all around you, beneath your feet, both the seen and the unseen. Feel how you have been transformed. Thank the spirits of place and end the rite with a reiteration of there being peace, if you made the call for peace at the beginning.

The ritual is done. Now it is time to walk the walk.

Meeting the Ancestors Ritual/Meditation

Below is a ritual that can also be used as a meditation to connect you to the ancestors through the breath. You can perform this as a ritual in your sacred space before your altar if you so wish. It is recommended to do this often, to deepen the connection to the ancestors. It is especially relevant to perform this at Samhain. You can also do this as a meditation, wherever you are.

If performing this as a journeying meditation in ritual, set up your sacred space. If doing this solely as a meditation, simply ensure that you won't be distracted.

We begin by closing our eyes and focusing on our breath.

Visualise the World Tree and a door in the broad trunk that connects to the Lowerworld. You walk toward it and open it, noting a silvery light coming from within. You follow this light down, down into the tree's roots where you find a chamber. In the middle of the chamber, you see a pool of water and you walk toward it. You bend down and look into the water and see your own reflection.

Now choose a bloodline to follow, whether from your mother or father's side. Choose a single parent and envision them standing behind you. You can feel their presence behind you and a line that links your heart to theirs. As you breathe, you breathe together—that line also linking your breath. Breathe with each other for a moment.

Now, see your parent's parents standing behind your parent with a connecting thread to your parent from their hearts, which then connects to you through your parent. Breathe with them, all three generations breathing together.

Continue focusing on your breathing, envisioning the lines stretching back behind you and all connected through the heart.

Now envision your grandparents' parents and their parents, back throughout the mists of time. Even if you don't know their faces, feel their presence behind you, stretching back and connecting to each other, breathing together through that single thread from your heart.

Take the time to really feel the mass of people behind you, standing silently and breathing with you, in and out, lit up out of the darkness.

Now, turn to face your ancestors, acknowledging them, breathing with them.

See the large mass of people before you as they are truly there, breathing with you. Some may look like you, some may look very different. Some may have their features dissolving into shadowy forms the further back you look. Let them all breathe with you, silent in a vast cavern of ancestors, the darkness all around you.

Now, listen to the message that your ancestors have to tell you.

Take a moment and allow one or more of your ancestors to come forward and speak to you. Honour them as they honour you. When they have finished, thank them and watch them return to their place, still connected through your heart and breath.

Now turn away, but still feel all your ancestors behind you, breathing with you. Know that they are a part of you and will always be a part of you. Hear the breathing of your ancestors behind you, feel their strength. You know who you are, where you came from. It is a great gift. You see your reflection in the dark pool of water and give your thanks.

And slowly, with each inhale, allow your ancestors to fade from the chamber, but not from your consciousness, generation by generation, until you stand alone once more. Though they are gone from your vision, they still live on in your heart and in your breath. Release the vision fully of your ancestors and return to yourself in the darkness of your mind's eye.

You stand up and bow to the pool of water and then turn back and exit the chamber. You follow the path you came in by, up and up through the roots of the tree, guided by the silvery light. You reach the door and open it and come out into the Middleworld once more.

Focus on your own breath and slowly begin to be aware of the sounds around you. Wiggle your fingers and toes, and when you are ready, open your eyes.

This is a very powerful meditation. It is also very healing and can leave you feeling very grounded and centred. You will have a stronger feeling of who you are and where you fit in the world.

Close down the ritual area and leave an offering if you've performed this as a ritual. If you've done this as a meditation, eat or drink something if necessary in order to ground yourself.

Ritual to Connect with the Realm of the Land (Serpent Energy)

Go outside and find a spot that sings to your soul, that you feel connects you most fully with the energy of the land. Walk to your spot in silence so that you can really still your heart and mind in order to feel the land's energy better without all the mental chattering getting in the way. What follows is the serpent meditation where you will be able to experience a similar feeling of connectedness that I felt all those years ago, through the serpent energy of Albion (the ancient name for Great Britain). The serpent energy may be different where you live, so allow that simply to be and do not force preconceptions upon the experience. You may see dragons, adders, or rattlesnakes or simply lines of undulating energy. Allow the energy of the land upon which you live to flow through you, to connect with you in an intentional way, and find your own relationship to that energy. First find out all that you can about the land where you live: the type of soil, rocks, and so on. Let that inform you and then see what happens, what form the serpent or land energy will take for you personally.

Set up your sacred space, if performing this as a ritual. If doing this as a meditation, ensure that you won't be distracted.

Focus on your breath, but do not force it in any way. Simply notice your breath, feeling it move through you, in and out, for about a minute. You will find that you slowly relax and then you are able to begin.

Close your eyes, if that is comfortable. Feel the ground beneath you. Feel yourself either seated or standing upon the earth and come into full awareness of your own being. Then, slowly, bring that awareness down, out of your body and into the earth. If you'd like, place your hands upon the ground and shift your focus downward, through your hands and into the land itself.

Allow the energy of the soil to come into your awareness. Is it deep, slow, rich, and full of clay? Is it sandy, arid, and quick? Is it rocky, a solid wall that slowly thrums? Wherever you are, whatever type of place you've chosen, bring your focus into the earth. Connect with all that this land has to offer. What associations can you make? How are these reflected in your own life?

You begin to feel a humming in the earth. It is the serpent energy, shifting, coiling, sliding through the land, finding its energetic pathways that connect power places and sacred sites, humming with a deep vibration. The intensity of the vibration indicates how close this ancient ley line is to your current spot. You feel a point of energy breaking away and slithering toward you, seeking you out. You in turn answer that call and send your will toward it, in peace and with deep respect. Softly, you touch that energy and feel the serpent of the land, moving through the currents of being, through all things, yourself included. Allow yourself some time to really see and feel this energy. Determine what shape it appears to you and how you can create a lasting relationship with it. Breathe with this energy; breathe with the serpent energy of the land. Feel it coiling and undulating. Feel how connected you are to this very spot and then spread your awareness of that connection a few feet, a few yards, half a mile, a mile, and more. Ride the serpent energy, ever flowing, across the land. Allow your awareness to expand, following the flow of the serpent energy.

Then, slowly, bring your awareness back to your own locality. You are in control: you are merely riding the energy lines to see where they go. You can ride them back easily to where you began, and the serpent within the land rises and caresses your being with a final soft touch. You then feel it retreating back into the earth, following its pathways, and its own intention. You bring your focus back to your own body, and when you are ready, open your eyes. You are where you began, upon this land, but your consciousness has grown. Give thanks to the land. You can honour it with these or similar words:

> Serpent energy of the earth,
> Flowing and fluid,
> The essence of all life in the realm of the land,
> I honour you for all that you are
> With all that I am.
> May I be the awen.

Feel within you what the realm of the land means to you, both within your being and all around you. Meditate upon thoughts of solidity, fertility, acceptance, energy, renewal, and more. Explore the realm of the land within and without.

Close down the ritual area and leave an offering if you've performed this as a ritual. If you've done this as a meditation, wiggle your fingers and toes and eat or drink something if necessary in order to ground yourself.

Ritual to Connect with the Realm of the Sea

Find a place by the seashore or a lake, river, or other body of water that you feel connects you most fully with the energy of the sea (or any body of water if you don't live near the sea). Ensure that you have checked the tides if on the beach so that you are safe. Take a moment and attune yourself to the water, the sounds, smells, and sights, and creatures of the water. Do this on dry land for safety's sake, but near the water.

Allow the energy of the sea/water to flow through you, to connect with you in an intentional way and find your own relationship to that energy. Find out all that you can about the sea/water where you live, where it comes from, its flow and ebb, the cycles of rain. Let that inform you and connect you the realm of the sea.

Focus on your breath, but do not force it in any way. Simply notice your breath, feeling it move through you, in and out, for about a minute. You will find that you slowly relax and then you are able to begin.

Close your eyes, if that is comfortable. Feel the ground beneath you. Feel yourself either seated or standing upon the earth and come into full awareness of your own being. Then, slowly bring that awareness out, out of your body and toward the water. If you'd like and if it is safe to do so, place your hands in the water and shift your focus outward, through your hands and into the water itself.

Allow the energy of the realm of the sea to flow into your being. Feel the ebb and flow of the tides in your life. Feel the emotional energies from the past and present in your being, flowing in and out. Hold a vision of your future self in your mind and see it as fluid and changeable. Feel the blessing of the water upon that vision of your future self, a blessing coming from the ancestors. Come back to the present moment and feel the vastness of the energy contained in the cycle of water, from evaporation into clouds, falling as rain, flowing through streams and rivers and eventually the sea. Feel the continuity in this cycle and allow it to infuse your entire being, knowing that the cycle is within you as well. Feel the water flowing in your body, in your blood through your veins. Feel the call of the ancestors in your blood and from the depths of the watery realms. Heed that call and make them proud.

Then, slowly, bring your awareness back to your own locality. You are in control: you are merely riding the energy of the tides and the cycle of water. You can ride them back easily to where you began, and the water blesses your soul with its embrace. You then feel it retreating back into the sea, following its pathways and its own intention. You bring your focus back to your own body, and when you are ready, open your eyes. You are where you began, upon this land, by the threshold of where the land meets the water, where the realm of the earth meets the realm of the sea, but your consciousness has grown. Give thanks to the sea. You can honour it with these or similar words:

Flowing energy of the sea,
Dark depths and shimmering light,
The essence of all life in the realm of the sea,
I honour you for all that you are
With all that I am.
May I be the awen.

Feel within you what the realm of the sea means to you, both within your being and all around you. Meditate upon thoughts of fluidity, abundance, giving, receiving, emotion, ancestry, and more. Explore the realm of the sea within and without.

Close down the ritual area and leave an offering if you've performed this as a ritual. If you've done this as a meditation, wiggle your fingers and toes and eat or drink something if necessary in order to ground yourself.

Ritual to Connect with the Realm of the Sky

Go to a place in nature if you can where the sky opens out before you in a vast expanse. It may be on an open plain or on a mountaintop. If this is impossible, you can perform this ritual beneath a large tree, looking at the branches high above you, reaching for the skies. Take a moment and attune yourself to the air around you, your breath, the wind, and the creatures of the air.

Allow the energy of the sky to flow around you, to connect with you in an intentional way, to inspire you, and to find your own relationship to that energy. Open yourself to the vastness that is the realm of the sky, of deity and potential.

Focus on your breath, but do not force it in any way. Simply notice your breath, feeling it move through you, in and out, for about a minute. You will find that you slowly relax and then you are able to begin.

Close your eyes, if that is comfortable. Feel the ground beneath you. Feel yourself either seated or standing upon the earth and come into full awareness of your own being. Then, slowly, bring that awareness out, out of your body and toward the sky. Raise your hands to the sky and feel the air around you, any wind or breezes playing along your body. Listen to the sounds of leaves rustling in the trees or soaring high overhead—any sound that the wind might make. Or simply enjoy the silence of a windless day, yet still feeling the air all around you, upon your skin, awake and aware to its energy.

Allow the energy of the realm of the sky to flow into your being. Feel the vast potential that lies in the limitless heavens, moving through and outward from the earth and the sea, outward from this planet and into the whirling galaxies, further and further out into the endless universe. See deity in this vastness and allow your soul to open toward deity, if you so wish. Allow that divine presence to fill your soul, knowing that the spark of all that has existed, that ever will exist, already lies within you. Remember that you are made of star stuff, of the same material. Remember that all existence is made of star stuff. Let the seed of this knowledge take root in your soul and connect you to all of existence through the threads of awen, shimmering and connecting the energies of life to each other.

Then, slowly, bring your awareness back to your own locality. You are in control, you are connecting to Source from a grounded place. You can ride the energy easily back to where you began, and the sky fills you with inspiration. You then feel the energy slowly receding, following its pathways and its own intention. You bring your focus back to your own body, and when you are ready, open your eyes. You are where you began, upon this land, surrounded by the realm of the sky, but your soul has expanded and connected with Source, with all existence. Give thanks to the sky. You can honour it with these or similar words:

> *Limitless potential of the skies,*
> *Unending beauty and inspiration,*
> *The essence of all life in the realm of the sky,*
> *I honour you for all that you are*
> *With all that I am.*
> *May I be the awen.*

Feel within you what the realm of the sky means to you, both within your being and all around you. Meditate upon thoughts of potential, of seeking and exploration, of connection and knowing, of inspiration and instinct. Explore the realm of the sky within and without.

Close down the ritual area and leave an offering if you've performed this as a ritual. If you've done this as a meditation, wiggle your fingers and toes and eat or drink something if necessary in order to ground yourself.

Druid Blessing to Incorporate Land, Sea, and Sky into Your Life

Once you have connected with each of the three realms individually, you can then perform a blessing upon yourself, your sacred space, your home, etcetera. This brings all three realms of land, sea, and sky into your life, layered one upon the other. With this ritual, you are opening up your awareness of all three realms existing with and around you all the time.

You can set up a ritual circle if you prefer and incorporate all the Druid ritual elements previously described. When ready, sit in the middle of your space and then recall the energies of the three realms that you previously connected with. Remember how you felt with each previous and separate ritual, each realm's energies. Once you feel wholly connected to each and can feel them all around you (and within you), you can then envision them as a triple layer of protection and blessing around you. Begin with the land and envision a sphere of the energy of land surrounding you. You might see it as a particular colour. Feel the energy of the land surrounding you and then bring the energy of the realm of the sea into the ritual, overlaying it upon the energy of the realm of the land. The realm of the sea's layer in the sphere will form a second skin on top of the realm of the land and may be a different colour. Connect with the energy of the sea and feel how it works against and upon the energy of the land. Feel the balance, the flow, the give and take between the two. Once fully connected, bring in the energy of the realm of the sky and envision this as a third layer surrounding you, of a different colour from the sea and land if you prefer. Connect with the energy of the sky, feel how it dances with the sea and resonates with the layer of the land beneath. Feel all three layers blessing you and protecting you, connecting you to all that is, has been, and ever shall be.

Then, if you'd like, you can say this, which I have included in both Gaelic and English, taken and slightly adapted to include the word "me" instead of "you," from the *Carmina Gadelica*:

Neart mara dhuit	Power of sea be with me
Neart talamh duit	Power of land be with me
Neart néimhe	Power of sky
Mathas mara dhuit	Goodness of sea be with me
Mathas talamh duit	Goodness of land be with me
Mathas néimhe.	Goodness of sky.

Feel the powers of the land, sea, and sky giving their blessing to you and your work. Know that you are part of a great cycle in an endless dance of time with the realms of land, sea, and sky.

When you feel ready, pull the spheres of energy into your being, integrating them with your soul. These energies have always been with you; you are now aware of them in your life, and with awareness you can now work with and be inspired by them. See them as layers in your soul or perhaps around your physical body. Let the energies fade into invisibility, integrated and blessing you each and every moment. When need arises, you can call upon these energies both within and without and bring them to their full power to aid you in your work toward harmony with the whole.

Close down the ritual with respect and as you see fit and leave an offering for each of the three realms.

Ritual to Enter the Lowerworld

In this ritual, we will ride the Hedge or the World Tree down to the Lowerworld to meet with the king of the Fair Folk, the god of the Underworld: Gwynn Ap Nudd. Perform this ritual by a tree that you are working with or a hedge if possible. If this isn't available, you can perform this indoors, perhaps with a potted tree, but it is best to try to connect with the land out of doors in as many rituals as possible. If you need to make a special journey to get to a place where you can perform this ritual, then see it as a sort of spiritual pilgrimage. Make that a part of your rite. Remember to always ask permission of the spirits of place where you'd like to hold a ritual. This ritual is best performed at night.

- Make the call for peace
- Delineate / create sacred space (prepare and create the nemeton)
- Honour the spirits of place
- Honour the ancestors
- Honour the three realms of land, sea, and sky
- Honour the four quarters and centre
- Honour the deities

Declaration of Intention:
I have come to seek out The World Tree, to ride down to the Lowerworld, to know myself better and to meet with the Guardian of the Cauldron, the Lord of Annwn.

Now take a moment and settle yourself by the tree, hedge, or whatever it is that you are using to travel between the worlds. Take nine deep breaths to focus, ground, and centre yourself.

Close your eyes and see an image of the tree near you, then overlay that image with that of the World Tree. See the two blending together, and then in your mind's eye, approach the World Tree. You see a doorway appear and you open the door. Inside is silvery light, not sunlight or moonlight, but starlight. A staircase leads down and you follow it.

The staircase opens out into a wide cavern. There are torches lit and a table set up for feasting. However, it is empty. You see an open door at the other end and walk across the great hall to reach it. You look out over a new landscape, similar to your own but different. There is a humming in the air, a buzzing in your ears, and all of a sudden you hear music and laughter behind you in the cavern. You turn around and the great hall in the cavern is filled with folk talking, laughing, eating, and dancing. They are beautiful and they all shine with a soft glow like starlight. You instantly know these people to be the Tylwyth Teg, the Fair Folk.

One approaches you and smiles. They greet you politely and you answer in turn. They guide you to the tables and offer you a place. You sit down and the music starts to play in earnest. It fills the hall and your soul and you sit, enraptured by the sound. When the final notes echo away in the cavern, a hush falls among the crowd and everyone turns to the cavern's entrance.

Outlined in the starlight, outside you see a tall, antlered figure of a man. Behind him, the stars of Orion's bow shine between the antlers, crowning him in all his glory. He steps into the hallway and moves from a dark, shadowy form to that of a great king, wearing a cloak of many shining colours that shift and fade in various patterns. He wears a great torc about his neck and his eyes almost seem to glow with a deep blue colour.

Everyone stands and bows their head and you do the same. The Great King of Annwn, Gwyn Ap Nudd, walks slowly to the high seat. He walks down the great hall and you feel his passing like a strong breeze against your skin, sending a tingling and slightly chilling sensation down your spine. He takes up his place upon his throne and suddenly a great cauldron appears before him. Nine maidens move from the tables to gather around the cauldron and softly they blow upon the still waters within. The cauldron flames to life and you feel a great sense of energy filling the room.

One by one, Gwyn Ap Nudd motions for certain people to move from their places in the great hall to stand before him and look into the cauldron. You watch as a few do so and then you feel his strange blue eyes upon you. You are called.

You walk forward, your heart beating in your chest. Standing before the king of the Faeries, you feel the heat of the cauldron before you. You bow your head to the king and then step up and look into the cauldron. What you see in the cauldron is your shadow self, the deep and dark aspects of your soul that require work and due diligence on your part. These are the aspects of your self that you may not like or that you wish to change. The king is showing you what you need to do. You see the long lines of your ancestors behind you and know that you have the strength to do this task, not only for your benefit, but for them as well.

The waters swirl and then are still and the image fades. You look up into the eyes of the Lord of Annwn and know that the challenge is yours and yours only to accept. What will you do?

When you have made your decision, you speak your intention to the entire gathering. You hear a murmur of assent and encouragement for the decision and a small smile reaches the lips of the king. He nods slightly and you know that your time here in the Lowerworld is coming to a close. Your work awaits you.

You step away from the cauldron and the rooms shifts and changes: the king, the cauldron, the people, the tables, and everything slowly fading from view. You are alone in the cavern once more and the silvery light glows from where you initially entered. You follow the light to a door that leads to a staircase that winds around and around, up and up. When you reach the top, you open the door and come back to where you started. You step out and close the door behind you, bowing to the World Tree. The image of the World Tree fades and you see the former image of the tree, hedge, or whatever it was that you used to connect to the World Tree in your own world.

Slowly you open your eyes and come back to the Middleworld fully. Wiggle your fingers and toes, say your name, clap three times if necessary to fully bring you back to the here and now. Eat something and then close down the ritual space, leaving an offering to the king of the Faeries: Gwyn Ap Nudd.

Middleworld Ritual

In this ritual, we will meet with the god Herne the Hunter. Herne is another antlered deity and is possibly another form of Cernunnos, the antlered deity depicted on the Gundestrup cauldron found in Denmark and believed to be of Celtic origin. The name *Herne* may be a cognate of *Cern*, as "horn" is to the Latin *cornu*. At any rate, we honour the British god Herne during this ritual and meet with him here in the Middleworld. Perform this ritual by a tree, hedge, or other liminal place, if possible.

Set up your ritual space and then proceed with the following.

Declaration of Intention:

I have come to seek out the World Tree, to ride through the Middleworld, to know this land better, and to meet with the Guardian of the Greenwood, Herne the Hunter.

Take a moment and settle yourself by the tree, hedge, or whatever it is that you are using to travel between the worlds. Take nine deep breaths to focus, ground, and centre yourself.

Close your eyes and see an image of the tree near you, then overlay that image with that of the World Tree. See the two blending together, and then in your mind's eye, approach the World Tree. You see a doorway appear and you open the door. Inside is silvery light, not sunlight or moonlight, but starlight. You immediately see another door on the other side of the trunk and you walk directly through it and back out into the Middleworld. Everything seems the same, but your senses are heightened and your focus is sharpened with intention.

You take a moment to look around, to feel how it is to be in the Middleworld in this state of heightened awareness. You then feel a presence behind you and you turn back to the World Tree. A shape is emerging from behind the tree, a large antlered shadowy form. He steps out from the shade and into the dappled sunlight and you see before you Herne the Hunter.

He is tall and his beard reaches down to his hairy chest. He is clad in leather breeches and a heavy torc is around his neck. Around his wrists are bronze bracers and in his hand is a long spear. You feel the primal power of the Guardian of the Greenwood, an ancient power, and you bow your head to him. From behind him you sense other beings, creatures of land, sea, and sky all together, swirling in a mass of colours: black, red, and white respectively. You look into the eyes of Herne the Hunter and they flash a bright green. As soon as the flash has come, it disappears and he steps aside.

The whirling mass of colours fades into a single colour and that shimmering energy approaches.

You look into the whirling mass and a shape emerges. It is an animal, of the colour of its corresponding realm: black for land, red for sea, or white for sky. A magical being, it solidifies before you and slowly approaches. You hear words in your mind, words from Herne himself:

"This is one of your power animals, one which I have called to you to help you in your work."

You look closely at the animal and make a gesture of friendship. The animal responds and you feel a fondness growing between you. The animal then approaches you very closely and you know that it needs to tell you something. You open your heart to hear what it says, and in your body and soul you hear and feel its message. The animal might merge into your body for a moment, to relay the message, or it may even speak with human words. The power of Herne the Hunter works in many ways, so simply accept the message that it relates to you and thank it with all due respect.

When you have received the message, the animal slowly fades from view, but not from your memory. You turn to thank Herne, but all you see is a dark shadow dissipating into mist that fades from view.

The World Tree awaits you now and you make your way toward it, walking through the door and straight back out into the Middleworld. You can feel your senses still a little heightened; you breathe and ground the energy into the land itself. You are here, now, and there is work to do.

Slowly you open your eyes and come back to yourself fully. Wiggle your fingers and toes, say your name, clap three times if necessary to fully bring you back to the here and now. Eat something and then close down the ritual space, leaving an offering to Herne the Hunter, as well as to your power animal.

Research all that you can about the animal that appeared to you, both academically and in folklore and myth, especially those of the land where you live. Know that you can contact your power animal anytime you wish through the World Tree and may even meet more, should Herne choose more for your work.

Ritual to Enter the Upperworld

In this ritual, we will meet with the goddess Arianrhod in her abode of Caer Arianrhod. She will show you, through her shining being, a higher aspect of yourself, the self that you could become, and the greatest potential that you can reach in your work as a Hedge Druid.

Set up your ritual space and then proceed with the following.

Declaration of Intention:

I have come to seek out the World Tree, to ride up to the Upperworld, to meet with the Lady Arianrhod of the Silver Wheel.

Take a moment and settle yourself by the tree, hedge, or whatever it is that you are using to travel between the worlds. Take nine deep breaths to focus, ground, and centre yourself.

Close your eyes and see an image of the tree near you, then overlay that image with that of the World Tree. See the two blending together, and then in your mind's eye, approach the World Tree. You see a doorway appear and you open the door. Inside is silvery light, not sunlight or moonlight, but starlight. You see a staircase going up and you follow that staircase until you reach another door. When you open the door, you are met with light all around you, light that has no source. It feels as if you are in the clouds and you feel the light winds upon your face. You feel free, and without fear you step out into this realm, your feet finding solid footing even though it seems nothing is there.

The clouds shift and change shape before you and suddenly you see a castle emerging from the mist. Above the castle you see a crescent-shaped constellation of seven stars, like the bowl of a great cup, shining its light upon the walls. You walk up to the castle and you know that you are at Caer Arianrhod, the abode of the Lady Arianrhod, a great lady of sovereignty.

The doors open and you step inside. You walk down huge silent halls until you come to another set of doors. Here the star constellation is engraved in silver upon the stone doors and you gently touch them as they shimmer with light. The door opens at your touch and you enter the room.

There before you sits the goddess Arianrhod, a great queen. Next to her throne is a shining spinning wheel that spins out silver thread. She holds the threads between her hands, inspecting it, cutting it here and there, thinning or thickening the thread as she deems fit. She looks up at you and you are pierced by her grey eyes. They are filled with the knowledge of the universe, of time and tides and the immortal energy that lies behind all life as you know it.

"Approach," you hear her say in your mind. You walk toward the throne, aware of the awesome power of this goddess. "You wish to glimpse your higher self, your truest potential." You nod, for you cannot speak in her presence, so awed you are by her glory. "Then look up at the stars and you will see what you need."

You follow her gaze upward into a dark, starry sky. The stars shine more brightly than you've ever seen them before. You recognise some of the constellations, but some of them are completely new to you. The stars glow brighter and brighter and then fade into an image of your true self, your higher self, that which you most wish to be, that which you most would like to attain. You see yourself living as such and what is needed in order to achieve this vision. You also know that you must meld this vision with that which you received in the Lowerworld of Annwn; that the two aspects of dark and light must meet within you, within the core of your being. Only then, when they are brought to consciousness, can you truly be all that you have ever dreamt, fulfilling your truest potential. The vision fades and your eyes fall once more upon Arianrhod.

"The way will not come without work. You must walk your own path; no one can do it for you. On this path, I lay a tynghedau, a condition. Only when you have come to terms and dealt with the shadow will you be able to reign sovereign in your own kingdom of the soul. Keep the vision I have given you and do the work. Your highest potential awaits you."

You feel her words ringing through your soul. They fill you with a clear energy, like starlight. You know that you will carry your vision of the higher self with you as you do the work necessary.

The goddess fades from view before you, and the last thing you see is the spinning wheel with the shining silvery thread before that too fades from view. You bow and then you find yourself back among the clouds with the World Tree nearby. You walk toward the tree and open the door, descending back down to the Middleworld. You go through the door, carrying the knowledge with you.

Slowly you open your eyes and come back to yourself fully. Wiggle your fingers and toes, say your name, clap three times if necessary to fully bring you back to the here and now. Eat something and then close down the ritual space, leaving an offering to Arianrhod. May your work be blessed!

Rite of Protection Using the Shield of Brighid

This rite uses what is commonly known as "The Descent of Brighid" from the *Carmina Gadelica*. This rite specifically calls upon the powers of the goddess Brighid and cannot be used interchangeably with another goddess. If you honour or work with other deities, you might consider using the poem as an example to write your own spell or charm of protection. Alternatively, you might just leave out all the references to deity. At the end of the poem, we find the term *luatha-luis*, whose meaning is not wholly clear and which is open to interpretation. It may mean a fast-acting, possibly poisonous plant. *Luis* is the rowan or mountain ash, a powerful and magical tree, whose berries are poisonous when raw, but delicious and nutritious when cooked.

You can perform this ritual every Imbolc, especially if you are a follower or would like to honour Brighid. Or you can simply use it as a rite of protection. You can perform this rite after undergoing a purification such as smudging or saining yourself with smoke from mugwort or vervain.

For this ritual, I would strongly encourage the entire formality of designating sacred space. This will lend focus to your intention, as well as invite the powers of the ancestors, the three realms, the spirits of place, and more to your rite. Choose something that symbolises protection for you, a talisman if you will: something strong and durable, something that will shield you physically, spiritually, and psychically. You can make a shield yourself, using whatever materials you prefer. This doesn't have to be a full-body protecting hunk of steel, but can be symbolic; you can make one out of papier maché to keep near your altar, should you so wish. You might wish to use something natural that you can carry with you, such as a stone or crystal, or even say the poem over a pendant bearing the triskele or triquetra symbol, reflecting the triple nature of Brighid. There are many ways you can use this—be creative!

Set up and designate your sacred space. Once you have done so, sit or stand for a moment and breathe, focusing your intention on what is to come. Visualise a glowing light beginning to emanate from within, centred on your chest. This light reflects the light of the moon or the light upon water or the light of a flame. The energy from this light is not hot but cool, flowing through you and filling you with strength and confidence, as well as compassion and love. Raise your arms to the sky, drawing down the power of the sky and the full moon. Then hold your hands out in front of you and draw in the power of the sea and the highest tide. Finally, hold your hands to the ground and draw the power of the land into yourself, the serpent energy that courses and connects everything to each other. Stand fully upright once more, noting how the light emanating from within you is even brighter now. Take that light within your mind and form it into a circle or sphere of light around you. Visualise that light encompassing you, shielding you. If you have a talisman to represent the shield, hold this aloft and still visualise the circle around you. Then say the following words, from "The Descent of Brighid" from the *Carmina Gadelica*, feeling free to adapt or leave out the Christian influence:

> *Brigit daughter of Dugall the Brown*
> *Son of Aodh son of Art son of Conn*
> *Son of Criara son of Cairbre son of Cas*
> *Son of Cormac son of Cartach son of Conn.*

Brigit of the mantles,
Brigit of the peat-heap,
Brigit of the twining hair,
Brigit of the augury.

Brigit of the white feet,

Brigit of calmness,
Brigit of the white palms,
Brigit of the kine.

Brigit, woman-comrade,
Brigit of the peat-heap,
Brigit, woman-helper,
Brigit, woman mild.

Brigit, own tress of Mary,
Brigit, Nurse of Christ,
Each day and each night
That I say the Descent of Brigit,
I shall not be slain,
I shall not be wounded,
I shall not be put in cell,
I shall not be gashed,
I shall not be torn in sunder,
I shall not be despoiled,
I shall not be down-trodden,
I shall not be made naked,
I shall not be rent,
Nor will Christ
Leave me forgotten.

Nor sun shall burn me,
Nor fire shall burn me.

Nor beam shall burn me.
Nor moon shall burn me.

Nor river shall drown me.
Nor brine shall drown me.
Nor flood shall drown me.
Nor water shall drown me.

Nightmare shall not lie on me,
Black-sleep shall not lie on me.
Spell-sleep shall not lie on me,
'Luatha-luis' shall not lie on me.

I am under the keeping
Of my Saint Mary;
My companion beloved
Is Brigit.[36]

Let the words sink into the air around you. Let them suffuse the light that encircles you with their power. When you are ready, draw the circle of light that surrounds you back into yourself, centred on your chest. If you have a special talisman that you'd like to infuse with this energy instead, draw the circle of light that surrounds you into your talisman. When all the light has gone where it should, stand for a moment and see how this makes you feel. You can test the circle of light by holding up your dominant hand and immediately bringing the circle of light back around your being. See it spring back up with ease, to surround you and protect you. If you are using a talisman, see it coming forth from the talisman. You can call and release this power as you wish, as you need. It is not something to be played with, but something real—an energy being focused around you. You are connecting with the power of Brighid.

---

36. "Supplication of the Saints 157–159 (AGHAN NAN NAOMH)," *Carmina Gadelica* online, Archive.org, accessed August 7, 2018, https://archive.org/stream/carminagadelicah-30carm/carminagadelicah30carm_djvu.txt.

When you are satisfied that you have the protection you need, it is time to reciprocate and leave an offering for what you have been given. As the lady of poetry, smithcraft, and healing, an offering related of one or all of these would be suitable.

Close down your ritual and renew this rite of protection whenever you feel it necessary.

She has performed the Rite of Protection. She feels the energies and the shieldings of Brighid flow through her. She knows that Brighid is with her, this day and every day, this night and every night. With courage and confidence, the Hedge Druid packs her suitcase and catches her train.

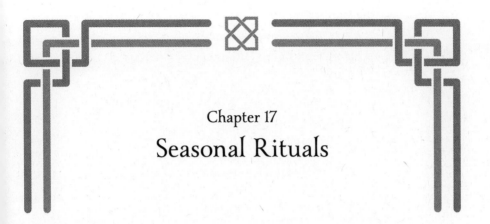

Chapter 17

Seasonal Rituals

Druidry works in tune with the seasons, helping us to remember that we are a part of nature. Modern Druidry celebrates eight festivals throughout the year, which are each a wonderful opportunity to take time out to stop and recognise what is happening all around us. This becomes all the more important the more hectic our lives become, and the benefits from performing these seasonal rituals can help us to go along with the flow of the seasons.

Imbolc

Imbolc is when the first signs of spring are returning to the land. By the calendar, it is from sunset on the January 31 through to sunset on February 1. It is a gentle festival, a soft awakening from the trials of winter. Though there may be hardship ahead, with cold weather and general uncertainty, we still honour the returning light, the longer days, the lambing season, and the first snowdrops. For this ritual you can make a Brighid's cross, which is a traditional symbol woven on this day to place upon your altar. Details on how to make the cross are found at the end of this ritual.

For this ritual, you will need:

- A small basket
- A representation of Brighid, perhaps woven from wheat or straw or a handmade dolly

- A wand, preferably of birch wood
- A candle
- A bowl of water
- Offerings (milk and butter are traditional at this time of year)
- A Brighid's cross

This ritual is a traditional one, where Brighid is welcomed into the home. If you prefer not to work with this specific goddess, you may replace "Brighid" with "spring" and leave out the basket, wand, representation of the goddess, and Brighid's cross elements of this ritual, simply welcoming spring and the blessings of renewal into your home at the beginning of this ritual and giving an offering as the sun rises the next day.

I prefer to do a good spring cleaning of the whole house before this ritual. Please note: this ritual is a bit different from the other seasonal rituals in that it specifically takes place indoors.

Set up your sacred space and ensure that you have everything at hand. You don't have to cast a circle or create a nemeton for this ritual. The entire house is the sacred space.

On the eve of Imbolc, at sunset on January 31, place the basket with the doll just outside your front door (or by an open window if in an apartment). Stand at the front door and take a moment to calm and settle yourself. Once centred, open the door and call out:

Brighid, Lady of Spring, I welcome you in!

Hold open the door and stand aside, feeling her answering call. Then go out and pick up the basket with the doll and carry it inside the home (or pass it out through the lintel of a window and back in again). Carry the basket and doll into your sacred space. Place it carefully in the centre of the space and stand or sit next to it, saying these or similar words:

Lady Brighid, I welcome you in. Grant your blessing upon this space from the heights to the depths, from the depths to the heights. In this time of new

hope, the light is growing and I am thankful. Blessings to you, Lady Brighid,
even as you bestow your blessings upon us all this springtide.

Light the candle and place it next to the basket.

May the blessings of a new dawn be upon us all.

Take the bowl of water and place on the other side of the basket.

Health, love, and prosperity be with us all.

Take the wand and place it in the basket, next to the dolly.

Lady Brighid, bless this wand, infuse it with your regenerative power: from
the land, from the sea, from the sky itself. Lady of Poetry, of Smithcraft, and
of Healing, bless and infuse this wand so that I may work in the world in
balance and harmony on my Druid path. Lady of the Sacred Flame, Lady of
the Holy Well, I honour you and your power, gentle and nourishing, strong
and compassionate.

Sit or stand for a moment by the basket and sense the power flowing
from Brighid into the wand. When you are ready, take up the wand and pass
it quickly through the flame (do not burn or scorch it!) and then dip it into
the bowl of water. Then hold it aloft and say:

Through the powers of fire and water, through the blessing of Brighid, the
Lady of Spring, and the Light of the World, may the work that I do reflect
her greatest gifts. May my work be filled with love, compassion, and honour
and may I be the awen.

Though it's not a traditional part of this rite, you can now trace the
awen symbol in the air before you with the wand, putting it straight to use.
See the symbol in the air before you and then allow the symbol to sink into
your body and your soul, filling you with inspiration.

When you are ready, give the offering, using whatever words you feel
appropriate. If you can, leave the offering next to a fireplace overnight and
then place it outside the next morning. Close down the ritual as you see fit.

Greet the dawn the next morning if you can. Welcome the new day, welcome the growing light. Take the Brighid's cross that you made and hold it up to the rising sun. Allow the energy of the sunlight to infuse the cross. See it blessing the turning cross, reflecting the turning of the wheel and the dance of the sun. Hang the cross in a prominent window of the home, to further bless your dwelling throughout the year. You can make a new one next year or renew the same one year after year.

How to Make a Brighid's Cross

Traditionally, rushes were used for making Brighid's Crosses: these rushes were pulled, not cut, from where they grew. However, not everyone has access to rushes and they can be tricky to use the first time, so I recommend using pipe cleaners—at least for your first attempt! They hold together easily and you can quickly see the pattern that is to emerge. You can also use paper drinking straws to be more eco-friendly. Also, ensure that you have four small rubber bands handy to finish off the sections. When you're more adept, do try making Brighid's Crosses with rushes, long grasses, wheat, or straw. Anything that is dry, such as straw or wheat, will need to be soaked for several hours first to soften them up enough to use so that they bend without breaking.

Take the first stalk and lay it upon the table. Take another and fold it in half. Holding the unbent stalk in one hand, wrap the folded stalk around the middle of the straight stalk and ensure that it is nice and tightly wrapped. The folded stalk should have its ends pointing out to the right. This folding part can be a bit tricky, as you will need one hand to hold the cross together and the other hand to add new stalks. Using a table may make it easier, as you can lay it flat.

Hold the join of the two stalks together between finger and thumb and turn the cross a quarter turn to the left (ninety degrees counterclockwise). Fold another stalk over the junction of the first two stalks so that the open ends point to your right once again. Push the stalks nice and close together, so that there are no gaps.

Continue rotating to the left and adding stalks until all are included. You can use as many as you wish; you will know when to stop. The finished product should resemble a four-armed cross that looks like it is rotating, for indeed it is a symbolic sun wheel!

Using the rubber bands, tie off the ends of each arm. (Alternatively, you can wrap them with extra pieces of stalks, tucking the ends under as you go to hold it tight.) Trim the ends so that they are nice and neat. There you have it—your very own Brighid's Cross!

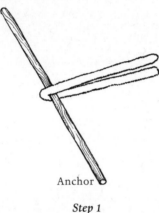

Anchor

Step 1

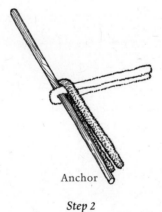

Anchor

Step 2

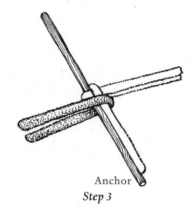

Anchor

Step 3

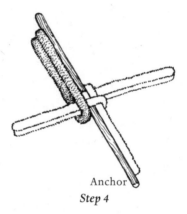

Anchor

Step 4

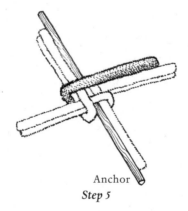

Anchor

Step 5

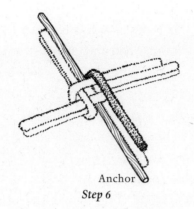

Anchor

Step 6

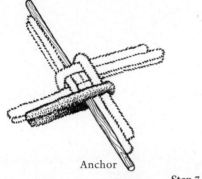

Anchor

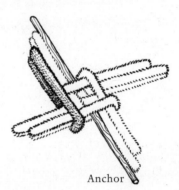

Anchor

Step 7

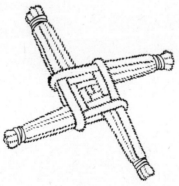

Step 8

Spring Equinox

For this ritual, try to find a place that is between two places: a threshold place, a liminal place. It might be on the seashore or a lakeshore where the water meets the land. It might be a hilltop, where the land meets the sky. Even a backyard can be seen as a liminal place, between your home and the wilderness, the indoors and the great outdoors, your boundary and that of your neighbour. You can choose a liminal time as well, such as dawn or dusk: not quite morning, not quite night. You may also choose to perform this ritual near a hedge (another liminal place) or by a tree if you wish to perform a hedge riding or travel the World Tree. This ritual is aimed at opening your mind and your self to wider perspectives as you stand on the balance point of light and darkness. This is an important time for a Hedge Druid, who seeks out liminal places and the Otherworld and uses the Hedge or the World Tree in their work.

There is nothing that you need for this ritual, no items at all, but you can always leave an offering if you so choose. Please ensure that it is biodegradable and compatible with the environment. Songs and poetry are always good options if you are unsure.

Designate the sacred space if you feel the need to do so. Some feel more secure within a ritual nemeton; others do not feel the need. Do what feels right for you. Take a moment or a few moments to connect with the place. Listen and feel. Allow the place to tell you its story. Connect with it and become a part of it.

When you are ready, stand and hold your arms out to the sides. Say these or similar words:

> *I stand at the threshold, in the liminal world between time and space.*
> *I stand upon the knife's edge;*
> *I stand upon the turning point in this liminal place.*
> *I honour the balance of day and night, of dark and light;*
> *Equal day, equal night.*
> *Grant to me Second Sight.*

Lower your arms, sit down if you wish, and meditate upon the area around you. If you're feeling adventurous, you can try the Druid's crane stance. Stand with one leg raised or on one foot with the other either pushed out in front or behind you. I've found that a good pose to adapt for this posture is the tree pose from yoga, where one foot is raised and placed on the inside of the standing leg, wherever it is comfortable. Using your hand, cover the eye on the same side as the raised leg while standing in this posture. This is an ancient posture said to be used by the Druids to see through and beyond the veils to the Otherworld. In this pose, you are half in this world, half in the Otherworld. It's a difficult pose to maintain and can be made more stable by holding a staff in your other hand, to help your balance.

Stand in this position for as long as you can. Allow yourself to open up to the place; allow it to give you insight. You can gaze at the clouds scudding overhead or the waves lapping the shore or the wind among the leaves of the trees. You might open yourself up to messages from the three worlds as you travel up, down, or through the World Tree/Hedge in your riding. Let your mind relax and open itself to what nature is trying to say to you. You may ask a question or have a problem that needs some inspiration in order to be solved. Allow nature to be your guide; allow the spirits of place to guide you. Allow the liminal nature of the time of the Spring Equinox to take you beyond light and dark, day and night, black and white. Find that balance point, where everything is perfectly held: in your body, in your mind, in your soul, and in the world around you. The answer will appear or you will get insight into your own nature and/or the nature of the world.

When you are ready, gently come out of this pose or rise from your seated posture. Hold your arms out to your sides once again and say these or similar words:

The balance shifts, the doors open
And we come through to the other side
The darkness recedes, the light increases
And we have no place to hide
Second Sight grants to me

Confirmation in times of uncertainty
The Wheel turns round, cycle never-ending
From darkness to light, this cycle I'm tending
Hail to the growing light, farewell to the long night
Hail to the awen and to the Second Sight

Give your heartfelt thanks to the spirits of place for their gifts. Honour every living thing for its own sake. Honour the times and tides of the Spring Equinox, of balance. When you are ready, give your offering, close down the ritual space if you created a nemeton, and thank the spirits of place once more. Remember and if you need to, write down what you learned and gained from opening up to the Second Sight. These insights may well carry you through the light half of the year, in balance and harmony until the Autumn Equinox.

Beltane

This ritual is not for the faint-hearted. For at Beltane, the portals between this world and the Otherworld are wide open and the Fair Folk are out in abundance. Here we will go out into a wild place and seek out a companion or guide of the Fair Folk: one that can offer advice, wisdom, and intelligence on the locality of place, what is needed, and what can be offered in return. Meeting one of the Fair Folk can be thrilling, but can also be a little scary. They are like us and yet not like us, as described in the previous chapter on the Fair Folk in part one of this book. They have different agendas and may or may not appear in human form. Yet Beltane is the traditional time for encountering the Fair Folk, as is Samhain. So here, with caution, we will attempt to meet one of them, to gain some insight into the work that we can offer to the Fair Folk as well as the spirits of place and what they may ask of us (and what we may receive in return).

This ritual is ideally performed outside, but can be accommodated for those who are unable to do so. You can perform this indoors at your indoor altar if you wish and take a similar journey in your mind to a destination of your choosing. Instead of a fire, you can have a candle upon your altar as the focal point.

You may prefer to fast during the day of this ritual if you are able (if in doubt, consult your medical health practitioner). Drinking vervain tea before the ritual or taking a few drops of the moon elixir (see end of this ritual on making your own moon elixir) might also aid in your working. It is important to ensure that you do not have any iron on your person or in the ritual area, as this is reputed to drive away the Fair Folk. If you feel the need for some protection against the Fair Folk, you can carry a pouch of St. John's wort upon your person, though this may affect some of the Fae who wish to communicate with you. This protective herb has its good qualities, in keeping the harmful away, but may also deter those whose intentions are entirely neutral or yet unclear.

Good places to hold this ritual are in wild places or liminal places such as a forest edge, the seashore, or a hilltop. Other places could be at ancient sites such as tumuli, barrows, or stone circles where it is often said the Fair Folk gather. You could also hold this ritual near a hawthorn or an elder tree, as these are trees associated with the Fair Folk. You may also choose to perform this ritual by a hedge. In any case, wherever you hold this ritual, ensure that the fire you create is safe and contained. Otherwise the Fair Folk might become angry with you and this is certainly not what you want! I've even performed this ritual in my own backyard, with great success after a Beltane rite with friends and consequently meeting one of the Fair Folk for the very first time: he came through the hedge and stood under an apple tree, clad in shades of brown.

For this ritual, you will need:

- An offering, such as butter or honey
- Somewhere where you can sit outside for part or all of the night and have an outdoor fire

- A mugwort smudge stick or cut and dried herb to be burned in a censer
- A handful of vervain
- Some food and drink for yourself

Designate the sacred space as you normally would. When doing so, focus on inviting those of the Fair Folk who are in tune with your intention alongside the spirits of place and who wish you no harm. That way, you may filter out unwanted attention from those who may not be so beneficial to you or your work. You might like to say something similar to what is offered below as you set up the space and after calling to the spirits of place:

I honour the time and tide and the beginning of summer. I also call to the Fair Folk, those who hold the knowledge and wisdom of this land and of the ages. Those who come from between the worlds, I seek your blessing on this rite and also your friendship. Those who are in tune with my intention, be welcome here in my rite.

Take as long as you need to settle and attune yourself to the place. Let yourself become a part of the landscape. Then light a small fire and gaze into the flames. Take your time with this ritual; it might take all night or at least a couple of hours. Allow yourself to really open up to the time and place and do not rush anything.

When you feel ready, take the mugwort smudge stick or burn some mugwort in a censer and sain yourself with the smoke. (Saining is like purifying—allow the smoke to rise and flow over all your body, cleansing your body and soul.) Once you feel cleansed and purified, sit down for a few moments and just breathe.

Now call to the Fair Folk, first throwing a handful of vervain upon the fire (or the censer, if performing this indoors). Say these or similar words:

I now call out to one of the Fair Folk, you who would be my guide, who would share with me the wisdom of the Otherworld. In return, may the work that I do benefit this world and the Otherworld and may there always be friendship between us.

Wait as long as is necessary. Someone will come to your call, whether in a human form or in animal form or as a light breeze or a wind that caresses you but touches nothing else. You might hear music or laughter without actually seeing anything. All these indicate the presence of the Fair Folk. Open your mind to any messages they might have to offer or simply become aware of their presence in your life in this place and time. At this initial meeting, a simple greeting might be enough and a lengthy communion unnecessary. You can work and converse with the Fair Folk at length in later rites and rituals, but for now you are simply opening up your awareness of them and of one in particular who wishes to work with you.

You may ask them for their name, but they may not give one to you, so don't be offended by this. Simply acknowledge them as they appear as your guide from the Otherworld. When your encounter is over (and it may be brief for this first time), slightly bow your head to them as the meeting comes to a close. Show gratitude toward them for making themselves known to you: give your offering in a suitable place for the Fair Folk and the spirits of place, acknowledging the beauty and gifts that have already been shared. Remember, don't say thank you, for that may put you in their debt! Simply give the offering with a feeling of gratitude.

When you are ready, eat some food and have something to drink and then put out the fire and ensure all safety precautions have been met. Close down your ritual space. Know that you can return to this place to commune further with your Otherworldly guide. In future meetings they may set tasks for you to perform in return for their wisdom. These might range from cleaning up litter in the area to coming at certain times such as the full moon or at special holidays. They might ask you for protection of their space in your world and you may need to seek out local authorities to communicate with and ensure that the place is protected and kept safe for generations to come. They might simply ask for further offerings of honey, whisky, or mead or poetry, song, and music. Work with them to the best of your abilities, ensuring that no harm comes to yourself or others, the Fair Folk included. Ensure that you keep up your relationship with them; do not take them for granted or ignore them or allow the friendship to cease due to laziness or apathy.

If you need to sever the relationship for any reason, return to the place where you initially held this ritual. You may be moving to another part of the country or have found another path. It is important to say farewell to your Faery companion and being polite to the Fair Folk is of utmost importance.

Making Moon Elixir

This is a wonderful little "potion" that can help open up your sight to the Fair Folk. Make a tea with vervain, strain, and allow to cool. Mix this with some spring water, preferably from a holy well or sacred water source and pour into a clear jar or container (not plastic). On the night of the full moon, bring the jar outside at sunset and allow the light of the moon to fall upon the brew, infusing it with that Otherworldly and magical light. If you can do this on the nearest full moon to Beltane or Samhain, you may find it doubly empowered. Hold up the jar and see the moonlight infusing the liquid. Say these or similar words:

> Light of moon and dark of night
> Open me to Second Sight
> Companion to Fair Folk I shall be
> Friendship between us, I and thee

Bring the jar inside just before the sun rises. If you are making a large batch to last you several months, add brandy, gin, or vodka that is about one third of the initial infusion. This will ensure that bacteria will not take over. If you're making a small amount to last only a month, this may or may not be necessary, though you should keep this in the refrigerator to prolong shelf life. You can decant a small amount into portable glass vials with droppers, similar to those used in the Bach flower remedies. Place a few drops under your tongue before ritual, to help you commune with the Fair Folk.

Summer Solstice Ritual

This ritual honours the strength and power of the sun in its full glory at the Summer Solstice, the longest day. It also provides the initial Three Cauldrons visualisation, which you can use throughout your journey on the path of the Hedge Druid.

For this ritual, you will need:

- A sprig of St. John's wort (to be collected just before the sun rises on the Summer Solstice or, if not possible, a small pouch containing the dried herb)

- A quartz crystal (Try to find your own in the natural landscape. They are readily available in many environments such as streambeds and seashores. I have several, which are beautiful and which may not be clear/translucent like the ones you can find in shops, but which come from the land where I live. If you must buy one, please ensure that it comes from an ethical source.)

- An offering

Find an outdoor place where you will not be disturbed and where you are able to see the rising sun. Designate your ritual space, should you so wish. Stand facing the horizon, where the sun will soon rise in the northeast. (If you cannot be outdoors, try to find a window that faces the rising sun; failing that, simply face northeast in your indoor ritual space. We must acknowledge that not everyone has the mobility to perform rituals out of doors easily.) Have your sprig of St. John's wort and your quartz crystal both at hand.

Take a moment to stand in the twilight of pre-dawn. Listen to the sounds around you: the awakening songs of birds and the dawn chorus, the sounds of the village or town waking up around you. Listen to the sound of the breeze, and feel the hum of the earth beneath your feet. Feel the magic that is in the air at this special time, the time of the longest day. Feel the lightheartedness of summer's ease and joy. Just before the first light touches the horizon, say these or similar words:

I stand here to greet the rising of the sun, on this the longest day. I honour the tides and times and the spirits of place. With the ancestors and the gods, my guides and the strength of my own being I greet the day.

Watch and wait for the sun to rise on the horizon. Watch the sunrise (but don't look directly at the sun after it leaves the horizon; let's be sensible!). As the red-gold light appears (if it isn't cloudy or raining) allow the sun to send a beam of light to light a fire in your head, your heart, and your belly. Visualise three cauldrons containing this fire in each location. Allow the light of the sun to fill these cauldrons with the magical golden light from the longest day of the year. See them alight with the golden rays of the sun to sustain you throughout the dark half of the year. (If the sun isn't visible, you can still perform this visualisation, for the sun is still there on the longest day, even though it may be hidden by clouds.) Remember this feeling, remember the sounds of birds around you, remember the light that infuses your very being.

When you are ready, take the sprig of St. John's wort and hold it up to the sunlight. Allow the sun to infuse the herb with the same energy and say these or similar words:

Midsummer's power in this hour
Captured in this herb of the sun
Light is flowing, light is growing
Strength for many and for one

See the sun's light infusing the herb. Next, hold the quartz crystal up to the sun and say these or similar words:

Crystal beauty, crystal fine
Sun's light be upon me and mine

When you feel the crystal to be infused with the light of the midsummer sun, put it next to the sprig or place it in the pouch. Later, you will hang the sprig or pouch of St. John's wort and the crystal in the heart of the home, to allow its energies to provide you, your hearth, and home with a strength of spirit and protection until next midsummer. Leave an offering in exchange for these wonderful gifts.

Take a few moments and simply meditate, feeling the power of midsummer flowing all around you. Close down your ritual space and carry the memory of the sun within your soul. If you can, later in the day stand outside at midday and also watch the sunset, honouring the different times of the day's passage. Feel the differing qualities of light during the day infusing you, and you can perform the three cauldrons meditation at all three times. Say a farewell to the setting sun of midsummer in the evening and acknowledge that now the tide has turned and the nights will begin to grow longer as the days grow shorter.

Three Cauldrons Meditation

Now that you have performed the initial Three Cauldrons visualisation, lighting the fire within and coming to a sense of the power centres in your body together with the magic and power of midsummer, you can revisit this meditation anytime you wish in your personal work. The lore of the three cauldrons comes from a poem entitled "The Cauldrons of Poesy" penned in the seventh century by an Irish *fili* (sacred poet). These three cauldrons are traditionally known as the Cauldron of Warming (or Incubation), the Cauldron of Motion, and the Cauldron of Wisdom.[37] They can be compared to the chakras in that they are energy centres held within the body.

The Cauldron of Wisdom is held within the head and is said to be on its lip when we are born. With experience and wisdom, training, dedication, and practice, this cauldron can be turned right-side up. It brings the gifts of poetry and art, awen and inspiration. The Cauldron of Motion is held

---

37. Liam Breatnach, "The Cauldron of Poesy," Ériu, Vol. 32, (Royal Irish Academy, 1981), 45–93.

within the chest, said to be lying on its side at birth. It holds our emotions and the way we are able to express ourselves, which again can be trained to turn fully upright. The Cauldron of Warming is within the belly and is found upright at birth in every person. This holds the essence of our health and again can be tipped through imbalances such as illness or near-death experiences. Through practice, we can find out how the cauldrons are held within our bodies and help to turn them to a position where they are able to hold all the gifts necessary for our health, emotional well-being, and the work that we do on the path of the Hedge Druid. Joy and sorrow are said to be the key elements that turn the cauldrons and so we must come to terms with the wide spectrum that lies between these two in order to understand how the cauldrons within our bodies are held and how we can work with them to our benefit. We are not banishing sorrow from our lives, but understanding it in order to appreciate joy.

In your ritual space, take some time to ground and centre. Feel the three cauldrons within your body and remember their associations. Feel how they sit within your body. I like to work from the belly to the chest and end with the head. You might prefer to work from the top down. See how each cauldron is sitting within your body and whether it is tipped or on its side, upside-down or in the correct upright position. If you find one in an incorrect position, examine your life, both recent and in the past, to see what may have made it turn into its current position. Then, with the strength of the Summer Solstice ritual flowing through you, remember also the joy of the rising sun, the sounds of the birds, the feel of a summer's day. Allow that joy to turn the cauldron upright and fill it once again with the light of the rising sun. Acknowledge the sorrow and balance it with joy. We are not seeking to banish sorrow, but to remember the balance in all things.

Lughnasadh Ritual

This ritual celebrates the gifts of the earth, honouring the Earth Mother or *Tailtiu*, as well as honouring *Crom Dubh*, the Pagan god who brought wheat to Ireland. It is a nice idea to go to a wheat field, if you can, both before and just after the harvest, to sit with the land, to feel the energy both before and afterward, and to hear the songs of the wheat and the land and how they differ in time. For the ritual itself, try to go to a high place in the landscape, a hilltop or wide-open space. If this is impossible, hold this ritual by an open window and have photos of wheat fields on your altar in your ritual space.

For this ritual, you will need:

• A loaf of bread

• A handful or sheaf of ripened wheat stalks (you can grow your own easily in a small pot over the summer)

• A flower garland

You can make a flower garland out of any flowers that you wish. Daisy chains are perfectly acceptable and easy to make. Instructions for making a daisy chain are at the end of this ritual.

Go to a high place and take a moment to settle, to commune with the spirits of place, to become part of the landscape and acknowledge the time and season. When you are ready, designate your sacred space if you so wish and then stand holding the flower garland in your hands. You will now honour the time of Lughnasadh and offer the flowers to the earth. Say these or similar words:

> Blessed Lady of the Earth
> Great Mother who gave all for her children
> I honour you, as your son honoured you
> As your daughters continue to honour you
> As all your children honour you.

Place or bury the garland of flowers upon the hilltop. Then, pick up the sheaf of wheat and say:

> Crom Dubh,
> The dark, bent one
> You who brought wheat to Ireland
> Who taught us how to work with the Earth Mother

Whose name has long been forgotten
And whose name now returns and is remembered
I honour you
As summer's sun wanes
And the first breath of harvest and autumn sighs in the wind

Place or bury the sheaf of wheat on the hilltop. Then, pick up the loaf of bread and say these or similar words:

From the gifts of the earth, we honour life
All that nourishes, all that sustains
The corn god is cut down with the sickle and the knife
As the summer's light dwindles, as summer's light wanes
Gifts of transformation, gifts from the earth
Bounty from the land, sea, and sky
We honour you for all your worth
Honouring the times and the tides

Break off a piece of the bread and offer it to the land. Break off another piece and eat it, acknowledging all that went into the production of this bread from the land that grew the wheat, the rain that caused it to grow, the sun that ripened it, the people who harvested it, and those who baked it (if you did not yourself). Feel all the powers of land, sea, and sky within the bread. Feel those powers both within you and without.

Meditate upon the cycles of life that provide nourishment to all. Then, when you are ready, close down your ritual space with gratitude for the gifts of the earth. Try to incorporate a sense of deep gratitude into all your workings and rituals during this harvest season.

How to Make a Daisy Chain

Collect enough daisies to create a circle the size that you would like. It doesn't have to be large; simply lay out the flowers and overlap the ends about an inch so that you have room to work with. Take up the first daisy and, an inch from the bottom of the stem, cut a half-inch slit into the stalk (you can use your thumbnail for this or a small, sharp knife). Pull the next flower through this slit and continue until you have finished the circle. Make a slit in the top of the very first flower that you used and connect the ends together by carefully pulling the last flower head through the stalk of the first.

Autumn Equinox

In this ritual, we will seek the wisdom from the five oldest animals, as the Celtic hero Arthur did on his quest to seek out Mabon, son of Modron. We will seek their guidance to help us keep our intention for the coming of the dark half of the year. We will clarify and vocalise this intention at Samhain, but for now you seek what you will need to support that intention. We will also honour the harvest and, if you can, celebrate afterward with a meal for friends and family, having your very own Harvest Home supper.

For this ritual, you will need:

• An apple
• A knife
• An offering

Find a liminal place if you would like to match up your Autumn Equinox ritual with your Spring Equinox ritual. You can also perform this ritual in your home or garden, celebrating the bounty of hearth and home. If you have an apple tree in your garden, this is an ideal place. You may use any tree or even decide to ride the Hedge for this work.

Spend some time attuning to the place and then designate your sacred space, should you so desire. Then take a seat, for we will be going on an inner journey to gain wisdom from five of the oldest animals: the Blackbird of Cilgwri, the Stag of Rhednyfre, the Owl of Cwm Cawlwyd, the Eagle of Gwernabwy, and finally the eldest of them all, the Salmon of Llyn Llyw. Ready yourself for this guided meditation. Read it through several times beforehand or record yourself reading it aloud so that you can follow your voice and the meditation in your working. You may wish to perform the crane stance for a few minutes beforehand, to help you access the realm of the Otherworld in your pathworking.

You find yourself in a wooded glade. It is dawn and the birds have just begun to sing. You set your intention: to gain wisdom from the five oldest animals, for them to inspire and carry you in your journey of intention as time begins its descent into the dark half of the year. As the nights become longer, we turn inward and seek out the inner wisdom of the soul, guided by the gods, the ancestors, the spirits of place, and the elements. So do we seek out wisdom from five of the oldest animals: the Blackbird of Cilgwri, the Stag of Rhednyfre, the Owl of Cwm Cawlwyd, the Eagle of Gwernabwy, and the eldest of them all, the Salmon of Llyn Llyw.

You find yourself standing on the edge of a forest glade, where you hear the song of a blackbird. You walk toward her and bow your head. She finishes her song and turns to look at you. "What is it that you seek?" she asks.

"Tell me if you know what wisdom I need in order to support my intention for my work in the coming dark half of the year."

The blackbird cocks her head to one side and then says, "You will need strength of body and of will; a sense of purpose. See that small nut right next to your foot? That was once an anvil, and every day I pecked at it, until it reduced in size to what you see before you. Years and years I persisted and so I prevailed. Now it is a natural part of this glade. Strength you will need."

You wait a moment to see if the blackbird has any further wisdom to impart to you. You may or may not receive further guidance. Accept what has been offered and thank the blackbird for her wisdom.

"There is another who can offer you more: the Stag of Rhednyfre. You will find him on the other side of the stream."

You bow your head to the blackbird and make your way across the glade to where a stream trickles beneath the forest canopy. You cross the stream and suddenly you see a stag before you, his antlers proud upon his head. You bow your head to him and say, "Tell me if you know what wisdom I need in order to support my intention for my work in the coming dark half of the year."

The stag stands silently, gazing deeply into your eyes. "You will need patience. See that stump just over there? That was once a small oak sapling, which grew to a mighty tree with a hundred branches. It has long since fallen, and from its many acorns this woodland has grown into what you see around you. All that remains from that first tree is this stump, and one day that too will be gone. But the oak tree did not rush in his growth and he did not hurry. Nor did his descendants. The forest grows at its own pace."

You wait a moment to see if the stag has any further wisdom to impart to you. You may or may not receive further guidance. Accept what has been offered and thank the stag for his wisdom.

The stag then says, "There is another who can offer further wisdom: the Owl of Cwm Cawlwyd. Seek her out in that ancient oak on the side of the valley."

You bow your head and make your way up a slope that opens out to a valley. A tall, ancient oak tree stands, looking out upon the valley. There are many gnarled branches in this tree and, looking up, you see a hole where an ancient owl is perched, hiding from the light of day. You bow your head to her and say, "Tell me if you know what wisdom I need in order to support my intention for my work in the coming dark half of the year."

"See this valley that lies out before me? This was once a wooded glen and then the race of humans came and cut it down for their enterprises. Then grew a second generation of woodland and then a third. Throughout all this time, I have watched and been a part of this. Just as the woodland keeps coming back, so too will you need persistence in your journey."

You wait a moment to see if the owl has any further wisdom to impart to you. You may or may not receive further guidance. Accept what has been offered and thank the owl for her wisdom.

Then the owl says, "There is another who can offer further wisdom: the Eagle of Gwernabwy. Seek him out on the cliff face over yonder."

You bow you head and make your way along the edge of the ridge, to where rocks gather and form a cliff. You see the eagle perched upon a rocky outcropping, the wind whipping around him. You bow your head to him and say, "Tell me if you know what wisdom I need in order to support my intention for my work in the coming dark half of the year."

"See this rock upon which I am perched? This was once a mighty mountain, and from its summit I could peck at the stars. But I have worn it down with my clenching talons to the rock face you see before you. All this time, I have never stopped looking or reaching for the stars. Just as my aspirations reach as high as the sky, so too do you need to reach for your goals and keep them focused in your mind."

You wait a moment, to see if the eagle has any further wisdom to impart to you. You may or may not receive further guidance. Accept what has been offered and thank the eagle for his wisdom.

Then the eagle says, "There is another who can offer you further wisdom: the eldest of us all, the Salmon of Llyn Llyw. Seek her out in the river that runs through the valley below."

You bow your head and make your way along the edge of the ridge to where the river flows deep in the heart of the valley. You see the salmon swimming in the clear depths and say, "Tell me if you know what wisdom I need in order to support my intention for my work in the coming dark half of the year."

"Come hither and sit upon my back and I will take you to a place of great peace and serenity. For that is what you will need in your quest, to carry yourself through the dark half of the year." You climb upon the salmon's back and she takes you to a place of quiet and peacefulness in the river. There is no sound but the soft running water, and a peace and calm settles upon you. You realise that the acceptance of things as they are brings about a great peace within.

You wait a moment to see if the salmon has any further wisdom to impart to you. You may or may not receive further guidance. Accept what has been offered and thank the salmon for her wisdom. She leaps high into the sky with you upon her back and when you land, you find yourself alone in the forest glade from where you started your journey. You turn to thank the spirits of place and then come back to yourself, seated within your ritual space, fully awake and aware.

It is a good idea to bring along a journal to record what wisdom you have received from the above journey. Then, when you are ready, take the apple and cut it halfway across the middle of the fruit, instead of from the stem to the base. You will see the star-shape within the apple, reminiscent of the human body standing with arms raised out to the sides. The five oldest animals are represented there. You also see yourself within the apple and then take a bite, knowing that the apple is also within you. Honour the harvest in whatever words you like and give thanks in deepest gratitude for the blessings that you have received. Take a moment to feel this truth and then give your offering. Your ritual is complete.

Samhain

In this ritual we set out our intention for the work that we will carry out during the dark half of the year. At this time when the veil between the worlds is thin, we can call upon the aid of our guides, especially those whom we met at Beltane and whom we have hopefully kept up contact with throughout the year. If you have not, you will need to re-establish the friendship if the other side is willing and make offerings as needed.

We have sought out what we will need in support of our intention at the Autumn Equinox and now we are vocalising that intention, to have it be witnessed by the spirits of place, the gods, the Fair Folk, and most especially the ancestors.

For this ritual, you will need:

• A pen or a pencil

• A piece of paper

• A fire or a candle

• An offering

• Something to burn the paper in

Before this ritual, throughout the month of October, think about what you would like to set in motion in your own life and in your work as a Hedge Druid. Narrow this down with focus until you have a short phrase or word that symbolises your intention. You will work with this intention throughout the dark months of winter, nurturing it and planning so that you can bring it out into the light at Imbolc and receive Brighid's blessing upon it using the previous Imbolc ritual (or any other god/goddess that you choose to work with in a ritual written in your own words).

You can work this ritual indoors or out. I prefer to work this outside, as at Samhain the hosts of the Fair Folk are abroad and many interesting things can happen! Animals might approach, strange breezes blow over you, sounds and shadows bustle in the hedgerows, strange clouds roil in the sky, and more (all of these I have witnessed first-hand on the night of Samhain). If you wish to be as cautious as possible, carry some St. John's wort upon your person to deflect the energy of any who would wish you harm. You can also perform this ritual in your designated sacred space, affirming that none can enter but those who are in tune with your intention. It is said that the Wild Hunt rides at this time of year, and so precautions are a good thing to consider. Finally, by being out of doors at a time like this, we are acknowledging the wild powers of nature and attuning ourselves to our own wild nature.

Designate your sacred space if you so wish. Spend more time and effort on honouring the ancestors, as this is the time when you can most easily reach out to them and vice versa. Perform the ancestor meditation in the ritual if you so wish. This is an excellent way to ground and connect to the powers of life that flow through you, harking back generation upon generation.

Then, spend a few moments settling yourself and reminding yourself of your intention for the work that you wish to carry out for the rest of the year. Think to the weeks just gone where you narrowed down the focus into a single word or short phrase. Now, call upon your guide from the Fair Folk to be with you, to aid you in your work and provide you with wisdom that you can carry back to your life, strengthening your work and your intention. When you feel that they have arrived (they might already have been with you from the very start of the ritual), bow your head and affirm friendship between you. Then ask them for their aid in providing you with a symbol to signify the entirety of the work that you wish do in the coming year. Repeat the word or phrase that you have come up with to symbolise your intention and listen for a response. You might close your eyes and then see a symbol in your mind's eye, or you might hear something that brings a symbol to mind. Your guide might give you something or hold something in their hands which symbolises your intention. When you have pictured the symbol and feel that it is right, draw the symbol on the piece of paper. Take your time and push your own energy into the symbol both as you draw and afterward, holding the drawing in your hand and setting it firmly with your intention. You can ask your guide to also lend their energy to the symbol, if you so wish. Repeat the word or phrase of your intention as often as you wish; nine times is a traditional number.

Next, take the paper to the fire and say the following or something similar:

Fire of transformation, fire of Samhain
Into your flames I begin again
I set my intention, clarify my desire
To be transformed by this sacred fire

By the powers of land, sea, and sky, by the friendship of the Fair Folk, by the strength of the ancestors, by the gifts from the gods, and by the blessing of the spirits of place, may it be so.

Place your paper into the fire and watch the flames transform it into ash. Know that your intention is being released, and visualise yourself fulfilling your intention as the flames consume all. Take a moment to rest and allow the magic to work. Honour your guide of the Fair Folk with these or similar words:

I honour you from the depths of my heart for your guidance and aid. May there always be friendship between us.

Place your offering with gratitude (but don't say thanks!) to the Fair Folk especially, as well as the ancestors on this sacred night. Honour the time when the veils between the worlds is thin and honour that there is more to reality than meets the eye. Allow yourself to feel the magic of Samhain, the ending of the old and the beginning of the new.

Close down your ritual and then if you wish, have a feast with friends and family. You can set out a plate for the ancestors and offer this up outside afterward. Light a candle in a window to guide the spirits who have passed on this year and acknowledge the cycles of life and death.

Winter Solstice

This ritual honours the sun's standstill on the horizon before the days begin to lengthen again and we see increasing daylight hours. You can perform this indoors, bringing greenery into the home and decorating your ritual space: perhaps have a fire laid with a yule log if possible. If you prefer to work outdoors, dress warmly! If working this ritual indoors, try to stay awake all night if possible. If working out of doors, this isn't necessary, as the effort you are making to be out of doors should suffice. We are going to stand strong in the darkness, holding our intention close to our hearts and finding courage to see the coming of the day and the rising of the sun. For this ritual, you will need:

- Two candles, if indoors
- A fire if out of doors and a candle or a second, unlit fire ready
- A bough of evergreen foliage
- An offering

In the darkness before dawn, designate your sacred space, should you so wish. Have a candle or a fire lit. Stand tall and hold aloft the evergreen bough, saying these or similar words:

The nights are long, the winds are cold
The year turns, the year grows old
Like the evergreen, we see life anew
In the darkest depths, despair eschew
We turn toward the growing light
We welcome it with hearts alight
We honour the darkness and its gift
Even as our hearts grow and lift
My intention I hold clear
My dreams and hopes I carry near
With the sun's rays rising on the new day
I have the strength and courage, fear to allay

Put down the bough and stand with arms outstretched overhead, feet apart and heart and soul open wide, saying:

In darkness, light
In despair, hope
In fear, courage to see the day

Douse the flame of the candle or the fire and sit for a while in utter darkness. Wait for the sunrise. When the sun begins to show itself on the horizon, light the new candle or the second fire, and in that action, see the turning Wheel of the Year flowing through you and the land. Perform the Three Cauldrons exercise that you began at the Summer Solstice. Feel the light of the sun within you. Give your offering to the spirits of place.

If you are performing this ritual indoors, try to remain awake and keep a vigil throughout the long night. Watch the rising sun. If you are performing this ritual outdoors, it may be impractical to remain out all night (and dangerous in the cold), so return indoors when you wish and then go back out and watch the rising of the sun. Repeat the last three lines of the ritual as the sun is rising and allow the words to fill your being with happiness and hope in the newness of the year and in the turning tide. Repeat at noon and again as the sun sets. Know that the darkness is necessary, that there is great learning and wisdom to be found there as well as in the light. Honour both light and dark within your soul and be sovereign in yourself whatever the season. Let your intention for your work seep into every part of your being. Keep the dream close to your heart, then live the dream.

The Wheel has turned once more and the closing of the year lies before her, the new year waiting just beyond the veil. The Hedge Druid thinks on all the work that she has done, the rituals that she has performed throughout the year, the intention of her work flowing through her. She reviews what worked and what did not and scrys into the flame of the fire for divination on the work of the coming year. The cycle continues: the flow of awen.

Chapter 18

Moon Rites

Just as we have seen with the seasonal rituals, having a set of rituals to honour the times of the moon and its phases puts us more in tune with the cycles of nature. Here we look at full and dark moon rituals in detail.

Full Moon Ritual

I use the full moon as the start of the moon month, as I believe that this was how the Celts would have reckoned the months. It is far easier to see when the moon is full than to wait all night to determine the dark moon (or new moon, as some in Western Paganism call it, though technically the new moon refers to the first crescent in the sky). Since the Celts reckoned their days from sunset to sunset, it makes sense to reckon the moon months from the time of the full moon, then follow its wane, through to full again.

We don't have much historical evidence of what our ancestors would have done, if anything, at the times of the full and dark moon—only a few charms and invocations found in the *Carmina Gadelica* along with references to the time when mistletoe was cut during the moon's cycle. Therefore what follows here are rituals that I have created to honour the full and dark moon respectively.

This ritual is best performed outside. If you can't be outside, then try to stand by a window so that the moon's light will shine upon you. This full moon ritual incorporates a version of "drawing down the moon," which is a term used in many strands of Modern Paganism when honouring the full moon. Have a large bowl filled with water nearby. Designate sacred space if so desired.

Take a few moments to become one with your surroundings. Allow the light of the moon to fall upon you, if possible. Let your thoughts, cares, and worries melt and be washed away by the cool light of the moon. When you are ready, hold your arms outward and upward toward the moon and say these or similar words:

Lady of the Silver Wheel
Whose turning in the sky illuminates the darkness
From light to dark and back to light again
I honour you for all that you are

Feel the light of the moon filling you with silver light. Feel its cool power: the power that causes the tides to flow, the power that flows through women's cycles, the power that oversees cycles of planting and harvesting. Let your mind fill with all the associations that you can think of when drawing down the moon into yourself. Then, when you are ready, chant these or similar words:

Bright moon of ____ (moon month name, e.g., "Wolf")
Blessed by your light
Bright moon so fair
Jewel of the night
Another cycle has come
Another cycle has passed
May all my endeavours be blessed
Endure and everlast

Pick up the bowl (I use a birdbath on my patio) or shift your position so that you can catch the full moon reflected in the water. Gaze upon the silver orb in the water and allow your mind to open to receive blessings and guidance from the Lady of the Silver Wheel. You might have a specific intention for your work this moon month, or you may want to receive guidance as to what you should be working on. Either way, allow the moon's light reflected in the water to show you—in your mind's eye or in physical reality—what it is that you need to achieve this cycle or to confirm your intention. Clarify your intention once confirmed and speak it aloud over the water, then blow gently across the water so that the moon's reflection ripples. Then stand tall, bow your head to the moon, and give thanks.

If you would like to perform further magic, to harness the power of the full moon, then feel free to do so. (Spellwork is covered in a later chapter.) Commune with the Fair Folk, should you or they so desire. They are usually quite active during the full moon.

Close down the ritual space and give an offering to the Fair Folk.

Dark Moon Ritual

This ritual takes place when the sky is void of the moon's light at night. We cannot see the moon because it is too close to the sun. So, this is a time of going within, a time of rest, and a time of meditation. It is a potent time, for just as at the full moon, at the dark moon the tides are at their highest and lowest of the month and the moon's effect on us is just as strong as when the moon is full.

You can perform this ritual indoors or out. Designate sacred space if so desired, and then sit down to meditate. Allow your body and mind to calm and relax, listening to the sounds of the night. Feel the darkness around you, holding you. Know that the darkness is not something to be feared, but that it is just another aspect of the cycle of the moon, the seasons, and tides. As a Hedge Druid, we learn to find our balance point in all of nature and so we work with the darkness as well as the light. This darkness provides us with rest and release and an opportunity to go deeply within.

The following is a guided meditation/pathworking that you can either read through several times or record yourself reading it so that you can follow it in practice. After a few times, you should become familiar with it and no longer need a reminder or recording.

It is a dark night. You find yourself upon a wide plain or isolated moorland. You see before you a ring of standing stones, outlined softly in the starlight. You walk toward the circle of stones and, before entering, you bow your head and offer a prayer. When ready, you enter the circle from a northern entrance and slowly walk just within the circle of stones clockwise, touching each stone in turn and connecting with its energy. When you have touched all the stones and feel their life force humming in tune with yours, you turn and walk to the centre of the circle.

In the centre lies a stone on its side and upon its surface is an indentation where a pool of rainwater sits, creating a small bowl. You bow your head to the stone and then lean over to gaze into the water. You see the stars reflected in the dark water and gaze upon their beauty. Eventually, the stars fade and another image may appear in the water. This may be an image or a symbol; it is of that which is holding you back from your work and your purpose. You acknowledge this symbol and then blow gently across the water. It ripples and then another image appears, one which will offer insight into how to overcome that which is holding you back. If the image is the same, there is nothing holding you back. You acknowledge this symbol and then blow gently across the water. It ripples and then you slowly see the stars reappear in the reflection.

Take a moment to consider what you have seen and how you can apply it to your work of this moon-tide. If you have veered off-track, allow these insights to help you find your way back until the next full moon. You might find that you are still on course and have had your intention and work confirmed if nothing is blocking you and your work. Sit within the circle of stones and feel their energy around you, grounding you, fixing your purpose deep within your soul. When you are ready, stand and, beginning in the north, walk the circle counterclockwise, touching each stone in turn and offering thanks. When you have reached the beginning, bow once more to the circle and then leave the circle of stones.

Slowly, the wide-open space dissolves around you and you find yourself back in your ritual space. Take a moment to settle and feel yourself fully back in your body, in this time and space. Thank the dark moon for its blessing and give an offering to the spirits of place.

The work is now up to you.

The Hedge Druid takes up her pen and journal and writes down all that she has seen in her dark moon meditation. She draws the symbols of the work that she is undertaking and records her thoughts and feelings and any other relevant information that came to her during her journeying. When she is finished writing, she softly closes the book and gazes at the candles upon the altar. She thanks the dark moon for the vision and gives her offering of rye bread and butter and a glass of wine. Afterward she takes some bread and wine for herself and thinks upon the work that lies ahead, contemplating various paths that lie before her.

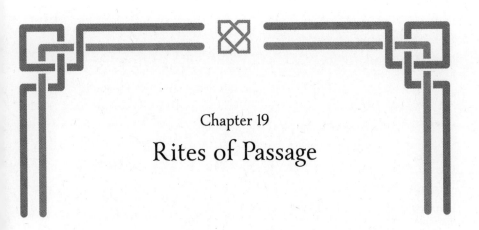

Chapter 19

Rites of Passage

Here are some rites and rituals that mark out events in our lives which we may wish to acknowledge. You can use these as a guide to create your own rituals, if you prefer.

Child Blessing

You can perform this ritual of blessing upon a child. It is not like a christening where you are indoctrinating them into a tradition; it is simply offering a blessing upon the child who is free to choose whatever path their life takes them. You can also perform this blessing upon yourself, perhaps at Imbolc or the Winter Solstice, as a form of ritual purification and blessing.

This ritual can be performed near a body of water or indoors if this isn't convenient/possible. Try to use natural water in this blessing, such as rainwater or spring water from a local source if possible. If performed outdoors near a lake or the sea, you can use that water. Fill a small bowl with the water for the ritual. Designate the sacred space if you so wish, and then recite the blessing chant below (which is an adaptation from the *Carmina Gadelica*) while touching a drop of water to the child's forehead:

A small wave for your form
A small wave for your voice
A small wave for your speech
A small wave for your luck

A small wave for your integrity
A small wave for your health
A small wave for your desire
A small wave for your courage
A small wave for your grace
Nine waves of blessing be upon thee.

You can also recite the following afterward, again from the *Carmina Gadelica*, if you wish. If you are performing this ritual in a group setting, it's nice to have everyone recite this together for the child; or if you are performing this for yourself, you can hold up representations of water, air, earth, and fire as you recite the following:

Deep peace of the running wave to you
Deep peace of the flowing air to you
Deep peace of the quiet earth to you
Deep peace of the shining stars to you

Celebrate the joys of life with friends and family. Honour your loved ones deeply.

Rite of Adolescence (Invocation of Personal Power)

You can use the following as a guide to create your own rite of adolescence for your child or for a friend's child, should they wish. This marks the transition stage from childhood to adolescence, that liminal time when they are no longer children and not yet adult. For girls, it could be after their first menses or for boys when their voice changes. You will have to discuss this with the adolescent as to when they feel it is right for them, without imposing your own will upon the situation.

This rite draws upon an adaptation from the *Carmina Gadelica*, where I have substituted and adapted the "Invocation for Justice" to an "Invocation of Personal Power." This honours the transition of power from external sources to the adolescent's own sense of self. This also acknowledges their changing bodies as well as minds and helps them to feel comfortable in their own skin during this phase of their lives.

Designate sacred space if you wish. This ritual is to be performed at dawn and just before the sun rises. Have the adolescent bathe their faces with dew, if possible, or with water from a silver, crystal, or glass bowl that has lain out all night. Just before they bathe their faces, they say:

I will wash my face
In the nine rays of the sun,
As the Goddess nourishes her son
In the rich fermented milk.

They will then say the following, as the sun rises:

Love be in my countenance,
Benevolence in my mind,
Dew of honey in my tongue,
My breath as the incense.

Power may be attempted over me
Power lies within
I am the white swan,
Queen/king/sovereign above them.

I will travel in the name of ___ (optional deity)
In likeness of deer, in likeness of horse,
In likeness of serpent, in likeness of queen/king/sovereign:
Strong will it be with me, strong in my own power and destiny.

If your child does not wish to name a god or goddess for this invocation, then drop "in the name of" and say no name, simply beginning with "In likeness of deer."

Give a gift to the adolescent, something that symbolises their burgeoning strength and power over their lives. Honour them for who they are, separate and whole in and of themselves. End the ritual with a picnic or indoor break-fast feast, with friends and family if desired.

Marriage/Handfasting Rite

This is a ritual that I have used for many years in my work as a Druid priest-ess. You can change or adapt it as you see fit to align with your own inten-tion. You may like to have a priest or priestess lead the rite for you if you are the one getting married, or you may wish to perform the rite between you and your partner yourself; the choice is entirely yours to make. You may also wish to include readings from members of the wedding party.

This ritual can be used either as a marriage ritual or as a handfasting ritual. Often here in the UK, there will be a legal ceremony where the paper-work is carried out and then another ceremony in which the marriage ritual will occur with friends and family as witness.. If done as a handfasting, this can be an act of commitment for a year and a day between the parties or for as long as their love shall last: the commitment being determined by the wording in the ritual itself.

For this ritual you will need:
- A horseshoe to hold the vows
- A stone to swear the oath upon
- Food and drink to share in ritual
- Rings for each partner
- Cord(s) (this will bind their hands together, so it may be a single cord or plaited cords of various colours and long enough to twine around both their hands several times)

To begin:
- Determine the bearer of rings and cord(s), place items on altar
- Guests form a circle
- Wedding/handfasting party process into the circle
- Designate sacred space, if so desired

Introduction:

We are here today to celebrate the union of ____ *and* ____ *on this* (number) *day of* (calendar month), *during the moon of* (enter moon month cycle) *and in the beauty of* (name the venue).

____ *and* ____ *will exchange vows with each other before their families and friends, this place, the* (wind, sky, rain, depending on weather), *and the ancestors all standing witness.*

Oaths will be proclaimed and rings exchanged to formalise proceedings.

Blessings will then be bestowed and later toasts and libations will be made.

The coming together of two souls is a very special occasion where soul touches soul, spirit touches spirit. In that touch, there is divine inspiration, where the spark of energy moves from a single source to a shared source, where we find our place in the web of life, together, with all of existence. Committing to walk this path with another is to be celebrated, done with respect and honour. May we know what it is that we witness this day and may we cherish it in our hearts throughout our lives.

Declaration of Intention:

____, *you stand here today to marry* ____; *you will exchange oaths. Your words will be witnessed by those present here. Do you stand here as a free person without influence of coercion or duress?*

They say "I do." Repeat for the other partner.

Exchange of Vows over Horseshoe

The wedding ceremony is linked in many ways with the horseshoe. The use of the term "groom" is directly correlated to the horse. The horseshoe itself is a well-known symbol of luck, the shape of the crescent holding in fortune and bearing the oath for the new couple. The couple will now take hold of either side of the horseshoe, to swear their vows upon it, which will be held within the crescent for as long as their love shall last.

The couple takes turns saying their own vows.

Swearing of the Oath:

You will now swear to uphold your vows by placing your oath upon this stone, to act as a foundation for your future together, to remind you of your words and actions, your intention and your honour.

The couple takes turns saying: "Upon this stone, I pledge my oath to uphold my vows."

Exchange of Rings:

Rings represent eternity, of the continual cycle and flow that is life and love. These rings are a symbol of that love that these two share, blessed by their feelings for each other and the sacredness of this day. Accept these rings from each other as a token of your love and honour, wear them with pride and always be mindful of this day.

The couple exchanges rings.

Binding the Hands Together:

This cord symbolises the union between you. Remember this bond and your vows and honour them and each other, for this lifetime.

Their hands are bound together. Hands will stay bound together until the end of the ritual, when they then can be taken off. If the hands are loosely bound together, then the cords can be taken off without undoing the knot and thus it is kept "sealed." If the knot needs to be undone in order to take it off, then redo the knot yourself or in the presence of the couple and ensure that your action is filled with the same intention as expressed in the ritual.

Simple Feast:

____ and ____, you have been graced with the gifts of the earth and sky. May you share these gifts with each other.

The couple breaks off a piece of bread and feeds it to each other.

You have also been blessed with the gifts of wind and rain, may you share these gifts with each other.

The couple brings a chalice of water/wine to each other's lips.

As you have been blessed by Earth and Sky, Wind and Rain, so too must you remember to give back, with joy and honour, at this very special time.

The couple places bread and water/wine by the altar.

Blessing of the Four Quarters of the Earth:

Priest/ess takes couple to the four quarters of the circle to be blessed by each quarter, beginning in the north and moving clockwise.

May your love stand the cold harsh time of winter. May the earth treat you well.

May your love last the sunrises of further years. May the sky watch over you.

May your love last the fires of change. May the sun's healing light be on you.

May your love flow as the waters deep. May you be as strong as the rivers flow.

May the spirit of the Earth Mother and Sky Father and the realms of land, sea, and sky bless your union with joy and abundance, with love and laughter, with strength and perseverance, and with honour and integrity.

Declaration of Marriage:

You have both taken vows before your families and friends with this place, the (wind, rain, sky…) and the ancestors standing witness. You have exchanged rings and received blessings; therefore, it is with the greatest of pleasure I declare that you are married.

The couple seals the ceremony with a kiss.

Close down the ritual.

Jumping the Broom:

Sometimes the couple like to jump the broom, which is an old folk custom to bring luck and fertility into the union. This is a fun way to end the ritual, with the wedding party forming two lines as an "aisle" and the couple running down the aisle to jump the broom at the end. It also makes a great photo!

Handy little note: If doing this ceremony on a hot summer's day, it is good to have the rings sitting in a glass or bowl of water, so that when the time comes, they can slip easily on the finger, which can swell up with the heat.

Another little note: if the relationship doesn't work out, try to have a Releasing Ceremony, where the couple can walk away from each other with honour. Only you will know what this will entail. If this isn't possible to do in ritual, you can do something on your own to find closure and release at least for yourself.

Funeral Rite

This can be a rite that you perform for another loved one or which you can keep and have at hand in the event of your own death. You can keep a copy with your will and other papers to be enacted upon your death, such as what type of burial you wish, what kind of casket (there are many wonderful eco-friendly options nowadays), what music you wish to be played, and so on. It is nice to write a poem from yourself, to be read to those that have been left behind. A heartfelt poem in the first funeral I ever performed was a poem from the deceased, read aloud by her daughter and entitled "My Wish For You." I think this is a wonderful sentiment to ease the grief of the mourners and is utterly heart-warming to hear it in your own words, so I have included this in the following funeral rite. Simply write what you wish those who are left behind to hear from you, with love and blessings.

To Begin:

• Designate sacred space, if desired or appropriate.

• Process into a circle.

Declaration of Intention:

Friends, we are gathered here today to honour the passing of ___, dear spirit to those gathered here, who passed away on (date). Let us gather together in a circle and hold hands, to connect our energies together in remembrance of her/him in peace and with love.

We honour the life that has passed and that lives on in the Otherworld. Though the spirit has passed over the Western Seas, we hold the memory in our hearts. We know that the deceased are still with us—in the air that we breathe, in the smiles and laughter of friends and family, in the earth beneath our feet. For this world and the Otherworld overlap, and we honour all our loved ones who have gone before and acknowledge the legacy that they and we will, in time, leave for future generations. In this, there is no end, only continuation in the cycle of life, death, and rebirth.

Allow readings and poetry, if any.

Remembrance:

If anyone wishes to share a remembrance of ____, in honour of her/his spirit, please step forward to say a few words.

Minute of Silence:

We will now have a moment of silence to send ____ our thoughts, our prayers, and our love.

Committal:

____ has departed from this incarnation but lives on in a flame as bright as any star in the universe. She/he has left to dwell in the Blessed Realms in the west where she/he will be granted rest and refreshment before being born again.

Mother Goddess, comforter of the dying, receive ____ into your arms and give her/him your blessed peace and comfort. Lord of the Underworld, may she/he be reunited with the memories of those who have gone before. For we know that when refreshed and rested amongst the memory of our dear ones, we will be reborn again through the grace of the Great Mother Earth who never dies.

Blessed be and fare thee well.

To Conclude:

- Lower the coffin, lay flowers
- Recite poem from the deceased
- Close down ritual

These are just a few examples of rituals and rites of passage that you can incorporate into your own tradition as a Hedge Druid. Read, research, and try out new things, discard those that don't feel right, and work intuitively, academically, and experientially. Then your tradition will be fully grounded and you can express the awen in a multitude of ways that work for you. Blessings on this exciting journey!

The child is sleeping in his mother's arms. The Hedge Druid takes the silver bowl filled with spring water and makes the symbol of the awen upon the child's forehead. He wakes up, his eyes sleepy, and looks into the eyes of his mother. She smiles down at him and speaks his name aloud for all to hear. The child gazes upon his mother's features for a moment longer, yawns, and then closes his eyes once more. All around, the love of family and friends flows through the ritual space and the Hedge Druid smiles at her nephew, repeating his name alongside the rest of his family.

Chapter 20

Daily Practice

For me personally, I feel that a daily practice is essential to maintaining the connection between the self and the natural world. Though we are never truly separated, our marvellous human brains can create a feeling of disconnection, which can be alleviated through a daily practice.

A daily practice could consist of taking time to meditate and/or contemplate aspects of the self, of the world, of the gods, ancestors, spirits of place, and other pieces of the great puzzle. If one follows a specific deity, one should try to connect to that deity, whether in communion as a mystic or in prayer as a devotee (or both). Remembering your roots is a very grounding experience and so honouring the ancestors every day can have a great impact on your life, whether you are honouring your ancestors of blood, place, or spirit. You might also give an offering as part of a daily practice, if you so desire. You might simply think of what there is to be grateful for and a mini-ritual of gratitude can become a part of your daily practice. Asking for blessings, both for yourself and your loved ones, for those whose voices are not heard, for those who are suffering; prayers of peace can all be a part of daily practice.

Paganism and Druidry have no liturgy in the broad sense, but we can create our own set of rituals and daily practices to help us remember that the spiritual and the mundane are one. Everything is both very normal and sacred at the same time. When we take time to pause and reflect on this concept and others within our tradition, we are raising our awareness of life and the world around us. We begin to act from a place of intention instead of a place of reaction. With daily contemplation and meditation, we also become more grounded and less easily caught up in our shadow selves: the unconscious and emotional responses to situations that usually have no bearing on the present situation. We can become aware of our soul wounds and celebrate our achievements. We can become more aware of how we live in the world and work toward the benefit of the whole, in a holistic worldview. Why else be Pagan, much less Druid, if we are not there to support the whole? We are there for the earth, for the gods, for the ancestors. We must be present and centred within ourselves in order to be of greatest benefit to the All. Druidry is all about service.

Therefore do consider a daily practice, if you haven't got one already. Think about ways in which you can take a few minutes or a few hours each day to connect with the world around you, to step outside of your head and be with the world as it is, awake and aware. Think about connection and you may find that your practice deepens with time and your inner strength grows with each and every day.

Day-to-Day Routine

Working alone in our own tradition has a great many advantages: we can study, work, meditate, pray, and perform ritual whenever we feel like it, whenever it strikes our fancy. In a group tradition, in order to get everyone together at the same time and on the same page, there may be a set time and place for ritual, as well as perhaps a study, prayer, and meditative structure for everyone to follow. In our practices as Hedge Druids, it is up to us to decide what suits our purpose and how best we can work in whichever capacity.

I prefer to have structure in my life. The purpose of this chapter is to demonstrate how we can incorporate our Druid practice into our daily lives and, if we prefer to have a structure, how to create that effectively. My own daily practice follows a repeating pattern each and every day. Some of the prayers I say every day, repeating the same words. This does not mean that they lose their significance over time, but they allow me to find new meaning to the words spoken each and every day and also give me a sense of continuity in my own tradition. What can be extremely beneficial is to create your own book filled with prayers, meditations, and contemplations for each and every day. You can organise this by the season and have four different themes for each, honouring the times and tides of life. Your daily prayers will revolve around these themes, and so perhaps for winter your prayers can include protection and inspiration during the long, dark months and/or prayers for others who are struggling during the season. You can come up with your own liturgy, should you so wish, though some would say that having liturgy in Druidry is anathema. I would disagree, finding it extremely beneficial to maintaining a daily practice; the point is that I create my own liturgy and do not impose it upon others. It is a structure for me and me alone. Here are some ideas on how to do something similar:

1. Start the day with an opening prayer as soon as you wake up. Every morning, I take a moment to be fully aware of myself in my body as the very first thing that I do. I then go outdoors or by an open window to take stock of the day and commune with nature. Watch the sun rise every morning, if you can, or just look out the window and notice what is different and what is the same as the day before.

2. Have an altar or shrine space where you can begin your day or to make offerings should you so wish. Write up some prayers that can be recited and are appropriate to the seasons. You can also bless your altar space and yourself each and every morning with water or incense. You might say something like "Lady Brighid, be with me this winter's day. Cloak me in your green mantle and let me be protected from harm. May the cauldron of inspiration warm my spirit, may my soul be kindled by your flame. May your light shine upon and bless others this day and may they have the warmth and nourishment that they need." Dip your finger into a bowl of water and say, "Drops of awen be upon my lips, upon my work. May the Lady Brighid guide me this day and every day."

3. Recite a prayer before each meal. You could say "I give my thanks for this food I am about to eat. May it lend health, strength, and nourishment to me. I give my thanks to the spirits of land, sea, and sky for their bounty."

4. Leaving the home, you could say a prayer for protection. "Power of sun and moon be with me, strength of fire and storm protect me, swiftness of wind guide me, flowing of sea nourish me, solidity of earth hold me, this day and every day."

5. Go about your daily activities with a Druid's perspective. Remember that you are part of the whole, in everything that you do. Recite the prayer before meals just before you have lunch; you can do this silently in your mind if necessary.

6. Upon returning home, say a prayer upon entering, such as "Thanks be to the powers of sun and moon, of fire and storm, of land, sea, and sky for being with me this day as I return to the sanctity and sanctuary of home." You could keep a small bowl of water by the door to dip your finger in and touch your forehead as you enter, blessing you upon entrance. This is also a great way to leave the worries of the world at the door and enter into your own personal space in a good frame of mind.

7. Meditate as often as you can. Find out whether you are suited for morning, midday, or evening meditations and try to incorporate that into your schedule as much as possible. If that means foregoing television for half an hour, please do it. You can usually watch your programmes on replay or record your favourite shows.

8. Close your day with an evening prayer, perhaps while watching the sun set. As you began your day with prayer, you can you finish it in the same attitude. You might even like to incorporate singing into your evening prayer. Perhaps you could sing the "Song of Amergin," to remind yourself of your connection to nature:

I am the wind on the sea;

I am the wave of the sea;

I am the bull of seven battles;
I am the eagle on the rock;
I am a flash from the sun;
I am the most beautiful of plants;
I am a strong wild boar;
I am a salmon in the water;
I am a lake in the plain;
I am the word of knowledge;
I am the head of the spear in battle;
I am the god that puts fire in the head;
Who spreads light in the gathering on the hills?
Who can tell the ages of the moon?
Who can tell the place where the sun rests? [38]

9. Just before you go to sleep, as you lie down in bed, you can also say a prayer, perhaps something like "Lady Brighid, I rest my soul in your blessing this night. Guard me and mine, this night and every night, by your beauty and grace, so may it be."

Grounding and Centring

Grounding and centring can be an essential part of daily practice. It can help us get through difficult times such as grief and help us to find a balance point where we are able to fully feel our emotions yet act in the most appropriate manner relevant to the situation. We are acting from a place where we are sovereign in ourselves, where what we say and do is from a place of intention rather than reaction.

So how do we ground and centre? There are many different ways of performing these actions, but here I will offer my own personal way of doing it. You can do it before or after your daily meditation and it complements that practice immeasurably. Daily meditation helps us to maintain the practice

---

38. Lady Gregory, *Gods and Fighting Men*, Sacred Texts, accessed February 15, 2018, http://www.sacred-texts.com/neu/celt/gafm/gafm09.htm.

of grounding and centring throughout the day and not just when we are performing the work itself.

I begin by taking three to nine deep breaths, fully feeling the air entering my lungs and expanding my body and then releasing the breath, ever so slightly pulling in the lower abdomen to expel all the air. After I have taken these breaths, I allow my breathing to return to its natural state, which can change depending on how I am feeling, my physical and mental health. Here, I am not trying to control my breath, but just to be aware of it. Is it high in my chest with short breaths? Is it deep and relaxed? Is it somewhere in between? I spend a few moments with just my natural breath and then I begin grounding.

Grounding is taking excess energy and releasing it from the body and mind. There are many ways of releasing this energy, and when we do release it, we're not necessarily releasing "bad energy"—just excess energy that is not helping us in any shape or form, whether good or bad. The idea is to return to a balance point, and so releasing excess energy helps us to achieve that state. Keeping in excess energy—perhaps energy that we've picked up from others during the day or from situations—can leave us completely stressed out, and so releasing this ensures that we keep an even keel. I visualise the energy being released with my natural breath, out of my body and mind. If I wish, I can return that energy to the earth, to the air, to the water, whatever element I wish to release into. I avoid releasing energy into a fire or flame for this exercise, because I use fire for more transformative magic and spellcraft. So, for me it's usually into the earth or air.

Once the energy has been released, I sink my roots deep into the earth in order to ground myself. This was an exercise taught to me by my teacher, Bobcat (Emma Restall Orr). I envision a tap root extending from the base of my spine, going down into the earth with every out breath. I spread my roots into the soil and then take a few moments to breathe, in and out, through my roots in the soil, allowing the cool, slow, natural energy of earth to fill and ground my being. When I am done, I breathe my roots back into my body on the inhale and then finish the grounding practice.

This is then followed by centring. Centring is where we return to our true self, our point of balance. It's the reset button of our soul. To do this, I envision the World Tree within my body, running through my centre. I feel my roots deep in the Lowerworld, feel my body firmly in the Middleworld, and my aspirations and goals reaching toward the Upperworld. A beam of white light connects all aspects of the World Tree within me and I breathe this light up and down my body, allowing it to fill every aspect of my being. When I feel fully returned to centre, I allow the image of the World Tree to blend with my soul, to be carried within me, inspiring and centring me wherever I am and in whatever I'm doing.

Another way that I centre is using prayer beads. I have a beautiful mala created by a friend that I use to recite a prayer over and over again, allowing the vibration of my voice in the chant to wash through me, body and soul. After I have gone through all the beads (108 of them) in the stillness and si-lence, I can feel my body and mind clean and clear, having reset myself and now being completely centred.

And this is pretty much all there is to my own practice of grounding and centring. It helps me maintain a balanced perspective during the good times and the bad times and also allows me to take some time for self-care and compassion. Try it in your daily practice, if you wish.

Having a daily practice such as this can deepen your awareness of the sacred, of the blessings and gifts in your life, and attune you to the natural world. I think it is a very important part of being on a Pagan path and espe-cially on a Druid path, to remember the connectedness that we have with all beings, all the time—that we are part of a whole and that we cannot be separate from that in any capacity. This can also provide us with comfort and sustain us during hardships. Having a daily practice can become a haven of peace and quiet in a tumultuous life or during a difficult period such as mourning and grief. It can provide a structure for our lives where before it may have lost meaning or integrity. That being said, some prefer a much looser structure than the one outlined above, and whatever works for the individual, as long as it is done with honour and integrity in a holistic sense, will be beneficial.

It has been a dreadful month. The Hedge Druid has known deep sorrow, trials, and tribulations throughout the long winter. But still she goes to her altar every day and lights her candle to Brighid, saying her devotional prayers. In this, she finds solace. In the words spoken daily, she finds her strength. The little altar is like her true north—it guides her through the darkest nights, the light of her goddess burning brightly in her soul.

Part Three
STUDY

Now we come to the work that will require focus and commitment to self-learning. In this section, we introduce elements of Druid studies that can be undertaken by anyone and expanded upon in their own time for those who wish to specialise in a certain subject. We will look at herbcraft, divination, the Druid alphabet known as ogham, and spellcraft.

Chapter 21

Herblore

Working as a Hedge Druid, it is essential that you know something about the plants that are growing in your own ecosystem. Even in the heart of a city you can find dandelions, chickweed, plantain, nettle, and other useful herbs. Learning to work with herbs helps you to be more self-reliant and connects you with the seasons, as different herbs appear at different times of the year. Some herbs you can grow yourself in pots indoors or on balconies or patios. Others are best collected in the wild in the early morning.

Collecting herbs was a sacred act, which we can see in several charms found in the folklore compendium of Volume Two of the *Carmina Gadelica*. There are charms to be said when collecting figwort, fairy wort, and St. John's wort. An example of such a magical charm is "The Yarrow":

I will pluck the yarrow fair,
That more benign shall be my face,
That more warm shall be my lips,
That more chaste shall be my speech,
Be my speech the beams of the sun,
Be my lips the sap of the strawberry.

May I be an isle in the sea,
May I be a hill on the shore,

May I be a star in waning of the moon,
May I be a staff to the weak,
Wound can I every man,
Wound can no man me.[39]

What I would suggest is reading through the various charms found in this volume and then creating your own in relation to the herbs that you would use for magical or medicinal uses. Say this charm over the plant before you harvest it. Ensure that you do not take more than half of the plant, otherwise it will have difficulty in recovering so that it may flourish for you and others for years to come. Also, it is wise to leave an offering—perhaps water or a simple prayer of gratitude for the bounty that you collect.

Before beginning work with any herb, consult a good herbal book or a recognised herbal practitioner. It is essential that you know exactly what it is that you are working with. Some herbs can be very bad for you when taken with certain medications or if pregnant. Ensure that all precautions are taken, and it is strongly recommended that you consult with your physician before taking anything internally. There are a number of good herbals to be found in the bibliography of this book.

Below I have listed herbs that are useful for both medicinal and magical purposes, according to the seasons. This is by no means an exhaustive account, as there are thousands of herbs used in all areas of magic and healing and I've not the space to cover them all in this work. These are those that I am familiar with and that are easily obtainable either from the land or from ethical and organic herb supply shops. If herblore is very appealing to you, then please do seek out a qualified herbal practitioner to learn more.

Spring Herbs

Chickweed—Stellaria media

Parts used: aerial parts (all above ground parts)

---

39. *Carmina Gadelica*, "The Yarrow," Sacred Texts, accessed January 29, 2018, http://www.sacred-texts.com/neu/celt/cg2/cg2046.htm.

Chickweed is excellent eaten fresh in salads or made into a pesto. It is very nourishing and also tasty. It also works as a skin soother: you can make a bath oil with it by infusing the fresh herb in olive oil for three days or blending the fresh herb with vinegar to apply it to rashes, stings, and itchy insect bites. It is best used fresh, but you can buy the dried herb in most herbal shops.

Magical uses: take internally in the spring to cleanse and purify the spirit, to refresh the soul after a long winter. You can make a lustral water (an infusion like you would for tea) to pour into your bath and cleanse your body or to sprinkle around the house to bless and purify.

Dandelion—Taraxacum officinale

Parts used: root and leaf

Dandelion is excellent to eat in the spring, with the leaves and flower heads being edible and very nutritious. Use like a spinach in salads. To treat warts, squeeze the white juice from the stem onto the wart once a day and be sure not to wipe off the old juice (it may darken on the skin— don't worry, it's working!). Do this for three to seven days and the wart should disappear. The root can also be chopped and dried and used as a delicious coffee substitute. Dandelion is an excellent tonic for the kidneys and can be drunk as a tea to flush out toxins from the body.

Magical uses: to bring courage and action (dandelion is from the French, *dents de lion*, literally meaning lion's teeth), to remember the light of the sun, and to help the body maintain the inner cauldrons upright.

Elder—Sambuccus nigra

Parts used: flowers

Elder flowers can be drunk as a tea or made into a cordial to help boost the immune system, as well as just being delicious. Blend with nettle as a tea to clear up nasal congestion.

Magical uses: elder is a sacred tree to the Faeries; if you would like to commune with the Fair Folk, you might scatter elder flowers around your ritual area. Never, ever burn elder wood.

Nettle—*Urtica dioica*

Parts used: leaf and root

★Do not take nettle root during pregnancy.

Nettle makes an excellent springtime tea, as well as a delicious and nutritious soup full of vitamins and minerals. You can blend it with spinach to make it go further if you don't have a huge harvest. Nettle is a natural antihistamine and so it's a good tea to drink during hayfever season or when you have a cold. Do not harvest the leaves after it has flowered, as it can then irritate the stomach lining.

Magical uses: use this plant to strengthen your resolve by drinking it as a tea. Can also be used in protection rituals, incorporating its sting when not approached correctly.

Summer/Late Summer Herbs

Heather—*Calluna vulgaris or Erica cinerea (bell heather)*

Parts used: flowers

Heather is an antiseptic, a diuretic, and a disinfector for the urinary tract. It increases urinary production, is expectorant, antitussive (cough suppressant), antiarthritic, antirheumatic, and sedative. Also used to treat kidney and bladder stones, cystitis, and inflammatory bladder conditions. Main uses are as a cleansing and detoxifying remedy, as well as being very helpful in treating rheumatism, arthritis, gout, and metabolic conditions. Hot poultice of it is used for chilblains (itching/swelling on hands or feet). Heather can be used as a mild tasting tea to treat coughs and colds. It's a great detox plant, which can also help boost the immune system to relieve the symptoms of arthritis and rheumatism.

Magical uses: burn as an incense to cleanse and purify. Drink internally in ritual as a tea to strengthen your own personal power.

Calendula—*Calendula officinalis*

Parts used: flowers

Calendula is anti-inflammatory and antispasmodic (soothes muscle spasms) and used for wound healing. Homeopathic uses are to apply to open wounds and stopping bleeding after dental work. Used for excessive pain and chills in damp weather. Best to gather in daylight in the summer when in full bloom and best used fresh, although it can be dried (it loses some of its external healing properties when dried). Also recommended for heart ailments. The juice mixed with vinegar heals the skin, our largest organ, so you can add it to a bath and have a nice long soak to ease skin complaints or rub on affected areas directly. Drunk as a tea, it comforts the heart and spirit. The petals can be crushed and used as a poultice for bruises, bites, and stings.

Magical uses: heals old wounds of the heart and soul.

St. John's Wort—*Hypercium perforatum*

Parts used: flowers and leaves

St. John's Wort is used for strengthening the nervous system or as a nerve tonic. It has an affinity with the solar plexus and therefore is useful for treating nervous disorder and for mental diseases of the central nervous system such as depression and insomnia. It is also good for nerve pain, neuralgia, back pain, sciatica; good for after surgery, lacerations. St. John's wort can be made into a tea to help strengthen the nervous system and also help alleviate seasonal affective disorder (SAD). *Be warned though:* St. John's wort can help ease the spirit when the sun is at its weakest during the winter, but this herb will also increase your sensitivity to sunlight and increase your chances of getting a sunburn, so be careful! Paradoxically, the herb infused in an oil such as olive or almond oil helps to treat sunburn like no other treatment I have ever tried. It's incredible!

Magical uses: warding off negative energy, protection from malevolent Faeries.

Hawthorn—Crataegus oxycanthus

Parts used: leaf, blossom, and berries

⋆Not to be used with other beta-blockers or heart drugs/herbs. Please consult a qualified herbalist if on heart/blood pressure medication of any kind.

Hawthorn flowers and leaves can be taken and drunk as a tea to help boost the circulatory system. The young leaves in the early summer can be eaten directly and are extremely nourishing, known in folklore as "bread and butter."

Magical uses: eases a broken heart; is also a Faery tree so a sprig worn on the person in outdoor ritual can open up lines of communication with the Fair Folk. Do not bring the blossom into the home, for bad luck will ensue.

Autumn Herbs

Elder—Sambuccus nigra

Parts used: berries

Elderberries are good as a tea with some honey when you have a cough and/or a cold. They help to boost the immune system and, when used with nettle, can clear up congestion. The berries are also antiviral, so when you have the flu, it can ease the symptoms. Alternatively, you can drink it during cold and flu season to stave off any threat.

Magical uses: elder is a sacred tree to the Faeries, and if you would like to commune with the Fair Folk, you can make a crown covered in the berries to meet with them in ritual. Never, ever burn elder wood.

Hops—Humulus lupulus

Parts Used: flowers

Hops are used as an estrogenic (acts like estrogen in the body) and enhances women's libido (decreases it for men). It is also used as a galactagogue. It regulates menses and menstrual difficulties, is a soporific and sedative for men, a stimulant for women, an antispasmodic, and a bitter tonic. Hops can be made into a tea (very bitter!) to help regulate menstrual cycles and alleviate symptoms of PMS. You can also drink a beer that is high in hops content to ease painful periods (drink responsibly).

Magical uses: spells and charms to increase love. (Note: it is wiser to accept and love yourself, thereby making you more confident and pleasing to others, rather than try to force someone else to love you. That goes against their own will and shall never end well.)

Lady's Mantle—Alchemilla vulgaris

Parts used: entire herb

*Consult your physician before taking if you are pregnant.

This herb can be infused in a tea to help ease pain, as it contains salicylic acid (where aspirin comes from). It helps to regulate menstrual cycles and hormones. It can be used during labour to ease and regulate contractions and afterward for toning the uterus.

Magical uses: honouring the feminine and sovereign queen in your own self.

Raspberry—Rubus idaeus

Parts used: leaf/berry

*Do not use the leaves in first half of pregnancy if prone to miscarriage; the berries can be eaten instead

Raspberry leaf is a lovely tea and the berries are wonderful picked fresh and eaten straight away or frozen and used in smoothies. As a tea, it tones the uterus and is beneficial for the last three months of pregnancy as a birthing aid. It also eases heavy/painful periods.

Magical uses: brings abundance and fertility.

Winter Herbs

Juniper—Juniperus communis

Parts used: berry

Juniper is an antiseptic, a strong diuretic, and a urinary tonic. It enhances labour two weeks prior to due date and is useful for treating cystitis and other UTI's. Juniper can be used as a tea, which helps to treat cystitis and other urinary tract infections. It is a strong diuretic, much like dandelion. You can also eat the berries, which when cooked down I'm told are lovely with game such as venison.

Magical uses: resolving emotional issues.

Rosemary—Rosmarinus officianalis

Parts used: leaf

Rosemary stimulates blood flow to the brain, so you can drink it as a tea to help aid your memory. It can also ease migraines and calm anxiety. As it is anti-inflammatory, it also helps with menstrual pain as well as toothache.

Magical uses: past-life recall, purification.

Skullcap—Scutulleria nodosa

Parts used: aerial parts

Skullcap makes a bitter tea that can be drunk to ease nervous complaints and tension. It is also good for muscle pain and cramps and helps to promote sleep. It combines well with other calming herbs such as chamomile.

Magical uses: protection, breaking addiction.

Valerian—Valeriana officianalis

Parts used: root

*Not for prolonged use.

Makes a nice (but rather smelly) tea to be drunk to ease nervous complaints such as insomnia, stress, migraines, and exhaustion.

Magical uses: sleep and dreamwork, trancework.

When using herbs in spells, always awaken and charge them so that they are in tune with your intention. It is letting the herb know that you wish to use it for a specific purpose. You can also do this when using the herb medicinally; in fact it is highly recommended! In magic and spellcraft when using an herb, you can simply hold it in your hand and feel the energy of the herb itself slowly stirring. Tell the herb of your intention and then push some of your own personal energy into the herb. Visualise the end result of the spell as you are doing this, and thus the herb is "charged" with your intention.

These are but a few common herbs that you can work with on your path as a Hedge Druid. I would encourage you to be familiar with at least a handful of herbs that grow near to you. Simple herbs such as nettle in a tea are both lovely and very nutritious, and harvesting it yourself can connect you to the seasons. Take a course in herbalism, if you wish; there are many out there and even interesting ones such as herbal first-aid! What you have in your kitchen cupboards could treat a variety of ills as well as boost your magical work.

She leans over the mug of nettle tea and inhales its deep, green scent. The first nettles of spring–this is a real treat compared to the nettles that she harvested last summer and cut and dried in her airing cupboard. The Hedge Druid takes a sip and lets the taste roll over her tongue. Not as sharp as the dried herbal tea, the fresh tea speaks of growing things, of sunlight and sap. She savours the taste and thanks the plant deeply for its nourishment.

Chapter 22

Ogham

O gham is often characterised and described as a mnemonic "tree alphabet" and is used by many in the Druid tradition. As a Hedge Druid,
it is entirely your choice as to whether or not you incorporate it into your
path. The pronunciation of the word depends on which part of Ireland you
are coming from and to which period in time you are referring (medieval
Irish vs. modern Irish, for example). Sometimes it is pronounced "oham" or
"oh-am," other times "ogam," and more.

The ogham alphabet consists of twenty letters, with an additional five
that were added at a different date to enable people to write in words of
Greek origin. There are sounds in the Greek language that are not found in
Irish and vice versa. The Druids spoke many languages, Greek being one of
them. And as we all know, some words just aren't translatable! Some Druids
use the extra five letters, some do not.

There is large debate over the origins of the ogham alphabet. The ear-
liest recorded ogham that we can find goes back to the third and fourth
centuries and was carved on stone. So the ogham is slightly less than two
thousand years old; however, the linguistics suggest that it is far older than
the carved stones themselves, and by the time of its recording in stone it
had already been in existence for perhaps a few hundred years, if not more.
Some myths describe the ogham as being written on wood. Heroes might
carve letters onto a branch during their quest to let others know of their

deeds and whereabouts. If ogham was indeed carved on wood as portrayed in myth, actual carvings on wood have not survived in the damp and rainy climate of Ireland, where it would have rotted quickly. Archaeologists have yet to discover preserved wood with ogham written on it. Ogham is also found in manuscripts from the Christian period.

The tree alphabet was described and popularised by Robert Graves in his work *The White Goddess*. However, this is just one of one versions of the 150 different types of ogham, described in the work *The Scholar's Primer*, a seventh-century work of Irish grammarians, written by a scholar named Longarad. The tree ogham specifically has taken root (if you'll pardon the pun) in Modern Druidry and Paganism, due to the proliferation of Graves's work and our love of trees. However, there is also pool ogham, which is derived from harbours, lakes, rivers, and other bodies of water. There is king ogham, named after kings as its name suggests. We also find trade ogham, where each letter is named after a specific trade. We've seen that it can be used in hand ogham, for signing without speech, alongside shin ogham and nose ogham. There is a colour ogham and even a bird ogham for all you bird lovers out there.

The Scholar's Primer (the texts of the ogham tract from the *Book of Bally-mote* and the *Yellow Book of Lecan* as well as the text of the *Trefhocul* from the *Book of Leinster*) suggests that the ogham came from the god Ogma, Oghma, or Ogham, however you wish to spell or pronounce it. It states that Ogma is the father of the alphabet and Ogma's wife is the mother (her name uncertain). We can find alphabets, runes, and writings derived from deities the world over, such as in the Norse or Egyptian traditions. A mythical account is but one of many.

The shape of ogham helps to make it easy to carve into stone or wood. It also makes it easy to sign with using your hands. It might have been developed in order to preserve a formally oral religious tradition, as the Roman Empire continued to expand and the fate of the Celts became less and less certain. Certainly travellers to the continent would have seen Latin inscriptions all over the place and may have been inspired to do something similar to save some vestiges of their own culture. In effect, this would indicate that it was of Pagan origin, rather than Christian.

You can find standing stones with ogham travelling up one side of the stone and over and down the other side, depicting lineages of kings. Sometimes they indicate which tribal territory they are from. Ogham has been used for many ancient secular signposts, if you will. Ogham was formerly used in a very mundane way, but today's Druids and Pagans apply a more mystical approach to it. Whether it was originally a mystical alphabet or not, we may never be sure. We can agree that ogham is magical in that as a written alphabet, it can connect us with the past, speaking to us from millennia past and allowing us to communicate with the ancestors. It frees us from space and time, as all written words do. They will live on.

Translating the ogham is another tricky matter. Linguists differ in their interpretations of each letter, and so if you want to use the ogham in your practice, you will have to find a translation that makes sense and works for you.

Many Modern Pagans and Druids use the ogham in a divinatory manner. In some myths we see the use of ogham in order to determine past events, what happened then, and so on. But today the preference is to look ahead into the future, much like any other popular divinatory system such as the runes or tarot. *Fidlann* is a term for "casting lots" and, as *fid* translates to "wood," this could be ogham divination. You can make your own set of ogham staves for divination purposes by carving the ogham onto a piece of wood. If you want to be very specific, you can carve the relevant ogham onto the relevant wood then cast the staves onto the ground or flat surface. From where they land and which ones are readable, you can divine what it is that you need to know. Below I've included the ogham alphabet:

Ogham Alphabet—twenty letters:

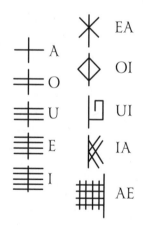

Ogham Alphabet—additional five letters (left) and typographic ligatures (right)

Here are the main twenty trees of the popular tree ogham in greater detail and some of their divinatory meanings. Some of these trees were known as chieftain trees and were protected under Ireland's indigenous Brehon law, which was in existence prior to the establishment of English common law. Brehon law/lore was a civil law officially formed in early medieval Ireland, stemming from an even earlier oral form. Brehons were similar to judges and memorised laws to settle disputes.

Name	Letter	Meaning
Beith (Birch)	┝	Sacred tree of Brehon lore; new beginnings, fast growth; associated with courage and the pioneering spirit; cleansing and purifying; a new phase in life; feminine energy and focus
Luis (Rowan)	┢	Sacred tree of Brehon lore, sacred to goddess Brighid; protection, perspective, and wit; Faery and Otherworld influence
Fearn (Alder)	┢	Sacred tree in Brehon lore; prophecy and sacrifice; associated with the god Bran; confidence; power and warrior spirit; balancing emotions; masculine
Saille (Willow)	┣	Sacred tree of Brehon lore; balance, harmony; emotions and healing; divinity and spirit; beauty
Nuin (Ash)	┣	Sacred tree of Brehon lore; strength and courage; righteousness; warrior and wisdom; inspiration; death; sovereignty
Huath (Hawthorn)	┤	Sacred tree in Brehon lore; Otherworld influence; challenge and transformation; honour; declaring boundaries; Faery tree
Dair (Oak)	┥	Chieftan tree in Brehon lore, above all others; strength; commitment; doorway; growth; divinity and sovereignty; truth; knowledge and wisdom; balance; associated with Brighid
Tinne (Holly)	┥	Sacred tree in Brehon lore; associated with the god Taranis; persistence, strength, and endurance in hardship; protection; warrior spirit; masculine energy

Name	Letter	Meaning
Coll (Hazel)		Sacred tree in Brehon lore; divinity and divine guidance; inspiration and awen; balance and alignment; potential; integration and relationship; wisdom; protection; divination
Quert (Apple)		Sacred tree of Brehon lore; Otherworld gifts and blessings; holistic well-being; healing; magic
Muin (Vine or blackberry)		Bounty and harvest; fruits of labour; cycles of growth, death, and decay; gifts and blessings; sacrifice
Gort (Ivy)		Tenacity and perseverance; endurance; connection and relationship with others; feminine energy
Ngetal (Reed, Broom, or Fern)		Skill of mind and body; independence; discretion; conscious choices; associated with Brighid
Straif (Blackthorn)		Magical aptitude and skill; Otherworld influence; protection; boundaries
Ruis (Elder)		Faery tree; Otherworld connection; sacrifice and atonement; equilibrium; transition; death; magic; protection
Ailm (Scots Pine or Silver Fir)		Sacred tree in Brehon lore; quiet wisdom and contemplation; calm and peace; new perspectives; inspiration; immortality
Furze or Onn (Gorse)		Fire in the head; fire in the belly; fertility; new ideas and plans; renewal; power; purification
Ur (Heather)		Cycles and regeneration; opportunity; connection; community; tribe; good fortune
Eadha (Aspen or Poplar)		Communication; movement; signal that a change may be required; sacrifice; death
Idho (Yew)		One of longest-living trees on earth; perseverance; quiet and calm; patience; endurance; regeneration; cycles of life and death; blessings; silence and quietude; immortality; the Otherworld

This is a brief glance into the ogham. A full account of the ogham is beyond the scope of this work and indeed there are many books solely dedicated to the ogham and Celtic tree lore and magic. I encourage you to seek these out, do your own research, and if this interests you, to dive deeper into the world of Celtic trees and their wonderful mysteries.

She throws the ogham staves upon the shingle beach before her. They rattle among the stones, and she uses those closest to her and whose symbols are the most visible for divination. She allows the sound of the waves pushing and pulling the rounded stones along the shoreline to lull her into a trance, and slowly the ogham begin to form a pattern in her mind, showing her what it is that she needs to do, what it is that she needs to know.

Chapter 23

Spellcraft

We have looked at Druid magic in the first section of this book, and here I will incorporate some spells that can be used in the Druid tradition. These spells are crafted through my own knowledge of the past and what is available in today's world. These are not "ancient spells," but workings that can help a modern-day Hedge Druid on his or her path.

Búad Channelling

This pre-spell preparation or channelling uses the energy of the landscape, *búad*, to connect the magical worker with the land and enable her or him to channel that energy into further work. This can be done at the start of any spellcraft to add further energy to the work.

Take a moment to connect with the energy of your own landscape. You will have already come to know it as best you can, whether it is forest or city, town or countryside. Through having made a connection with the land upon which you live, you will be able to harness some of that energy in your own work. If possible, go out into nature nearby and perform this where you will be able to feel the wind on your skin, the ground beneath your feet, and see the heavens above you. Name the place that you are connecting with in your mind, to further solidify its connection to you. Feel the ancestors, both human and non-human, who have walked and who make up this land. Feel the spirits of place all around you. Connect with a local land deity, if you so desire, and speak their name.

Hold out your hands and feel the energy of the land. You might wish to tap into nearby ley lines or simply put your hands upon the earth and draw up the cool, dark, earthy energy into your being. You may visualise this energy as a serpent that runs through the land (this is especially apt in the British Isles). If you are working near water, draw that energy into your being, or if you are working on a hilltop or other high place, draw in the energy of the wind and the sky above you. Feel that energy connecting within you, mingling with your own personal power. Draw it down deep, into a deep well within your soul, slowly circling with this energy. You can carry this energy within you back to where you would like to do the spellwork (at home, for instance, if you are in a city park) or, if you are ready, go straight into it and use this energy right away. Leave an offering afterward to the spirits of place.

Cles Channelling

This pre-spell preparation or channelling uses the energy of a particular place in the landscape, or *cles*, that has been used and combined with human energy. It might be a circle of standing stones, for instance. You don't have to travel to Stonehenge or Callanish in order to work with this type of energy. If you have enough space in your backyard, you can create your own stone circle—I certainly have! It doesn't have to be large; simply large enough to sit or stand in. Think of it as more of a temple, but one that is open to the land, sea, and sky. You can use wooden posts or flower borders. Be creative. It might be a simple outdoor altar under a tree or, if you cannot go or work outside, an indoor altar or temple room might work for you. Through repeated work in connecting with the búad energy of that particular place and infusing it with your own energy, you will have built up enough of a "temple" that you can build the cles energy that will then be contained in the temple, allowing you access to this form of energy easily enough when required. This may take a few weeks or months. Always consult the spirits of place before building any sort of temple area. They may or may not agree to this, and it can help or hinder your work if you go against their wishes.

Breathe deeply in your temple space. Designate sacred space, if you so desire. Feel the energy that has collected within this space, energy which now builds upon itself as well as infuses with your own energy. See the temple space humming or glowing with that energy. Adjust your own energy so that it is in tune with the cles energy, and then draw that energy into your being. Feel it mingling and blending with your own energy and being drawn into a deep well within your soul. This pool whirls and swirls slowly with energy, and you can carry it with you back to where you will be performing the spell or go straight into the spellwork *in situ*. Always leave an offering to the spirits of place afterward.

Gathering the búad or cles energy can be used to bless, charm, infuse, and boost magical workings.

Talisman Magic

This is a very accessible form of magic. It is also quite simple. You can use items that you have found in nature, such as a piece of wood from a specific tree (perhaps working with ogham meanings) or a special rock that you picked up while on a walk. You can also make your own talisman, modelling something out of clay, perhaps with a symbol of the work that you would like to do or ogham associations. You might make a small bag or pouch and fill it with herbs to lend their energy to your magical work (see chapter 21 for appropriate herbs as well as charging them with energy). You might make a small dolly as a representation of yourself, say for healing, courage, or protection. Whatever you decide to use as a talisman, ensure that it has been ethically sourced/made.

Beforehand, you may have channelled búad or cles energy. If not, simply work with your own energy, without these additional "boosts." Hold the talisman in your hand and feel the energy/energies swirling in a deep pool or well within you. Gather them up from within, and when you are ready, push them out into the talisman. You might simply see this energy streaming from the well within you directly into the talisman or you might hold your other hand over the talisman and visualise the energy streaming from your hand into the object. You might place the talisman on a table and use a wand to direct the energy. The choice is yours. As the energy pours from you into the object, see it awakening with power. When enough energy has been stored, stop the energy flow and pick up the item.

Sit with it and state your intention over it. You might like to say these or similar words:

Talisman of magic
Talisman of might
Grant to me my desire
For (your desire, e.g., "courage" or" protection") *this day and night*

Holding the talisman, visualise yourself working and filled with this energy. Programme this intention into the talisman through the visualisation. Then, when finished, blow gently across the item to bless it. Carry it with you when needed or place in the home or wherever suits you and the spell best.

Spell of Protection for the Home

For this spell you will need:

• A small drawstring bag
• Charged herbs of St. John's Wort, mugwort, and oak bark

Designate sacred space, if so desired. Into a small drawstring bag, place the charged herbs of St. John's Wort (for protection), mugwort (for magical power), and oak bark (for lasting effect). Ensure that you have charged these herbs with their own intention. Infuse this talisman with búad or cles energy, if you so desire, as well as your own intention (see Talisman Magic above).

Carry this talisman throughout every room in your home. In every room, recite the following, which is an adaptation from the *Carima Gadelica*:

(Optional god/goddess, or I) *bless this house*
From site to stay,
From beam to wall,
From end to end,
From ridge to basement,
From balk to roof-tree,
From found to summit,
  Found and summit.

See the energy of the talisman filling the room, offering protection. When you have carried it through every room, carry it three times around the outside of the house if you are able. Then, hang it or place it in the heart of the home. Leave an offering for the spirits of hearth and home afterward, and you might even like to leave offerings as a daily practice to ensure their cooperation.

Spell of Invisibility

There are times when we need to cloak ourselves from certain dangers. Walking alone at night or coming across people who might wish you harm are some examples. Working out of doors in the landscape, you might also like to use this spell to ensure that you are not interrupted in your work.

Visualise yourself throwing a cloak over yourself, which covers you completely. See this cloak shimmer and then cause you to fade, to blend in with your surroundings, rendering you "invisible." Softly recite aloud or in your mind the following:

I bind to myself today
The power of sky,
The light of the sun,
The brightness of the moon,
The splendour of fire,

The flashing of lightning,
The swiftness of wind,
The depth of sea,
The stability of earth,
The firmness of rocks.
—Adaptation of "The Deer's Cry" (*Fe-fiada* charm)[40]

See yourself blending with and being supported by all of the above. Feel the elements of earth, air, fire, and water working within you to shape and shift you into a blend of your environment. Hold this for as long as you need to. And if you are in danger, move swiftly to safety, and don't forget to drop the visualisation afterward, so you don't get run over crossing the street!

Spell for Healing

For this spell you will need:

• A candle

• A bowl of water

• Willow (you can buy willow bark from most herbalists, if you cannot obtain a few leaves or bark yourself)

Take your candle and bowl of water. On the candle, inscribe the ogham of willow (saille) and visualise the healing energy of the willow tree infusing the candle with its power. Place the candle in its holder and hold the willow herb in your hand. Awaken and infuse the willow with energy and then sprinkle in a circle around the base of the candle or candleholder (some candleholders have room for this just around where you insert the candle without the herb actually coming into contact with the candle itself, which is ideal as we want the candle to burn all the way down without setting fire to anything). Take a moment to look at the candle and herbs and speak aloud

---

40. Mary Jones, "Lorica of St. Patrick," Celtic Literature Collective, accessed February 7, 2018, http://www.maryjones.us/ctexts/lorica-e.html.

your intention. Then, take a moment to build up energy once again within yourself and strike a match, lighting the candle, saying:

Fire, aid me in my work.

Take the bowl of water and hold it in your hands. Feel the energy of the water and push some of your own energy into it. When it is brimming with energy, place it next to the candle or just before it and say:

Water, aid me in my work.

See the primal powers of water and fire blending together. Visualise their energies channelling the intention of the spell and releasing it out into the world. Then say this, adapted from the *Carmina Gadelica*:

Bone to bone,
Flesh to flesh,
Sinew to sinew,
Vein to vein;
As Brighid healed that
May I heal this

If you wish to leave out the goddess Brighid, simply remove that line.

See yourself in a healed state and hold this image for as long as you can. When you have done all that you can, take a moment and rest from your work. Allow your mind to clear and settle; think on nothing, allowing the spell to do the work from now on.

Let the candle burn all the way down. If you need to leave the candle burning but cannot be in the same room, place it in the bathtub or shower (away from shower curtains) and close the door so no pets can come in and investigate. Let the magic flow.

How to Craft Your Own Spells

You have now seen some examples of how magic can be worked in the Druid tradition. As it is a growing tradition, with new knowledge and techniques influencing it all the time, you can certainly feel free to write up your own spells, using whatever tools you desire, whatever components and techniques you feel best suit your practice. Here are some guidelines as to how to go about writing and performing a spell.

First off, intention is everything. You must have a very clear intention of what it is that you wish to achieve. As well, many in the Druid tradition would say that you should only resort to spellcraft if you have tried and exhausted all other more mundane means. So, if you'd like to bring more abundance into your life (i.e., more money), you can't just expect it to fall into your lap. You will need to look for better-paying jobs or look into other routes of obtaining better pay in return for services. You might look for better investment opportunities or how to save money each month by recording all transactions and then going over them in detail, to see what you can eliminate. When we are trying hard in the physical world, then we can also add energy from the spiritual and magical realms to our work. If you are unsure as to whether your intention is clear or whether it needs some work, you can always practice a form of divination, such as the ogham, to help you in determining the correct intention and form of address (i.e., the spell itself).

Once you have clarified the intention, then it is time to do some research. There are many good books available on European magic and folklore, and these can provide inspiration for you in your own spellcraft. Having studied magic and folklore in my own locality of East Anglia, I feel more in tune with those magical practitioners from the past, as well as the land itself. Immerse yourself in research, in folklore and mythology, and you will most definitely be inspired in your own spellcraft. You do not have to follow old lore to the letter (many of these involve things which would be abhorrent today, like burying a live frog in an anthill in order to collect the "toad bone" to be used in magical workings), but you can see where they were coming from and adapt the working to something that is correct for today's day and age, if you so desire. You may like to use ogham or other symbols in your work and so you will need to know what each means, both academically and in your own mind, for you might have a slightly different interpretation based upon personal experience.

Think about the repercussions of the spell as well. Is it likely to have a negative outcome on anyone in its completion? If so, you will need to determine for yourself the ethics of the situation. Try to envision as many possible outcomes for the spell as you can. You can then word the spell correctly, to ensure that it is ethically sound when it comes to its execution.

Next comes writing the spell itself. It's very useful to actually physically write down the spell, from start to finish, so that you have it set in your mind. Often when we write things down, we retain them better in our memory. As well, if halfway through the spell you forget what comes next, you can check your writings and carry on.

Then it's time to gather the components, if any, that you will need for the spell. Ensure that you have everything at hand that you will need. You don't want to break your concentration and focus halfway through the work to rummage around your cupboards for the mugwort that you forgot to bring into your ritual space. Make sure you list every component for the spell when you are writing it down.

Then you must determine an auspicious time, if any, to perform your working. You might like to perform a certain spell at the full moon, to benefit from the power that can be drawn in ritual and spellcraft. Or you might prefer to work at the dark of the moon, to use those energies which may be more suitable. You might like to check the tides, to find out when the highest and lowest tides are or check for astronomical and astrological influences. You can even use divination, if you'd like, to find out what the best time for this spell would be. The Celts certainly did; Queen Boudicca herself released a hare before going into battle to determine whether she would be victorious and have the aid of her goddess, Andraste (whose name means "victory"), with her. She did, for a while at least!

Finally, it's time to perform the spell itself. You will need to be uninterrupted, so turn off phones, tell housemates that you are to be left alone, and prepare yourself for the working to come. You might like to meditate beforehand, to clear your mind and ensure that you are working from a clear perspective. You could also sain (smudge) yourself to "purify" or prepare you for the work (mugwort is ideal). You might also like to channel some energy such as búad or cles energy.

So, broken down, here are the parts in order, that you may want to consider when writing your own spells:

- Intention—what is the intention of this spell?
- Divination—do you need to perform a divination to confirm the intention or outcome?
- Research—take your time in informing yourself; use your wit and intelligence.
- Repercussions—what, if any, negative repercussion may take place as a result?
- Write down the spell—in your own words, word for word.
- Gather all spell components—write these down as part of the spell so that you can tick them off to ensure that you haven't forgotten anything.
- Determine the timing—the Druids were big on auspicious times, so let that influence you too if you so desire.
- Perform the spell—no distractions; preparation such as meditation, cleansing, or saining and channelling energy are ideal.

Take some time after you have done your spellwork to rest and reflect. Try not to think too much on the work in the coming weeks, but allow the magic and your intention the time to work. Usually you will notice a difference within a moon's cycle, depending on the spell that you cast. If you wish, you can boost the power of the spell by visualising the outcome during certain times of the day, adding extra energy to the work, but please don't fixate on the outcome all day long. It helps as well to journal your work so that you know what has been successful and what hasn't. By recording this, you might try something slightly different the next time, with which you might have great results. A small alteration may be all that is needed, such as timing or a certain herb or your intention. It's hard to remember all these things, so by writing down the spell and its results, you can check on the progress and adapt your future work if necessary.

The spell is done. The Hedge Druid sits back, watching the sun rise over the lake. The mists shift in serpentine patterns as the heron calls across the still water. The magic has been put into action. The dawn star blesses the magic with its shimmering light. The Hedge Druid stands and bows to the lake then makes her way back to her camp to have some breakfast and write in her journal.

Part Four

SKILLS AND TECHNIQUE

In this final section, we turn the focus inward, preparing ourselves for doing the work in the world, in leading a life dedicated to the service of the environment, our community, the gods, the ancestors, and so forth. We will begin with a look at ethics and then move on to the subject of peace in Druidry, a concept that goes back to ancient times. We will also look at how to use the voice and body in ritual and in everyday life, as well as how to work as a teacher, leader, and/ or priest from a place of balance and service.

Chapter 24

Ethics

In this chapter, we will explore issues related to living and working ethically in the Druid and indeed all Pagan traditions. I am not saying "you should do this" or "you should not do that," but instead I am looking at issues in working with anger, hurt, and vengeance, as well as peace and working in service.

Working with Anger, Hurt, and Soul Wounds

Treat others as you would like to be treated. Such a simple phrase, yet so hard to comply with when we've been hurt or wounded in any way. Our first reaction is to hurt back, to wound in return. Yet is this how we would like to be treated? What if the person who hurt you didn't even know that they had? But what if it was completely intentional—is it then justifiable to perpetuate the cycle of hurt? How do we, as Druids, work with anger and soul wounds in today's society? How do we work with honour?

We don't really know how the ancient Druids worked with the concepts of honour or revenge. We have an account of how the Druids stood on the shores of their sacred isle at Anglesey, just before the Romans invaded, and called down their magic and their might, black-robed women with wild hair brandishing torches and running between the Druid ranks. What those men and women were doing we just don't know, but we can be fairly certain that they were protecting their land from invaders. Whether or not their magics would have been invoked without provocation is a total unknown, but here we have an example of defence rather than offense. Boudicca wiped out Colchester and London in retaliation for the rape of her daughters by the Romans after performing divination with a hare (if the hare ran one way, it was favourable, the other way, unfavourable). Whether or not that great queen in history was a Druid or was advised by them is debatable. We know that some ancient bards apparently had the power to cause boils to appear on the faces of those whom they satirised. Did their victim deserve it? And who gave the bards the right to judge and condemn? Some were said to be able to shout loud enough to cause miscarriage in women throughout the land. What would one have to do to provoke the death of innocents? Is this justifiable in any situation?

But that is ancient history, myth, and legend. How do we, as Druids today, work with feelings of anger and the concept of revenge? How do we deal with people hurting us, with our rights being taken away? How does the word "honour" factor into our everyday lives?

It's difficult, especially when we have such a quick means of communication in our world. Emails and opinions can be shared without a second thought. People can comment, cut down, undermine, say whatever they feel like in the virtual realm, and not really suffer very many consequences in the real world. Governments lie to us outright and have been caught out in their lies and still there is no justice. Even the most kind-hearted person begins to feel the anger and rage boiling within, battling with compassion and love for the world that they live in, for the world they would like to see. How can we deal with these emotions? If someone is attacking us, how do we as Druids protect ourselves and yet find justice? How can we ensure that the balance is maintained?

The first idea that we need to let go of is the idea of revenge. We do not need to hurt someone when they've hurt us. We would like to, we might desire to hurt them in response, but we don't need to in order to continue in our daily lives. We have to work out the difference between our desires and our needs, as with so many other aspects of our lives. It's perfectly human to want to hurt someone when they've hurt us or upset us or someone we love. It's up to us how we act on those feelings, however. We have to be emotionally responsible.

Pride is an oft maligned trait in the human race. Pride can be the reason many people seek to hurt others, trying to "save face" or avoiding confrontation with those aspects of themselves that they so dislike. Instead they wage a war outside of their inner worlds so that they don't have to own up to their own shadow selves. Yet pride can also be a good thing. Our pride can be part of our self-respect. In this way, pride will not allow others to walk all over us, but neither does it seek to destroy others who don't agree with us.

As Druids, we work in service: to the gods, to the ancestors, and to the community. We know that we have to give back, that we have a responsibility in this world to ensure that the ecosystem in which we live is functioning well. A balanced, diverse, healthy ecosystem is where there is a give and take and where relationship is the key matter of the discussion. Those relationships must work together, must find a way to honour each other in order to flow smoothly, to be efficient and benefit the whole. As Druids, it is the whole that concerns us most. The whole is what we work in service to, rather than the self. When we heal the whole, when we work holistically, then we also benefit the self. It's not altruism, it just is. We must first understand the self, the reasons why we behave the way we do, and in that understanding, we find compassion for others. In finding that compassion, we heal the whole. And the cycle continues…

When we are in positions of power, acts of anger and revenge can be even more devastating to the whole. We must learn how to work honourably with our power, out of self-respect and out of respect for the rest of the world. Without all our relationships, whether they are with other humans, the bees, the mountains, or the rivers, we would simply not exist. We don't live in a bubble or a vacuum. We need others in order to survive. We must learn to work with others, even if we disagree with them or cannot understand them. When others hurt us, we need to ride the currents of emotion and keep the bigger picture at hand in order to work honourably. We need to let go of our destructive sense of pride and ego and build on the best aspects of both. We need to work from a strong and balanced sense of self and yet be able to let that sense of self go into the light of utter integration for the benefit of the whole.

Wiccan, author, and activist Starhawk writes in her book *The Twelve Wild Swans: A Journey to the Realm of Magic, Healing, and Action*:

> We let go of vengeance out of love and concern for our larger community. To be a true leader, we must be able to look at each of our acts and say, "How will this affect the community? Is it worth dividing the community for me to be proved right? Would I not be destroying the very source of support and healing that I most need?"
>
> And we relinquish revenge because we hold a vision of healing, for ourselves and for the world. ... We cannot serve a broad vision by being petty and spiteful.[41]

If we are to be leaders, priests, or upstanding members in our community, allowing our actions to speak as loudly (if not more) than our words, we need to relinquish forms of revenge and focus instead on healing. We don't need to make someone look bad, to punish someone, to destroy them or perform character assassinations. We can't push out people simply because they disagree with us. People *will* be annoying, *will* try to pick fights, *will* be aggressive or antagonistic. We don't have to respond like for like. If we are to work as Druids in the community, we need to let go of our desire for the above when we are hurt and instead focus on the need for healing in the community as a whole.

This doesn't mean that we allow people to walk all over us. Whether it's an individual, a government, or whatever else, we can still stand up for what we believe in. We can speak out against injustices: we can march in protest or start a campaign, raising money and supplies to help those in need. When it becomes personal, we can simply ignore it and get on with our lives, doing the work that needs to be done, having compassion both for ourselves and perhaps even for the person who is antagonising us. We know that work still needs to be done, and getting distracted because of false pride or ego is not

---

41. Starhawk, *The Twelve Wild Swans*, (Harper One, 2001), 130.

helping the whole. We can work with our feelings of anger and injustice and then see where they fit in the grand scheme of things. We can always ask ourselves: will this benefit the whole?

It requires us to look deeply at ourselves first and foremost. When we are able to do that, we can begin to work honourably. We see our own failings and we have compassion for ourselves. We see those same failings reflected in others and we have compassion for them. We know that we live in an extremely damaged world and that perpetuating the hurt and anger will only damage it further. We will stand up for what we believe in. We will speak out against bullies and those who would tout their privilege. We will seek political and social reform. We will endeavour to find the balance, to find a fairer system where the term "justice" actually means something. We will work to nourish and strengthen this planet that we live on, even as it nourishes us. And we will focus on working in relationship with everyone around us, deeply immersed in our own sense of self-respect and honour.

And in doing so, we relinquish the notion of revenge and instead focus on healing for ourselves and for the world. That is the power of the Druid.

The Dark Night of the Soul

Taking care of our thoughts and feelings is essential to maintaining our equilibrium. We have to work with emotional responsibility and take charge of our behaviour rather than letting impulses, reactionary behaviour (which is often improper), and the deluge of other destructive human emotions rule our world. We have to come to know our shadow side, to come to terms with the good and the bad and to feed that which will sustain us and not that which will destroy us. We acknowledge the necessity of destruction, but we need not feed it to our own detriment. We do not ignore negativity but rather work with it in order to better understand our own sense of self, and in doing so, better understand others in the process. We all have destructive and negative thoughts, but what defines us is whether and how we act upon these thoughts. Sometimes it is necessary to work with destruction, but often we do not seek the way in which it will cause the least amount of harm. For us Druids, we need to remember the balance of the whole as we strive toward holistic living and becoming a beneficial and nourishing part of an ecosystem. We have to remember our place within the whole and take responsibility for the role that we play in our life and in the lives of others.

There are far too many people who—knowingly or not—vent their emotions, their failures, their worries, anger, or stress upon others. Let us not be like them: let us not unconsciously or consciously add to the suffering in the world. We have to take a long, deep look at blame: at whom we blame for our emotions, our behaviours. Only when we do so can we begin on the path to emotional responsibility. Certainly, there will be external factors beyond our control, but here in the gentler West, the life that we live is essentially up to us to determine. We're not suffering the ravages of war or famine for the most part, though poverty is accelerating at an incredible pace and homelessness is a real issue and concern for many around the world. There are also many who may suffer from ill health—physical or mental or both. But in working to take the reins and guide our souls toward integration, we must first of all be willing to do so. We must want health, healing, and wholeness, for it will not happen without our effort. We must work through the dark night of the soul and see the dawn.

We not only have to look at who we are blaming, but also when we blame ourselves for our suffering. That is not to say that we give ourselves a *carte blanche* and do not take responsibility for suffering that we have caused to ourselves and others. Rather, we acknowledge and then move on from there instead of staying stuck in the well of stagnant waters in our soul.

The world provides us with examples each and every day of how not to be: from world leaders insulting each other over social media, the bad behaviour of colleagues, the trials we endure from friends and family and more. Seek out the darkness within and without and work with it in order to reclaim the energy that lies in the shadow. For it is in the darkness that the seeds wait for the warmth and light of spring. The darkness is nourishing if we allow it to be, if we are able to seek the calmness and centredness necessary before transforming the energy into something that will grow and flourish. In the darkness lies potential. Take a long, deep look at your own self, and in doing so, come to know your own dark night of the soul.

Choices

Choice is often something we don't we think have. Yet we make hundreds of choices each and every day, from what we are going to eat and what we are going to do to how we are going to interact with the world.

Choice is at the heart of my own personal ethics. I choose whether or not to behave in a certain way. I try to fill my life with intentional behaviour rather than reactionary behaviour. I don't always succeed, but at least the attempt is there to be conscious of how I am working in the world. When something doesn't go our way, when someone is mean, rude, or demeaning to us, it is our choice as to how we will respond. We have a personal responsibility that involves this choice, which is centred on this choice.

Yet, often we act like we don't have a choice. Someone is nasty to us and we are nasty back. Someone cuts us off the road and we flash our lights and get upset for the next fifteen minutes of our journey. Plans don't work out and we get all in a bother because of that. In these situations, it's not that we don't have a choice but that we choose not to acknowledge the fact that we do indeed have a choice. It's easier to not acknowledge the choice, most of the time, in order to vent off steam at someone or something, to project anger and irritation at something that is totally unrelated. Jung stated that what is unconscious controls us—and this is so very true. When we acknowledge that we do have a choice, we are becoming conscious and our behaviour and lives become so much more intentional rather than reactionary.

I decided a long time ago that I would much rather live an intentional life. Bad things will happen, but it's in our ability to respond with *all* our ability or responsibility that shows the kind of person we wish to be. When I had some very trying encounters with people in very emotional and stressful situations, it was entirely my choice as to how to respond. From an integrated, Druidic perspective, I also saw that I had the choice to either prolong or encourage more suffering in the world or step back from that and not allow myself to go down that road, instead working with empathy and compassion to benefit the whole rather than simply satisfy myself. It didn't mean that I liked the person any more for what they said or did right then and there in that situation, but it did mean that I wasn't going to exacerbate the situation and create more suffering for myself or for others. I was working with intention, conscious of my response, the reasons for their behaviour, and the reasons why they upset me as well. This made the unconscious conscious and I was able to proceed with complete sovereignty of my own words, thoughts, and actions, as well as my soul.

This personal sovereignty is a large part of Western Paganism. We see it in our myths and legends, in the quest for the grail, in the tales of goddesses and the land itself. When we are able to move through life from a centred and conscious perspective, awake, and aware that we do indeed have choices, then we are coming at life from an angle that makes us indeed a part of the whole, working toward the benefit of the whole. We're questing that which will make us whole: the holy grail. Relationship is at the heart of Druidry, in that relationship with the world is at the core of everything that we do. We are not separate, we cannot ever be, and what we do affects myriad other forms of life.

So remember that you have a choice. When life gets sticky, take a moment and think about what choices you have. It's not easy—I'll be the first to admit that—but with a single breath in a confrontational situation, you can reset your boundaries, come to terms with and remember your sovereignty, and accept that you have a choice in how to respond.

Duty and Service: The Life of a Druid

For me, Druidry is about living a life in service. Many people confuse the word "service" with being subservient: being beneath someone else in a lower position, lowering yourself for others. Service has nothing to do with this and everything to do with using your skills, wit, and intelligence to benefit the world around you. Relationship is at the heart of Druidry, and service to Druidry requires good relationship. There is equality, a give and take, in order to maintain a sustainable relationship. We work to serve the whole: the ecosystem, our community, our families, our ancestors, our gods, our planet. Our work as Hedge Druids is not just for ourselves, even though it may be a solitary path.

To work in service requires an open heart, a sense of duty, and also discipline. Too often when things are rough, people can lay aside their spiritual practice, feeling that they need to do so just in order to survive or that they simply can't be bothered. When we do this, we are stating that the theory and foundation of our religion or spirituality is just that: a theory. It's not something that needs to manifest. When something just remains a thought, a theory, then it is completely intangible and unable to create change in the world. At these points in time, when we are stretched to our limits, when we are in pain, when the world seems to be crumbling around us, this is when we need our Druidry the most. We may not feel like doing ritual, but this may be exactly what we need. We may not want to meditate, but again, that may be just what clears up our thoughts in order to proceed, to find the way forward. This is where discipline kicks in, as well as duty. When we just don't feel like it, we can remember our ancestors, remember their struggles, their fears, their failings, and know that we can do better; we can give back for all that we have received. With relationship at the heart of Druidry, we must learn what we owe to the world and not forget this very important concept. Only then will we truly understand the concept of duty and manifest it in the world, living a life in service.

I am blessed in so many aspects of my life. That is not to say that my lady Brighid does not throw me onto her anvil every now and then and pound the heck out of me, stretching me and reforging me anew. But in service to her, I work with the gifts that she provides me, with the challenges that lie before me, and see them as opportunities to reforge relationships or to understand why they don't work and walk away. I learn where I can be of service, where my skills and talents lie, and then use them to the best of my ability, living my truth. Above all else, Brighid keeps reminding me to live my truth.

In the midst of despair, when all seems dark, I stop and take a look around. I see the blackbird singing in my garden at sunset, listening to his call that takes me beyond this world and into the Otherworld. I see the deer eating the birdseed that falls from my feeder. I watch the clouds turn from white to gold and then deepest pinks and orange, a wash of colour that delights the eye and feeds the soul. I remember to look for and see the beauty in the world, in the small things and the large. I remember that I am part of an ecosystem and that I have a duty to give back. This gives my life meaning and it is also the meaning of life.

As a Hedge Druid, I walk a life of service. This service provides my life with meaning. I owe it to the land that nourishes me to protect it, to give back for my many blessings. I owe it to my ancestors, without whom I would not be here today. I owe it to my gods, who provide me with such deep inspiration that words cannot even come close to describing my relationship with them. Knowing what I owe, I walk the path of service in perfect freedom; for freedom is found when we release our self-centred perspective and take the whole of nature into our hearts and souls. We are nature.

It's not just for us. It's for all existence.

Not again. This time is one time too many. The Hedge Druid fumes, anger radiating from her. Another of her favourite spots has been destroyed, this time it is a hollow way, sacred to the Fair Folk. The trees that formed the hollow have all been cut down so that horses can ride through where the hollow once stood, instead of on the land and the permissive bridleway that the landowner previously agreed to. The shock of the sight brings tears to her eyes. How could someone do such a thing? For over fifty years, the villagers have walked down this hollow, its mystery and magic enchanting all. Now gone, all gone. A curse fills the Hedge Druid's mind and she opens her mouth to utter it into the late afternoon sunshine. But she stops as the first word leaves her lips. To curse the landowner would be vengeance. To pray for

healing and to re-establish the bonds with the Fair Folk are more important. The Hedge Druid reaches into her pocket and pulls out some seeds and herbs as an offering and prays to the Fair Folk. She will come back later, once her emotions are more settled, and think more on what she can do.

Chapter 25

Peace

Peace is an important aspect of Druidry. It is only when we have peace within ourselves that we can truly work from a place of honour in relationship to the rest of the world. When we have peace, we are not striving. There are so many things that we may intentionally or unintentionally strive for: recognition, power, fame, and more. Finding worth in ourselves and in our work leads us toward a peaceful coexistence with the rest of the world. It is working with deep intention. It helps us navigate the obstacles that we may discover in our life's journey, in good relationship.

Peace and Sovereignty

I see sovereignty and peace as being inextricably entwined. We cannot have one without the other. Sovereignty is obtained when we come to a deep understanding of ourselves and how we work in the world mentally, physically, and emotionally. When we know ourselves, when we understand why we do the things that we do, when we can control our thoughts and feelings and live lives of intention instead of reaction, then we are truly sovereign of our life. This comes from a deep well of peace, where we find that inner core of ourselves that is silent and still, that sings our soul song in its purest form. It is our personal truth. Neither sovereignty nor peace can be conferred from without; both must begin from within.

Peace is related to truth. We have to be willing to be open and honest with our selves, to see through our many layers of delusion in order to understand our very being. We have to see the good and the bad, acknowledge all these within ourselves—and through this acknowledgment, gain some control, some sovereignty, over our behaviour. Too often we run from the truth, whether it is the truth about ourselves or the truth about something like climate change. To face these truths requires us to change, to possibly suffer, in order to bring about that change. We don't like change. We don't like suffering. Yet we cannot escape either of these things. To truly live means to live a life that has good and bad within it; let's transcend those notions of good and bad and just live. When we do that, we move beyond suffering. We face our truth, and in facing our truth, we find peace.

Peace is achieved when we manage to step beyond our selves, to switch off that inner chatter, that constant thinking instead of being. This does not mean that we become robots with no thoughts, feelings, or emotions. Rather, we do not attach to them, we do not spend so much time with them, entertaining them as they go round and round in our minds. We step outside of that, moving beyond our own story in order to see the story of the world around us as it unfolds in every moment. This peace can be achieved with discipline, with daily meditation, with time spent out in nature. There is no limit to our ability to learn what this means each and every day. Little by little, we come closer to joy. When we realise the world is more than just us, we find peace.

We cannot control how others behave. We only have control over how we behave in the world, how we act and react to others. We can lessen our reaction to others to a more intentional way of being through mindfulness of our thoughts, our bodies, and the world around us. When things like pride and anger are not getting in the way, we can see things for what they really are. We have no need to threaten others, to undermine others, to make them suffer. We realise that in doing so we are only doing that to ourselves, through the interrelatedness of nature. Letting go of the ego's need for validation, for constant chatter, for endless self-centred thinking, we can dive into the still, calm pools of reflection where peace is found. We find that we can contemplate the self without recrimination or judgement. When we can do that with ourselves, we are able to do that with others. When we do this, we are working mindfully, with compassion and understanding.

It can be difficult when others deliberately try to shatter our peace, to shake our foundation and inner sovereignty. But we cannot control them and can only have compassion for them, as they are so caught up in their suffering that they feel it necessary to spread it out into the wider world. We can instead find our true sense of self-worth, our inner sovereignty, and let that light shine out in the world. We are our actions as well as our words. Our deeds are what are lasting in an impermanent world.

We can be at peace even in a world that seems to be going to hell in a handbasket. We can be at peace when others are trying to cut us down. We can be at peace in a world that is so materialistic and consumer-driven that it is making itself extinct. That peace is the core of our being. We know ourselves and, in that knowledge, can remove the reactionary behaviour that might lead us off the path of peace in our personal sovereignty. That peace is within each and every one of us if we are willing to see it and acknowledge it, to work to gain sovereignty of our souls. Through the opening of the eyes and the soul, we find that still, deep pool of being and of knowing and there we reign supreme.

Peace, Justice, and Permaculture

"Conflict resolution" consists of two words that very much need to be taken into consideration in today's political, social, and economic climates. I would like to add a third word, which is "honour." When we are taking into consideration the bigger picture, the benefit to the whole, changing our perception to a more holistic one, then we are on the path toward honourable conflict resolution. Where each part matters, where each part has value, much akin to the animist's view of the world wherein all of nature has inherent value, this worldview can help us to provide the solutions necessary in order to solve some deep problems. Too often it is easy to criticise; we often forget we must also offer solutions.

I teach my apprentices about the concept of ethical leadership, how we can work and explore ways in which groups with differing opinions, mindsets, politics, and worldviews can still operate cooperatively. Many aspects found within permaculture are a brilliant source of inspiration. Druidry is all about relationship and relationship is also at the heart of permaculture. Nature works cooperatively in order to provide a functioning homeostasis. Yes, there are brief flashes of competition here and there, but for the most part every aspect of nature works with others in order to survive.

If we look at mycorrhizal fungi, those tiny filaments of connecting threads that run underground connecting tree to tree in a forest, connecting many other plants and fungi, we see in a microcosm paradigm that everything is connected. Furthermore, there have been studies wherein it was found that, through these connecting threads, plants could help other plants, working cooperatively instead of competing for the best space and light. Trees in the sunlight could and did collect nourishment and nutrients that were then sent to trees in the shade that had little or no access. They did not even have to be of the same species: trees and other plants simply helped each other.

Unless we are hermits, we will have interaction with other humans. What we need to relearn is how to do so in a beneficial way, without falling into modern-day society's obsession with competition. It's not a dog-eat-dog world out there. Much of patriarchy and capitalism revolves around this idea of competition, and we need to let that go in order to find more balance in society as a whole. So how do we work with people whose perception is so different from our own? How can be bridge the gap, find the language, work honourably and sustainably with one another?

If we are working with a group and that group begins falling apart with bickering or power struggles, we need to look closely at how that situation came about in the first place. If we are in the role of leader, then it is up to us to communicate with all involved and find out just what is going on, getting different perspectives on the matter. We then need to look at the situation from a different perspective altogether, which is where permaculture can help us to widen our perception further, outside the human element, allowing the authority to come from nature.

If there is a problem in a garden, a proponent of permaculture would look deeply into the issue. If there is a mould or a damaging/invading insect in the garden, the solution would not be to just tackle the mould or the bug. Instead, one would look at the conditions that allowed such a thing to occur, looking deeply into the issue without any bias. Only then can more than one solution be offered and perhaps one that is more effective.

If we relate that to group dynamics, we could be more successful in addressing more than one problem at a time. If there is conflict within the group, we could solve a single problem by kicking out the ones who are perceived to be creating the conflict. But then another person might take their place, doing the same amount of damage. If we took a permaculture perspective, we would also look at the reasons why such a thing was allowed to occur, and the reasons could be many and varied. We may find that if we address the climate and conditions that created the tension in the first place, it would all stop and no one would have to leave. Only when all issues are addressed will there be any honourable conflict resolution.

As a Druid, I take my inspiration and my authority from nature. Nature is my teacher. Through nature I learn how to function in my environment and how to take the lessons that I have learned in my own locality and apply or adapt them to any location that I find myself in. Talking to the spirits of place, the ancestors, the gods, I can get a feel for what it is that I owe in return for what I have been given. I can work toward balanced, reciprocal, sustainable, and inspired relationship.

That doesn't mean that there will never be conflict. But when there is, we can see each conflict as a challenge and opportunity to learn more about ourselves and about the world. We don't need to have everyone like us and we don't have to like everyone, but we can learn how to operate in a society where we want or desire very different things. And where honourable conflict resolution is unobtainable, perhaps through continuing abuse or damage to our own well-being in any shape or form, we can learn to extract ourselves from the situation and find a new path forward. Much as when I am walking in the forest and see a patch of nettles, I will not walk through them, trying to find a relationship with them; I can honour them for what they are, but still avoid them. Some things simply will not work together, no matter how much we would like them to. Acceptance is a large part of permaculture and of peace of mind.

When we are working in such a manner, we will find peace not only for ourselves, but hopefully for others as well. Justice only arises when we have found some semblance of peace in ourselves and in the world. When we work holistically, honourably, in a desire to be utterly integrated—then we truly walk the path of the Druid.

The Hedge Druid is hurt and betrayed, her peace shattered all around her. She has been let down once again by her work colleagues and knows not what to do or where to turn. There has not been any peace in her life for weeks, as she struggles through the situation with daily attacks upon her work and no one to intervene. She steps through the hedge at the bottom of her garden, and there before her is a small muntjac deer. They look at each other for long moments, the deer and the Druid, both frozen in place and in time. Slowly, the Hedge Druid exhales and realises that there is a whole world out there beyond the situation and regains sovereignty of her soul. She knows who she is and that is what matters most. The little muntjac twitches an ear and then bounds away. The Hedge Druid smiles and thanks the deer for its wisdom.

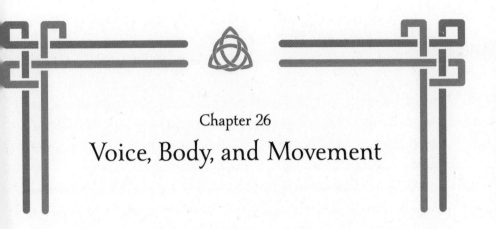

Chapter 26

Voice, Body, and Movement

In this chapter, we will look at how to use the voice and body in ritual. How we speak and how we move can have a great effect not only upon our own psyche but also affect our ritual. We need to be mindful of what we are saying and how we are saying it. We need to be aware of our bodies and what they may be trying to tell us (and others). If we are conscious of how we move, we can alter that, if necessary, to bring a more graceful aspect overall into our rituals and our lives as a whole.

Voice

As we have seen already in the magical techniques used by the ancient Celts and the Druids, we know that the voice and the spoken word had great meaning. Druids were said to be able to hurl down curses and cause boils to erupt on the faces of their foes, and their great shouts could cause infertility and miscarriage in women. How we use our voice, not only in magic and ritual but also in everyday life, has a profound effect not only on our own self, but on everyone around us.

Human beings are terribly vocal creatures. It's how we most express ourselves now, after much evolution. We're becoming less adept at the more subtle forms of communication, such as body language, intuition, and what is known popularly as the "sixth sense." Words and speech have taken over and as such we must learn to use them properly.

How conscious are you of your own voice when you are speaking? Very rarely, apart from when we are standing up in front of a crowd or trying to whisper in hushed tones to a friend, are we aware of our voice when speaking. Using the voice to its full extent can have a great benefit on your work as a Hedge Druid. Becoming aware of how you use the voice, which is simply another tool in the kit, helps you to understand how you can work better in your own tradition and will have a knock-on effect in everything that you do.

Take a moment and truly become aware of your voice. Say something along the lines of "I, (state your name), honour nature." See how you feel when you say your name, when you declare your love of nature. Now try to change the tone and meaning. Try to be more assertive. Try doing it with anger, then sadness. Do it as if you were speaking to a newborn human child or a kitten. See how this changes instantly how you feel inside yourself.

When doing Druid ritual, it is important to use the correct tone if using spoken word. We needn't be word-perfect in ritual and of course we will stumble on words or forget what we wanted to say, but the intention and the meaning will be there, expressed through our tone. I have been in public Druid ritual where the gods were called in a loud, shouting, and commanding voice, tinged almost with anger. I think that this may have been an attempt at projecting the voice so that everyone could hear, alongside perhaps the ego's drive to be a mighty Druid, but it did make me smile. No one likes to be shouted at, especially the gods, and I certainly didn't feel any answer to that particular request. I've also been in situations where it is difficult to hear the person talking in ritual, and this can have two very different outcomes: it might make everyone quiet down and listen intently, or it might just mean you miss everything that they are saying.

As a Hedge Druid, you might not think that it's too important in your own ritual work whether or not you are loud enough, as you're the only one around to hear it. You may be entirely correct; however, the tone still matters in what you are saying, even if the volume doesn't. Sometimes speaking louder does have a more commanding effect or create an increase of confidence in ritual. Sometimes it may just make you feel silly. Like all ritual, it is the intention that matters first and foremost, but we must also be aware of the delivery of that intention.

If we are praying, how are we executing that prayer? Some prayers are simply recited in your head, but others may be whispered or spoken aloud. When speaking aloud, become aware of your voice as a tool in the process of prayer. Use it as a gift, a great gift that allows you to connect with deity, the ancestors, or the spirits of place. Do not take that gift for granted. Feel the words moving through you, vibrating your vocal chords, coming out of your mouth and into the silence around you. Feel how the words and sounds change and charge the atmosphere. Becoming aware of this change is essential to effective prayer and also magical workings. Hold the intention deeply within your soul and allow the words to express that intention, with the tone modifying to suit the situation and the need. Try speaking into a deep silence where you can actually feel with your body as well as your mind the way the sound shatters the air, causing ripples and waves of effect throughout. Try it in utter darkness. Try it in a rushing wind, where the sound gets ripped away as soon as the words leave your lips. Try speaking in the pouring rain or during a blizzard or thunderstorm. For the adventurous, try it under water!

In ritual, you need to adapt and find the right tone to suit the intention, bearing in mind the effect and repercussion your words will have on you and everything around you. This also occurs in everyday life, and it is a very interesting exercise to spend a day becoming fully aware of your voice, what you say, and how you are saying it in your everyday routine. You might even prepare for this by spending the day before in silence, which again is a very interesting experience. When you do speak, follow the sound of your voice, the reaction the words create, the change that occurs between you and who you are speaking with. Become aware of your voice: is it smooth and soft, measured and graceful? It is loud and heavy, tinged with laughter or sadness? Also be aware of what it is that you talk about regularly. We might be surprised about how much we complain or how little we laugh. We might realise just how much we talk to our cats or how little we need to say in the company of old friends or family.

Many people dislike the sound of their own voice. As the voice is a tool, it is something that can be worked with; so, if you dislike the sound of your voice, be conscious and change it to something that is preferable to you and the work that you are doing. It's not too terribly difficult to make slight adjustments that make the process entirely more pleasing for yourself. Taking the time before you speak to adjust your tone, to perhaps find an even, measured tone with a hint of musicality, something that conveys grace and confidence or peace and mindfulness, can have a great impact on every conversation. As with everything, it is practice that allows us to become more skilled in this endeavour. Slow down the words, think before you speak in everyday conversation, think on the tone and delivery of how you would ideally like to be heard, and then do it. You may just surprise yourself with the results.

You may like to try this exercise in your own home with a partner. Go to a room on the other side of the house and say something in your normal voice. Then ask your partner if they heard what you said. Then shout the same thing and see what their response is. (You may have just shouted "Did you hear me?" which works just fine!) Next, bring your focus down into your chest, into your solar plexus or your diaphragm, whichever you are more comfortable envisioning. Allow that area to expand, allow your throat to expand, and now say the same thing again, without shouting, but still projecting your voice. Envision your words reaching your partner. See what their response is. If you don't have someone to try this exercise with, find a place that has a good echo for similar results.

Now take this exercise outside and instead of a partner go to a wild place. See if you can make your words reach the clouds above, without screaming at the top of your lungs. See if you can make your voice reach deep down into the ground, reverberating along the lines of energy running through the earth. See if you can connect your voice to the realms of land, sea, and sky. See how small you can make your voice and whisper secrets into a crumbling old oak tree. See what it may whisper back.

Use your voice wisely. Choose your words carefully. And above all, re-member intention is everything. The word "intention" comes from the Latin *intentio*, which can have three meanings: a stretching, straining, tension; an ex-ertion, effort, application, attention; or a purpose, an intention. Try to let go of the straining and tension and focus instead on the application and purpose, and you will surely succeed.

Body and Movement

Just as the voice is a wonderful tool that can be used to great effect, so too is the body. Becoming aware of how we move in ritual and in everyday life can help us to find more peace in mind and in body. Conscious movement is something that we need to take into greater consideration, both in our daily lives and also in ritual practice. How we move can affect how we feel, just as our voice can affect how we feel.

As a short exercise, walk across the room as you normally would. Now, try it again but this time imagine that you are a regal queen. Now try it again as a gorilla. See the difference? By becoming conscious of our move-ments, we can change how we feel and move out of the "ordinary" reality into something deeper. By doing this consistently, we can bring this into our everyday lives to achieve a state of grace in mind and in movement all of the time.

This is where mindfulness comes into play. If we have been doing a ba-sic breathing meditation, we will have come into an awareness of our bod-ies when we are in that practice. What we now need to do is to bring that mindfulness out into ritual space. When standing in ritual, how are we hold-ing our bodies? Are we standing tall or are we slumped in on ourselves? Are our shoulders hunched up and tight? How strong is our core?

Here is an exercise to try to bring awareness into the body. I use this ex-ercise in my dance company, to help ensure that good posture is maintained and body awareness comes into play. Stand or sit upright (without using the chair back, if possible) and bring your awareness into your body. If standing, stand with your feet hip-width apart (the width of your hip bones, not the exterior of your hips). Keep the knees soft, don't lock them in. Tuck the pelvis in just slightly by engaging about 10–20 percent with your lower belly (i.e., pull in just below the navel a little bit to stabilise your core and take strain off your lower back). Begin with the breath and feel your chest expanding on the inhale, the muscles across your back also expanding. On the exhale, consciously pull your navel in slightly toward your spine, to engage your core in the activity. Feel the muscles working across your back. Do this for a few breaths and see how you feel.

Now, ensure that you are still standing or sitting nice and upright, but not rigid. Keep awareness of the breathing and roll your shoulders back and down. Elongate your spine, if you can. Tuck in the chin ever so slightly, to lengthen the back of the neck. Keep the focused breathing and see how this makes you feel. Do you feel taller? Is there more room to breathe in your body? Do you feel different emotionally?

Keeping this posture, but not getting rigid with it, try walking around a little bit. With each step, roll through from the heel to the ball of the foot, really feeling each step. Take off your shoes for added sensitivity. Ensure that your core is slightly engaged and keep the shoulders back and down, the spine long. Notice how different this feels from your usual gait. Take your time getting used to the feel of this posture.

Now try leading with different areas of your body, just for fun. Instead of being in this grounded posture, try leading your body with your head, your belly, your arms. (Practice this somewhere where you won't be embarrassed!) Now pretend you are a ballerina and take a graceful turn, leading with the right arm to turn clockwise and vice versa. How does this make you feel? Take longer steps than normal, then shorter steps. Find the balance between the two where you feel confident and graceful. Then, in your grounded and aware posture, with each step become conscious of your arms. Allow them to flow and fall softly along the body and not be rigid or held tightly. When turning, to feel really elegant, lead ever so slightly with your wrist, arms still at your side but turning the wrist in order to turn the whole body afterward.

This exercise should bring in a good awareness of how you normally move and how you could move and hold yourself with some practice. Dance classes always help in achieving body awareness and are a great form of exercise too.

Speaking of exercise, as the body is a tool that can help us, we must ensure that we take very good care of it so that we can use it most effectively. Eating and exercising right go a very long way to ensuring that our bodies are well looked after. As Druids, we honour nature, and that includes our own bodies: so give up smoking, only drink in moderation, eat right, and exercise. We honour that we come in all shapes and sizes and what matters most is that we are as healthy as we can be.

In ritual, with a greater sense of body awareness, we can bring a grace and fluidity into our movements and have a greater sense of control and satisfaction. At the start of a ritual, don't just strike the match without thinking before lighting that candle; feel the match in your hand, breathe deep, and strike with intention. Light the candles with awareness. Don't just throw the match away, but place it mindfully in a little tray. If creating/designating sacred space, move around the circle with full awareness. Remember your walking exercise and bring that into play. Combined with the voice, when we move our bodies with conscious intention, our rituals and our lives can be so much more satisfactory and filled with grace.

The Hedge Druid sits in the wood, her prayer beads in hand. She chants with each bead passing through her fingers, allowing the vibration of her voice to fill her body and her mind. When she is finished, she is floating on the vibration of the sound, in tune with the Great Song of the universe, the Òran Mór of Brighid. She feels more deeply connected to her body, her mind, her soul, and to all nature. Mindfully, she rises and bows to the trees around her, honouring her environment. With graceful movements, she begins her slow dance in celebration of nature's beauty, beneath the boughs of the sleeping beech trees.

Chapter 27

Teacher, Leader, Priest

In my work as a teacher, my intention is to facilitate a way for those who want to not only follow a path based in an earth-based tradition but also for those who want to be an active seeker and participant on the Druid path. I want to help guide those who would be "carriers" of the tradition, rather than "followers." It is my intention that this book does the same. The way that we become carriers of the tradition is through personal responsibility, service, dedication, and ethical leadership. The path that we choose may be different from others; however, the inspiration remains the same. In our work for the land, in living a life of service, we might choose to work with animals or with herbs. We might decide to become celebrants for the community, offering our services for weddings, handfastings, funerals, and more. We might work in prison ministry or as an activist. We might inspire others through teaching, through our words and deeds. We might decide to become a teacher, a leader, a priest for the community. The path that we choose in which to share our awen is a reflection of our own selves.

When we become an active member of any community, the issue of leadership will more often than not come to the fore. What we seek is not power, but to provide an example of how to live the awen, to make that inspiration manifest in the world with honour and with integrity. In doing so, you are also living your truth. In leadership, we seek only to lead. It's not about power in any regard. We can lead without even touching upon issues of power. Simply by doing the work and walking the talk, we provide an example. That example is perhaps what best describes our leadership abilities. We don't seek to control others, to have power over them. Instead, we can work with them, to create a shared source of power, if we must. We could also simply be the awen, be the inspiration. Either way, when we consider leadership, we must also consider ethics.

Sometimes it is necessary for us to take the lead in a situation. Where we see that a change must occur, we must look deeply within to see whether we have the skills needed to tackle the issue. If we find that we do, we then look at the responsibility involved and whether or not we have the ability to respond. We must have this ability and not simply work from a place of desiring to create and affect change in the world or in our lives. Intention is wonderful, but we must also be able to make that intention manifest.

What does it mean to "lead"? Simply put, it means taking the first step in a situation, perhaps creating a path where there isn't one and walking your talk. Notice the words *lead, path,* and *walk* all relate to movement, to going forward. Leadership is about moving forward in a situation, with responsibility, honour, and integrity.

If, for instance, you see that a new housing development is proposed in your local area, you know that it will cause great suffering to the environment, and you have the ability to respond to the proposed plan and the energy to do the work—then you can make the choice based upon your passion, your intellect, your integrity, and your honour. If you know that there are rare lizards or toads or butterflies that will be destroyed, then you can put this knowledge to good use, to defend a part of nature whose voice often goes unheard in today's society. So, you can go to parish council meetings to see what the plans are. You can talk to people in the community to inform them of the situation. You can create flyers or get signatures from people who are in agreement with your intention. You can then bring all this to meetings with the parish council and the developers. You can contact local wildlife trusts and charities. You can take the reins in organising a group of people to help defend the landscape against the proposed planning. You can also look for alternative venues for the planning to go ahead that will cause less damage to an ecosystem. The possibilities are as numerous as you are capable of imagining.

This will require you to step in and take the lead in a situation. You may be on a solitary path as a Hedge Druid, yet you share this world with others. You may be utterly confident in your abilities or you may be learning along the way. Both situations are perfectly fine; it's how we learn and grow. What is important thoughout is that you have taken *personal responsibility*. We have looked at emotional responsibility already and this is another tool that you can add to your kit when you decide to take on any sort of leadership role. We have learned to ride the waves of our emotion so that we can see the world and any situation more clearly, to see it as it truly is, without the distorted lens of personal perception based on past wounds and history. We are able to act rather than react to any given situation.

This is the first step to ethical leadership. We have to be able to look deeply inside ourselves at our motivations and our egos. We have to come to terms with all that we don't like about ourselves and all that we do like. We have to learn the art of transformation, to confront and turn the shadow aspects of ourselves and bring that energy into something that changes us for the better and does not leave us in the dark, unaware of our motivations and reasoning in the world.

Ethical leadership requires clear intention, free from ego. It also requires a great amount of patience, because we will be working with others whose intention might not match our own. It is not exactly our intention to make everyone agree with us, per se, but to provide information, to provide inspiration, to help solve problems in our community. Just as in Welsh lore Gwion Bach received inspiration from the cauldron of Ceridwen and then became Taliesin, the Radiant Brow, the most famed of poets—so too must we drink from the cauldron of awen and use the knowledge and wisdom gained to further shine the light into the darkness of the unknown or the unconscious.

When working with others, we have to let go of notions of "power over," as activist and author Starhawk has written about, and instead work on "power with."[42]

"Power over" is all about control. It is firmly rooted in a wounded ego, which seeks to dominate another in order to feel better. For whatever reason, and there are many, many reasons why people behave the way they do, this seems to be the standard view of power in the Western world. In our capitalist society, in our dog-eat-dog world, we seek power over another in order to get our way. What we desperately need to do is extract ourselves from this way of thinking and into a more holistic view where we are not only looking to benefit ourselves, but to benefit the whole, the entirety. This is a major point in Druidry, for we know that we are part of an ecosystem and are trying to find our place within it. As Hedge Druids, the responsibility lies solely with us.

To do this, we use "power from within." This is how we use our knowledge and ability coupled with our ethical and moral codes to work from a place where ego and soul wounds have no bearing on the present moment. It is also based on our love and reverence for the natural world and allowing that love to inspire us in our ethics. Though we are created from our past experiences, when we find power from within we have personal sovereignty from which to work.

"Power with" is how we work with others, how we inspire others into action, how we use the awen to solve a problem. The ancient Druids were holders of great power, advising and influencing kings and queens. Though we may not have that influence any longer, we can look to how we influence people and consider the ethical implications therein. The key to using influence ethically comes from a sense of equality. When we work from a place where we don't assume or think that we are superior, we are able to respond better. As soon as we think we are superior, our pride is speaking and tainting the entire situation with judgement and false perception.

---

42. Starhawk, *Truth or Dare: Encounters with Power, Authority and Mystery*, (Harper and Row, 1990), 9.

Though it is better to want to create a world where the environment comes first and foremost, to think that we are better because we hold this point of view simply exacerbates the situation and allows our pride to create an "us and them" mentality. When we have this point of view, it creates a huge divide between people, which is often very hard to overcome. We have stopped trying to communicate and simply declared them "wrong" while we are "right." The lines of communication are broken and when we cannot communicate in any form, we cannot relate: therefore we have no relationship. Druidry is all about creating relationship, and therefore we need to communicate responsibly and with clear intention.

We know that there are no black and white answers, for the most part. All shades of grey fall in between. We must learn the arts of listening and of working with compassion. It can be so difficult in human interaction and communication. I've said it before and I'll say it again: you don't need to blow out someone else's candle for yours to burn all the brighter. We can use words and speech to interact with each other respectfully. We need to look deeper into compassion; for compassion, unlike pity, requires a total lack of judgement on the individual's part.

Compassion is both the easiest thing and the hardest thing in the world. To learn the ways of compassion, one must first release the notion of the self, the ego that one clings to, in order to see that we are all related, that we are all connected. It's all about relationship. We are all equal. We are all part of an ecosystem. We can learn how to live more compassionately.

Compassion requires us to listen, to try to understand. In all things, we must try to understand. It can be so hard when we are confronted with people in positions of power that we see abusing that power each and every day, creating hateful speech, creating discord and division for their own agendas and for their own egos. Even so, we have to work to understand these people and use compassion in order to try to find a language that works, to establish communication and hopefully a relationship. It doesn't always work. We may come across situations in our leadership, like racism, sexism, and a host of other human ills. Hateful speech and attitudes are learned behaviours. The good thing about that is that it can be unlearned.

In ethical leadership, we have to look deeply at our own energy and how it can be best used in any given situation. We often spend so much of our energy needlessly. Disputes, arguments, feuds, grudges, and long-held anger and frustration are just some examples. We need to choose our battles wisely, for they are not all worth fighting.

Sometimes there is nothing we can do. When faced with ignorance or denial, we are often facing an impassable wall upon which we can either hurl ourselves time and time again or simply shrug and walk away. It is not our duty to make the ignorant wise or to force someone into changing their mind. That can only occur from within. Our energy is a precious resource that must be used wisely. There are many fights that are worthy of our time, but we don't have to attend every argument that we are invited to. We can live our lives and simply be the example we wish to see in the world around us. Sometimes, that is all that we can do. Acceptance of this is hard, but crucial in many situations.

Think about the energy used in holding a grudge against someone for a few days, a few weeks, a few months, or a few years. How could that energy have been better spent? How much energy is involved in a family feud—from all sides involved? How much time is wasted arguing on social media, trying to prove your point and making a stranger change their mind? How much energy is spent talking behind people's backs, trying to get people "on your side"? Is it really worth it?

Even if it's something you truly believe in, proselytising the issue doesn't really do much. In fact, it can even have the adverse effect of pushing away those who are either in agreement or disagreement: they're simply tired of hearing your message over and over again. That's not to say that we shouldn't have opinions and that we shouldn't share them, but when we spend so much energy shouting into empty space, then maybe it's time to rethink the situation. We need to engage with others, to ensure that relationship is there; otherwise we're just trying to push against the wind.

We need to find the balancing point between standing up for ourselves and learning when we are expending energy needlessly. Walking away is not losing. It is opening up a new path for you to find better things to spend your time on. We have to stop thinking in terms of competitiveness, of winning and losing. Perhaps even stop thinking in terms of battle and fighting and instead work on cooperation and compassion. Remember, as part of an ecosystem, we're here for the benefit of the whole.

It's all about intention. We just need to have the right goals in mind when we are engaging others in any given situation, especially if we have taken a position of leadership. Choose your engagements wisely. This present moment is what really matters. Live it instead of losing yourself in a battle that doesn't or shouldn't even exist. Life has difficulties enough already. Be kind, be compassionate, and be mindful. You may find the battles beginning to lessen and a peace of mind settling deep within. Relationship and engagement take the place of battles and fighting. Enjoy that, for that is what life is all about.

Ethical leadership will lead to some confrontation, for certain. How we engage with the confrontation defines us. Ethical leadership as a teacher, a leader, and/or a priest is also a wonderful way for us to truly walk our talk, to experience actually *living* our spiritual tradition rather than just thinking about it. It begins to make manifest what it is that we truly hold dear in our own personal lives. When worked with honesty and integrity, what results from this can be wholly transformative, both for the individual and for the wider world.

When we are working with ethical leadership, we need to clearly look deep within ourselves first and foremost. We need to ask ourselves the questions: What is my intention? How does it benefit the whole? What are my opinions on the matter and how do they differ from others'? How can I engage with a different opinion or perspective with compassion and integrity? How can I relate to this person/situation with allowing my past to influence the present in a negative way? How can I create relationship? How is power working in this situation?

When we look deeply at these questions and can answer them frankly and with honesty, then we can begin on our path to ethical leadership. Then we can truly walk the walk of being a teacher, a leader, a priest in our Hedge Druid tradition. We can lead by example, whatever path our lives take.

The Hedge Druid checks her emails. There is an email from someone who has taken the time to thank her for the work that she has done and for the inspiration she has provided on that person's path. She smiles, glad that she has been able to help, the praise making the work worthwhile. But then she catches herself and knows that the work that she does is not for praise, but for the benefit of the whole. But the praise is nice, she concedes. She writes a thank-you email back, honouring the soul who has taken the time to connect with her. "May we be the awen, all of us," she writes.

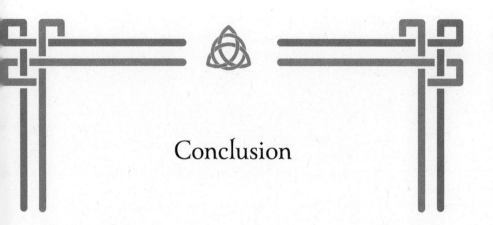

Conclusion

I sincerely hope that this book has touched you on some level and that the awen shared on these pages resonates with you. It has been a joy and a pleasure to share what I have learned and what I am still learning on this Druid path with you. I know that I will never stop learning, and each and every day, something new comes into my life and inspires me in my own tradition. The blessings of each new dawn are a true gift and one that I hope to use wisely, making my ancestors proud. I hope to honour the spirits of place, the gods, and the Fair Folk in all that I do, and I hope that the songs of the land will forever sing to my soul. It's hard work, keeping up that relationship, but it is well worth it. Some days are better than others; some are overflowing with inspiration and beauty. In my own work as a Hedge Druid, I ride these currents of life and death, of rebirth and regeneration, moving ever forward while paying attention to the experience of the past and being present in the moment.

Working and walking the path of the Hedge Druid may seem lonely sometimes, but know that you are not alone. The birds are singing, the earth hums beneath your feet. The bees are buzzing and the wind is whispering secrets untold. There are countless relationships to be had all around you, even if you are walking a solitary path. It takes great courage to walk this path, but know that you are supported by everything around you, if you only open yourself up to seeing and feeling those deep relationships and your place in the world. Your life has great meaning, as does that of the ant and the eagle, the cloud and the stream. What will you do with it?

May the road rise up to meet you.
May the wind be always at your back.
May the sun shine warm upon your face;
The rains fall soft upon your fields
And until we meet again,
May the gods, the ancestors, and the spirits of place
Hold you in the palm of their hands.
—Traditional Irish blessing, adapted

The sun is setting as the Hedge Druid comes out of the forest. She steps out into the meadow and sees the village before her. The sounds of children playing and dogs barking are carried on the breeze. She turns to face the forest edge once more, that boundary and liminal place where her work carries great importance. She knows the secrets of this world and the Otherworld, and her work in both worlds holds deep meaning for her and those to whom she works in service. She bows to the trees and then turns three times clockwise, uttering a short incantation. Now fully returned to the Middleworld, she brings the knowledge that she has gained from the Otherworld into her everyday life, to enchant and delight her world.

Here is the path that leads from the forest. Here is the path of the Hedge Druid.

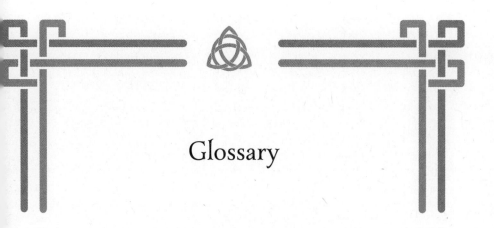

Glossary

Some of these words will be unfamiliar, particular to Druidry, or from another language. Here I've put together a glossary with pronunciations to help you understand the words and their meanings. The initial letter "c" is always a hard "c," pronounced like a "k." Therefore, it is "Keltic," not "Seltic." Some pronunciations may differ, depending on the region. Some pronunciations, such as the "ch" in Ablach, are sounds not heard in modern English, but come from restricting the air from the back of the throat and pushing it out without voicing the sound. An "ll" in Welsh is even more difficult; it involves spreading the tongue out to either side of the mouth and pushing the air out the sides by your cheeks, again without voicing the sound.

Abred (Ah-bred)—another name for the Middleworld

Alban Arthan—Winter Solstice, Welsh for "light of winter" or "light of the bear"

Alban Eilier (Alban Eye-leer)—Spring Equinox, Welsh for "the light on the earth"

Alban Elfed—Autumn Equinox, Welsh for "light on the water"

Alban Hefin—Summer Solstice, Welsh for "the light of summer"

Amergin—Irish bard/poet, known for the "Song of Amergin"

Andraste (Andrasta)—Celtic goddess of victory, known and honoured in East Anglia by the Iceni tribe

Annwn (Annoon)—Welsh, Celtic Otherworld/Lowerworld accessed through travelling below the earth, into the ground, or into a mound or hill

Arianrhod (Arian-rode)—Welsh goddess of the moon, the stars, "Lady of the Silver Wheel"

Autumn Equinox—festival celebrated by Druids on or around September 21

Awen (Ah-wen)—Welsh, divine inspiration

Awenyddion (Awen-ithion)—Welsh, "one who is inspired," used as a term for sect of magical workers in the Welsh tradition

Bard—professional storyteller, historian, poet, one of the three grades of Druidry

Belenus—Celtic/Gaulish deity of the sun

Beltane—festival celebrated by Druids on April 30–May 1

Blodeuwedd (Blow-die-weth)—Welsh, goddess created from flowers who was magically turned into an owl

Brigantia—goddess of the British Isles, a form of Brighid (see below)

Brighid—(also known as Brigit, Brigid, Bride, Braint, Ffraint Brighde, Brig, Brigantia) goddess known throughout the Celtic world; in modern-day most well known as goddess of poetry, smithcraft, and healing

Bíle (Bil-eh)—sacred tree found in each of the ancient five Irish kingdoms

Búad (bu-ath)—Irish, power found in the land

Caer Sidi (Kai-er See-dee)—fortress of the Fair Folk, also known as Annwn

Cailleach (Kal-ee-ack)—Scottish and Manx goddess of winter, wild weather, renewal, ancestral goddess

Calan Gaeaf (Kalan Gay-ev)—otherwise known as Samhain or Halloween (see Samhain)

Cauldron—motif found in Celtic mythology, also a ritual tool used by Druids today

Ceridwen—Welsh goddess of magic and brewer of the cauldron of awen

Cernnunos (Kare-noon-ohs)—Gaulish deity famous for being an "antlered" or "horned" god, Lord of the Animals

Ceugant (Kai-gunt)—another name for Annwn or the Lowerworld

Cill-Dara—ancient name for Kildare, Ireland, where Brighid's shrine can be found, translates to "Church of the Oak"

Cles—Irish, energy found in stone circles, ancient groves, tumuli, etc.

Clooties—ribbons tied onto the branches of trees in a magical working

Coventina—Romano-British goddess of wells and springs

Crane bag—from Irish myth, owned by the god of the sea, Manannan, used by Druids today to hold and transport their ritual tools

Crom Dubh (Krom-dove)—Irish god of the harvest

Culdee—Christian monastic and eremitical communities of Ireland, with ties to the pre-Christian Druids

Dagda—Irish god, "father god" associated with fertility, magic, abundance, and strength

Daire—Irish epitaph of the god Dagda, translates as "oak" or "abundance"

Draoi (Dree)—Irish for "Druid"

Draíocht (Dree-ockt)—Irish, spells and magic

Druid (Drew-id)—the oldest word that we have for a priest in the pre-Christian Celtic tradition

Druidecht (Drew-ee-ockt)—Irish, Druid magic

Druid's Egg—a fetish (power object) said to be used by the Druids and others to give them luck and success

Dúile (Dwee-la)—nine directions in Irish which translate as above, below, outside, inside, through, sky, sun, land, and sea

Emain Ablach (Ah-um ablach)—another Irish name for the Otherworld, "Island of Apples"

Epona (Ee-pone-ah)—Romano-British goddess of horses, agriculture, and fertility

Faery—a type of being from the Otherworld that sometimes interacts and communicates with humanity

Fair Folk—a euphemism for Fairies or Faeries

Fe-fiada (Fay-fee-ada)—Irish, a cloak or mantle spell of invisibility

Fetish—a power object, an object imbued with magical properties, can be made or found in nature

Fianna (Fee-anna)—warrior band that protected Ireland

Fili (Fee-lee)—special caste of magical worker in Ireland, sometimes referred to as "poets"

Fith-fath (Fee-fah)—see Fe-fiada

Geis (Jesh)—Irish, a magical oath taken upon oneself or laid upon by another

Glam dicin (Glam Dee-keen)—Irish, a mighty, magical shout, often used to curse

Gofannon (Goh-va-non)—Welsh god of metal-working

Gwion Bach (Gwee-on Bach)—he who imbibed the drops of awen from Ceridwen's cauldron and became Taliesin, the greatest bard

Gwyl Awst (Gwil Owst)—Welsh word for the festival of Lughnasadh, celebrated on July 31–August 1

Gwyn Ap Nudd (Gwin ap Neath)—Welsh god of Annwn, the Lowerworld, said to live inside Glastonbury Tor

Gwynfed (Gwin-ved)—another name for the Upperworld

Haegtessa (Hay-tessa)—Saxon word for "hedge sitter"

Hagazissa—German word for "hedge sitter"

Herne—god and figure from British mythology, also known as Herne the Hunter

Imbas forosna (Im-mas Vorosna)—Irish form of sensory deprivation to gain inspiration

Imbolc (Im-molc)—otherwise known as Oimelc, Irish word that translates as "of milk" or "in the belly," festival celebrated January 31–February 1

Immrama—Irish "to journey over water," used in guided meditation

Llŷr (Hleer)—Welsh god of the sea

Lowerworld—one of the three worlds found within the World Tree

Lughnasadh (Loo-na-sa)—harvest festival celebrated by Druids on July 31–August 1

Manannán mac Lir—Irish god of the sea

Middleworld—one of the three worlds found within the World Tree

Morrigan—Irish Celtic goddess of war, healing, and sexual passion

Nehalennia—Dutch goddess of the sea

Nemetona—British goddess of the sacred grove, sanctuary

Nemeton—a sacred grove where Druids were said to worship; now also a magical or sacred space created for ritual use

Nodens—Gaulish and Brythonic god of the sea, hunting, and dogs

Nwyfre (Noo-iv-re)—Welsh, energy such as "the life force"

Ogham (Oh-am)—often characterised and described as a mnemonic "tree alphabet," but of which there exists over 150 variations

Ogma—Irish god who invented the ogham, also known as "the honey-tongued" and patron of many scholars

Ovate—one of the three levels in Druidry, consisting of healers, seers, prophets, and diviners

Sain/Saining—to bless, usually with smoke (akin to smudging)

Samhain (Sow-ehn)—festival celebrated by Druids on October 31–November 1, an ancient Celtic fire festival

Scrying—a form of divination, such as gazing into a bowl of water or a pool of water or gazing into the flames of a fire

Sickle—tool with curved blade, used to cut herbs and also used in magical ritual

Sidhe (Shee)—Irish term for the Fair Folk or Fairy/Faery

Silver Branch—ritual tool found in myths and used today by Druids to signal working with the Otherworld or working "between the worlds;" consists of a branch from a tree (usually apple) adorned with silver bells

Staff—ritual tool used by Druids in much the same way as a wand, to direct energy; also helpful when out walking the countryside

Summer Solstice—festival celebrated by Druids on or around June 21, honouring the longest day

Tailtiu (Tale-tee-uh)—Irish goddess of agriculture and fertility

Taranis—Gaulish/Brythonic god of thunder

Tarb-feis (Tar-fee-ish)—Irish, ritual sacrifice of an animal whose flesh is then eaten

Teach-an-alais (Tech an allish)—Irish for "sweat house"

Tech Duinn/House of Donn (Tech Doo-in)—where souls gather after death, perhaps then moving on to other realms; identified today with Bull Rock, an islet off the western tip of the Beara Peninsula, Ireland

Tlachtga (Clach-tah)—Hill of Ward in Meath, the ancient central kingdom of Ireland; sacred to the Druids and the place of the high king

Tuatha Dé Danann (Too-ah-ha Dey Da-nan)—Irish, "people of the goddess Danu," a pantheon of Irish gods and goddesses

Tylwyth Teg (Tull-wit Taig)—Welsh name for the Fair Folk, Fairy/Faery

Tír na hÓige (Teer na hoy)—another Irish name for the Otherworld, "Land of Youth"

Tír na nÓg (Teer na Nohg)—another Irish name for the Otherworld, "Land of the Young"

Upperworld—one of the three worlds found within the World Tree

Ynys Afallach (Inish Av-ah-hlee-ach)—another Welsh name for the Otherworld, "Isle of Apples"

Ynys Afallon (Inish Ava-hlon)—another Welsh name for the Otherworld, "Isle of Apples"

Bibliography

Black, R. *The Gaelic Otherworld: John Gregorson Campbell's Superstitions of the Highlands and Islands of Scotland and Witchcraft and Second Sight in the Highlands and Islands*, Birlinn Limited, 2005.

Breatnach, L. "The Cauldron of Poesy," Ériu, Vol. 32, Royal Irish Academy, 1981.

Broadhurst, P., et Miller, H. *The Sun and the Serpent: A Journey of Discovery through the British Landscape, its Mythology, Ancient Sites and Mysteries*, Mythos, 2001.

Burl, A. *A Guide to the Stone Circles of Britain, Ireland and Brittany*, Yale University Press, 2005.

Carr-Gomm, P. *Druid Mysteries: Ancient Wisdom for the 21st Century*, Rider, 2002.

Cater, K. *The Shortest Day: A Little Book of the Winter Solstice*, Hedingham Fair, 2014.

Chappell, W. *The Ballad Literature and Popular Music of the Olden Time*, London: Chappell & Co., 1859.

Daimler, M. *By Land, Sea and Sky: A Selection of Paganized Prayers and Charms from Volumes 1 & 2 of the Carmina Gadelica*, Lulu, 2011.

Forest, D. *The Druid Shaman: Exploring the Celtic Otherworld*, Moon Books, 2013.

Forest, D. *Gwyn ap Nudd: Wild God of Faery, Guardian of Annwfn*, Moon Books, 2017.

———. *The Magical Year: Seasonal Celebrations to Honour Nature's Ever-Turning Wheel*, Watkins, 2016.

Freeman, M. *Kindling the Celtic Spirit*, Harper One, 2001.

Green, M. *Exploring the World of the Druids*, Thames and Hudson Ltd, 1997.

Gregory, A. *Gods and Fighting Men: The Story of the Tuatha De Danaan and of the Fianna of Ireland*, CreateSpace Independent Publishing Platform, 2014.

Herne, R. *Old Gods New Druids*, O Books, 2009.

Hopman, E. E. *A Druid's Herbal for the Sacred Earth Year*, Inner Traditions Bear and Company, 1995.

———. *A Druid's Herbal of Sacred Tree Medicine*, Inner Traditions International, 2008.

———. *A Legacy of Druids: Conversations with Druid Leaders of Britain, the USA and Canada, Past and Present*, Moon Books, 2016.

Howard, M. *East Anglian Witches and Wizards*, Three Hands Press, 2017.

Hughes, K. *The Book of Celtic Magic: Transformative Teachings from the Cauldron of Awen*, Llewellyn, 2016.

Hutton, R. *Blood and Mistletoe: The History of the Druids in Britain*, Yale University Press, 2011.

———. *Stations of the Sun: A History of the Ritual Year in Britain*, 2001, Oxford University Press, 2001.

———. *The Triumph of the Moon: A History of Modern Pagan Witchcraft*, Oxford University Press, 2001.

Kelly, F. *Early Irish Farming*, Dublin Institute for Advanced Studies, 2000.

King, G. *The British Book of Spells and Charms*, Troy Books, 2015.

———. *A Guide to Early Irish Law*, Dublin Institute for Advanced Studies, 2011.

Kirkey, J. *The Salmon in the Spring: The Ecology of Celtic Spirituality*, Hiraeth Press, 2009.

Kondratiev, A. *Celtic Rituals: An Authentic Guide to Ancient Celtic Spirituality*, The Collins Press, 1998.

Kynes, S. *Star Magic: The Wisdom of the Constellations for Pagan and Wiccans*, Llewellyn, 2015.

MacEowan, F. H. *The Mist-filled Path: Celtic Wisdom for Exiles, Wanderers and Seekers*, New World Library, 2002.

Macleod NicMhacha, S. *Queen of the Night: Rediscovering the Celtic Moon Goddess*, Red Wheel/Weiser, 2005.

Magee Sutton, M. & Mann, N.R. *Druid Magic: The Practice of Celtic Wisdom*, Llewellyn, 2013.

Markale, J. *The Druids: Celtic Priests of Nature*, Inner Traditions, 1999.

Matthews, C. *Celtic Devotional: Daily Prayers and Blessings*, Gill & Macmillan Ltd, 2004.

Matthews, C. & Matthews, J. *Encyclopaedia of Celtic Wisdom: A Celtic Shaman's Sourcebook*, Element, 1994.

Matthews, J. *The Celtic Shaman: A Practical Guide*, Rider, 2001.

———. *The Summer Solstice: Celebrating the Journey of the Sun from May Day to Harvest*, Godsfield Press, 2002.

McGarry, G. *Brighid's Healing: Ireland's Celtic Medicine Traditions*, Green Magic, 2007.

NicMhacha, S. M. *Queen of the Night: Rediscovering the Celtic Moon Goddess*, Weiser, 2005.

Oliver, N. *A History of Ancient Britain*, Weidenfeld and Nicolson, 2011.

Pearson, N. *The Devil's Plantation: East Anglian Lore, Witchcraft & Folk Magic*, Troy Books, 2016.

———. *Walking the Tides: Seasonal Rhythms and Traditional Lore in Natural Craft*, Capall Bann, 2009.

Pennick, N. *The Sacred World of the Celts: An Illustrated Guide to Celtic Spirituality and Mythology*, Thorsons, 1997.

Restall Orr, E. *Living Druidry: Magical Spirituality for the Wild Soul*, Piatkus Books Ltd, 2004.

———. *Principles of Druidry*, Thorsons, 1998.

———. *Ritual: A Guide to Life, Love and Inspiration*, Thorsons, 2000.

———. *Spirits of the Sacred Grove: The World of a Druid Priestess*, Moon Books Classics, 2014.

Roberts, A. *The Celts: Search for a Civilization*, Heron Books, 2015.

Ross, A. *Pagan Celtic Britain*, Routledge, 1974.

Seal, J. *Hedgerow Medicine: Harvest and Make Your Own Herbal Remedies*, Merlin Unwin Books, 2008.

Seal et als. *The Herbalist's Bible: John Parkinson's Lost Classic Rediscovered*, Merlin Unwin Books, 2014.

Starhawk. *The Earth Path: Grounding Your Spirit in the Rhythms of Nature*, Harper Collins, 2005.

Starhawk. *Truth or Dare: Encounters with Power, Authority and Mystery*, Harper Row, 1990.

Starhawk. *Webs of Power: Notes from the Global Uprising*, New Catalyst Books, 2008.

Starhawk et als. *The Twelve White Swans: A Journey to the Realm of Magic, Healing and Action*, Harper Collins, 2000.

Struthers, J. *Red Sky at Night: The Book of Lost Countryside Wisdom*, Ebury Press, 2009.

Telyndru, J. *Avalon Within: A Sacred Journey of Myth, Mystery and Inner Wisdom*, Llewellyn, 2005.

Thompson, R. *The History of the Devil—The Horned God of the West: Magic and Worship*, Home Farm Books, 2013.

van der Hoeven, J. *The Awen Alone: Walking the Path of the Solitary Druid*, Moon Books, 2014.

van der Hoeven, J. *The Crane Bag: A Druid's Guide to Ritual Tools and Practices*, Moon Books, 2017.

Weatherstone, L. *Tending Brigid's Flame: Awaken to the Celtic Goddess of Hearth, Temple and Forge*, Llewellyn, 2015.

Weber, C. *Brigid: History, Mystery and Magick of the Celtic Goddess*, Weiser Books, 2015.